Through Afghan Eyes

Survival during the Soviet-Afghan War and Warnings to the West before 9/11

SHER AHMAD

Sher Ahmad

Lynnwood, Washington

First Printing 2015

Printed in the United States of America

ISBN-10: 0986260800

ISBN-13: 978-0-9862608-0-3

Library of Congress Control Number: 2014921609

DEDICATION

I dedicate this book to my mother, Bibi Zahra, and my father, Hajji Mahmood, for their unconditional love to me and my siblings. Their advice about truth, honesty, and respect for humankind is still like music to my ears.

To Bibigula Ahmad, my wife and lifelong friend: you have always loved, supported and respected me during the past forty years, and have raised and given total love to our four children, their spouses and our grandchildren.

To the millions of refugees around the world who have been forced to leave their native homes due to their religion, political opinion, nationality, social group, ethnicity, or because of war.

CONTENTS

ACKNOWLEDGMENTS

I am deeply grateful to my wife, Bibigula, and my children, Pashtana, Mirwais, Yonus and Setara and their spouses and children--our grandchildren. They have been my inspiration and supporters of my life's work. To our family friends, Ken and Verena Hardman, thank you for your tireless efforts and countless hours editing this book, and for more than 20 years of unconditionally helping my family. Dr. Mose Durst, your learned comments are very much appreciated.

Since this book is a short collection of my life stories up to 9/11, and the people who are a part of those stories are too many to name for the limited scope of this book, I must apologize to them in advance for not listing all their names. I hope they will understand. That being said, I am very indebted to Dr. John H. Mowbray and Mrs. Kay Mowbray and nurses such as Anna Claire, who at CARE-MEDICO in Kabul, provided the professional care and support for my wife, Bibigula, during her illness in May 1978, at the outset of Afghanistan's darkest days. Without their efforts and dedication, she would already be in the graveyard.

My gratitude also goes out to Sanford Caudill, my family friend and former boss at USAID in Kandahar, who taught me life skills and exemplified the best of what an American can be in a developing country. To my friends, Gordon and Janet Stinson and the churches in Birmingham, Alabama, thank you for sponsoring my family as refugees to live in the world's greatest country, the United States of America.

PREFACE

Before immigrating to the US as refugees in 1985 during the Cold War, my wife and I lived, worked, and raised our young children in Afghanistan through the nightmares of coups, the Soviet invasion and civil war. Escape through Pakistan to the US allowed us to begin a new life. The problems of the past are not always easy to escape, though.

While working for two years as a humanitarian aid officer in Pakistan prior to immigrating, I warned US Embassy officials of anti-US extremism incubating in Afghan refugee camps in Pakistan. More than 15 years later, especially in the months leading up to 9/11, I warned local US officials again of the signs of emerging extremism in South/Central Asia and of international extremists recruiting in Northern California. But who would listen to me?

The global shock of 9/11 and its aftermath drew me back to Afghanistan as a Senior Cultural Advisor for US and NATO commanding generals and their staffs. Progress was made, but it would evaporate with each new rotation of commanders and troops.

As an Afghan and an American, I am deeply distressed about what has happened in the land of my birth. What is to come is even more foreboding for the next generations, not just in Afghanistan, but also in the US and for the global community.

At this stage of my life I am compelled to tell my stories. I worry for the safety of our communities, that they will increasingly be under the shadow of terrorist threats. I fear that terrorists will be even more successful in pitting Muslims and non-Muslims against one another, and Muslims against Muslims.

My memoir provides a window into the larger geopolitical history of Afghanistan in the twentieth century to just after September 11, 2001. This history reveals that since WWII, the US and other countries have been prone to making essentially the same tragic mistakes in Afghanistan.

Since 9/11 little economic and political progress has been made in Afghanistan even though billions of dollars of foreign aid and military assistance have been invested there by the US and other nations. Afghanistan remains ranked at the bottom among the poorest and most corrupt countries in the world. Greater progress could have been made if the US would have learned from its foreign aid mistakes there during the Cold War, and from its involvement in the Soviet-Afghan War and its support of mujahideen warlords.

When Soviet troops were withdrawn from Afghanistan in 1989, a devastating civil war led by warlords engulfed Afghanistan. A civil war could erupt again with the drawdown of US and NATO forces from Afghanistan. In almost full circle, it also appears that the US and Russia are descending into another Cold War.

My stories of survival present mission-critical insights that decision makers and field personnel in the US and Western government, military, and humanitarian aid agencies can use to prevent making the same agonizing mistakes in Afghanistan. These insights and lessons are transferable to other countries, especially those embroiled in insurgencies with complex ethnic, tribal, and extremist rivalries such as Syria and Iraq, and where millions of people have been internally displaced or have escaped to neighboring countries as refugees.

Writing this book forced me to remember many traumatic events and was often painful. I found it very difficult to mentally relive every detail of being held captive by terrorists for 13 days in a Pakistani airliner with more than a hundred other passengers. It had taken me a long time to recover from that experience. Remembering and retelling other life stories was also difficult for me. As you read on, you will know why.

SHER AHMAD

1

MY HOME

I was born in our family compound at the foot of Elephant Mountain, in the northwest corner of Kandahar City, Afghanistan, in a village called Kalacha e-Mirza Ahmad Khan. That has been our home since 1885, ever since my grandparents moved there from the Tubah Mountain, about 110 miles east of Kandahar City, on the Afghan side of the Afghanistan-Pakistan border.

Elephant Mountain got its name because it resembles the massive body of an elephant. During the Soviet occupation and Afghan civil wars, it provided a natural fortification that helped our families to defend themselves from attacks.

Hajji Rawouf, my grandfather on my father's side, was a famous Islamic teacher, not a mullah, but like a scholar with a PhD in theology. He was fluent in his native language of Pashto, as well as in Hebrew, Farsi (Persian), and Arabic. Grandfather promoted education and sent all of his children to school. Pursuing education and public service has been a strong tradition in our family since the founding of Afghanistan in 1747 by Ahmad Shah Durrani. One of our ancestors was a close friend of his.

Grandfather was not interested in wealth. During his life, the Afghan Government awarded him a gift of a large plot of land for his service as a community leader and freedom fighter during the Second Anglo-Afghan War. He never went to look at the land, though.

I don't remember Grandfather because he passed away soon after I was born in 1946. My parents described him as a tall man, stern in manner, but very kind to his family. For many years he made pilgrimages to Mecca until he lost his eyesight in old age. In his early years Grandfather walked with others from Kandahar to Mecca five times and back. As the years passed, he took the luxury of riding a bus and a boat, and finally, in his golden years, he traveled by plane to Mecca. The last time Grandfather traveled to Mecca he did not return, and my family doesn't know whether he made it to Mecca, nor where he died.

My father, Hajji Mahmood, was born in 1903 and had three wives. My mother, Bibi Zahra, was his youngest wife. She bore 13 children in our family compound where all my siblings and I were born. As was the custom, women in our extended family helped my mother deliver us into this world. Only four of her children, including me, grew into adulthood. My other nine siblings died in infancy or as young children. I have had eight other half-brothers and half-sisters. Two of my children, Pashtana and Yonus, were also born in my family compound.

Our extended family of aunts, uncles, and cousins lived together in 14 compounds facing one another, separated by a small street in front, and next to farmland and orchards. In each compound many rooms connected to a courtyard or garden in the center, like the hub of a wheel. Each compound was protected by tall, thick walls made of mud, stones, and bricks. In the midst of the compounds stands our family mosque.

This photo was taken in 1980 after the Soviet invasion. It shows the three-story home where I was born. The two people standing on steps at its base are my  cousins. Not long after this photo was taken, they were killed by the Soviets.

During most of my childhood our home had no windows. Each room had thick mud walls with a small hole in the roof where the sunlight streamed through. In the evenings and during sunless days or hours we relied on kerosene lamps to provide light in our dark rooms. During the winters I did my homework while the sunlight pierced through the hole in the roof. There was no table or chair in the room. I sat bent on my elbows and knees on the burgundy red carpet, made of ordinary Afghan wool, to read and write. As the sunlight moved, I moved with it. For at least six years I studied on that carpet. After two years my baggy pants, handsewn by my mother, were thin and reddish at the knees. When I entered the seventh grade, my father installed windows in all the rooms so there was enough light for me to study. That made a big difference in my ability to learn. We kept that carpet as a family treasure until my wife, children, and I escaped to the US in 1985.

I have fond memories of my days in Kandahar when I attended the Fazel Kandahari Elementary School. It sat on two acres of land at the base of a small, rocky mountain. It was a fun mountain. During the wintertime we often climbed up and slid down its polished side made smooth by centuries of children sliding down. It was really exciting! When we arrived home with our torn baggy pants after a day of sliding, our mothers were upset with us. But we were kids. Another fun place in the summertime was the Public Garden near my school. Within it was a three-level swimming pool made of stone and concrete. After school we went swimming there. While it was fun, we became even hungrier afterward.

It was in the first grade that I first heard the word *refugee*. It was a day in 1952 when I was six-years old. Our school principal, Mr. Aziz Barakzai, brought into our classroom a father and mother with their two children who were younger than me, about two and four-years old. Mr. Barakzai, a light-skinned man with blue eyes and a beard, explained, "These folks are Palestinian refugees. They are homeless and have no food. So if any of you can give some money, they will buy food for themselves." I didn't have money to give them and felt very bad for them, especially for the two children who I thought must be very hungry. I knew what hunger felt like. Every day I was hungry.

From the age of five through high school, I woke up early and

3

hungry every day. I determined myself to get up using my internal alarm clock, which I still use today. I had no watch and there was no clock in our home. During daylight we measured time by the shadow cast from Elephant Mountain in relation to our compound. After sunset the stars would begin to appear and we determined time by them. At midnight the stars were like millions of sparkling dots. We would say, "The scorpion is here, the archer is there," and so on. There was no pollution.

After waking in the morning, I immediately walked to the cows kept within our compound walls and led them to the canal. From there I crossed through the neighbors' wet farmlands for about one-and-a-half kilometers to cut alfalfa with a sickle and then carried the alfalfa bundles back home. I cut my fingers many times and you can still see some of the scars on my hands.

After finishing those chores I walked to my school, about three kilometers from our home. There was no road to the school, so with my brothers, cousins, and other village children we zigzagged through the neighbors' farms. In a developing country like Afghanistan the irrigation system in farms was very primitive. Walking through the farms meant that we had to step in the mud throughout the year. In the winter the rain caused lots of mud; in the summer the farmers watered their fields, so we walked in mud in the summer too.

Each one of us had one pair of shoes for the entire school year. To protect our shoes we bundled them with our books in a cloth that we tossed over our shoulders. When we needed to run, we folded the sheet and strapped it diagonally across the front of our bodies. Since the school was far away, we had to run in our bare feet in the cold winter weather and in the scorching heat in the summer. Rocks and sharp camel thorns were always our enemies.

When we arrived at school, we washed our feet in the nearby canal and wiped them, but our feet had become swollen from the long walk, making our shoes so tight that it hurt a lot to put them on. It was so painful that tears would come to my eyes.

If we were five minutes late, the principal, Mr. Abrahim Khan, a chubby man with big, bushy eyebrows and a beard, standing at the school gate, beat our hands with a stick. It hurt a lot. We had to leave home early to get to school on time to save ourselves from being beaten by Mr. Khan. We barely had time to eat breakfast.

Carrying our books for three kilometers to school was difficult and I was always hungry. The food we normally ate at home was cooked soup or rice. Since we had no containers, we could not take it with us for lunch. There were no local village shops to buy fast food or quick snacks. In the summertime, though, we picked mulberries, beans, raw corn, and ate them on the way to school. Usually the farmers allowed us to freely pick them from their farms. Eating the raw vegetables, though, upset our stomachs.

We had to study hard. Our teacher was Mr. Nabi Khan (no relation to the principal). He was pleasant-looking, tall, and light-skinned. If we didn't correctly complete our homework or didn't know the previous lesson, or did not behave well, he sternly beat our palms and fingers with a stick. That was the law throughout Afghanistan. Mr. Khan was likeable, even though he beat us.

Our school building had been constructed with stone, gypsum, and bricks by prisoners from the Kandahar men's prison located just a few blocks away. We were lucky because it was new and modern with many classrooms and a library. About 500 students from the first to the sixth grade attended my school where boys and girls were taught in separate classrooms. In my classroom there were 30 students. It was like all other classrooms. There were three rows of tables and benches, four windows, and a door connecting it to a clean, wide hallway. Grapevines on trellises hung outside the windows and provided protection from the hot sun in the summer.

Unfortunately, other schools in Kandahar were not as nice as ours. The Fazel Kandahari Elementary School also had a large farm in the back where wheat was grown. In the front was a beautiful garden full of roses, tall poplar trees, mulberry trees, apple trees, and apricot trees. There was also a volleyball court and soccer field. All sixth graders were given a small plot of land, seeds, and tools to grow vegetables. Our little gardens were also graded by the teacher.

Paper, pens, and pencils were scarce. I was given one pencil for one entire school year. I always broke my pencil into three pieces. I did that because I was afraid that if I kept it as one piece, I might lose it. Then I would have nothing to write with since I couldn't afford to buy another pen or pencil.

In 1988 when we lived in Fremont, California, I shared this story about breaking a pencil into three pieces with my daughter's class at Brookvale Elementary School. My intention was to impress upon the students how lucky they were and not to take their school supplies for granted. However, my kids got upset with me because it was embarrassing for them.

When I was in the fifth and sixth grades, after school I learned the English ABCs and numbers. My older cousin knew English and wrote words on a piece of paper for me. I practiced writing them by scratching them in the dirt with a big stick. That was the beginning of my path to become an interpreter and translator for English-speaking Westerners, and for the last king of Afghanistan, King Mohammad Zahir Shah.

2

STINKY ESCAPE FROM THE KABUL MILITARY SCHOOL

A strange thing happened at the end of my school year in 1959. I was 13 years old and in the sixth grade. My classmates and I were in the courtyard of my school compound waiting to be called one-by-one into the principal's office. When it was my turn, I walked in and saw military officers and school officials sitting around tables. Lt. General Mir Ghosadin looked at me while thumbing through my school records. He told his assistant to write my name on a list. I was dismissed and walked back out to the courtyard. All of us were curious about what was happening. The principal finally came to us and we asked, "What was that all about?" He answered, "All of you whose names are on the list are going to the Air Force to become pilots." It sounded reasonable to me as a sixth grader. Since I saw my name being written on the list, I said happily, "Oh good!" I don't remember how the others felt about it. So I prepared myself to go to the Air Force School in Kabul. However, I did not understand how that was possible since I was only in the sixth grade and needed to finish high school.

After school, when I arrived home, I explained to my mother what had happened. She walked to her brother's home who lived nearby and who was an officer and a doctor in the Army. When she told him what I had reported to her, he said, "Oh yes, that's very good. The Air Force School is very good." It was a high school which prepared boys to enter the Air Force Academy. In Afghanistan at that time, a boy had no choice in the type of school he attended. So it appeared to be a real opportunity for me. That would soon change, though.

A Shocking Discovery

After traveling over three-hundred miles and three days in a bus, my classmates and I arrived in Kabul. Very unexpectedly we were told that we would be trained to become sergeants in a six-month anti-aircraft course. We were shocked. Sergeants in those days were illiterate and had a very bad reputation. We had been drafted and this was our introduction into the Army.

It was late May. In my group there were 124 students from Kandahar. At the camp we were shown rows of uniforms and boots on the floor. Everything was sized for adults and was way too big for me. My feet shifted inside the oversized, heavy boots. The pants and shirts were baggy. We all protested and began planning how to escape. Some of the boys were beaten up by the instructors when they made fun of the sergeants. During our first hours there, I asked a sergeant, "Will I wear a uniform like yours?" He answered, "Yes!" I was so angry at what was happening to us that I impulsively spat in his face. He jumped up from his chair and started chasing me. The other boys taunted him, yelling, "Hey dog, stop chasing him. We will beat you up!" The sergeant did not catch me.

We arrived on a Monday. The following Thursday we were given time off and I walked to visit my brother, Wahid, who lived nearby and attended a civilian mechanics school operated by Germans. I explained to him what had happened. The next day, Friday, was prayer day. On the street I met other students who had come with me from Kandahar and we decided to escape from the camp. Wahid, however, told me that until he made contact with our father, I should continue at the military school. He assured me that I would not be forced to complete the anti-aircraft training.

My Father's Appeal

Wahid delayed until late July to send a letter to my father. After receiving the letter, he immediately traveled to Kabul. My father went directly to the office of General Latif who was head of the school and commanding general of the anti-aircraft division of the Afghan Army. My father explained to him that I and other kids sent from Kandahar were too young to manage older soldiers and that we were top students. I was number two in my class. My father appealed, "How will these young teenagers, 13 and 14 years old, control 22-

year-old common soldiers? The students sent to the military school from the other provinces are much older and less educated." The general told my father that eventually there would be more courses for us to take and that my classmates and I would be sent to the Soviet Union for training. When my father informed me what the general had said, I protested, "No!"

The general, respecting my father's position as a city councilman in Kandahar, told my father that he would try to resolve the situation for all 124 students. Two weeks later, I escaped by bus back to Kandahar because dozens of my other classmates had escaped from the military school. My father asked me to return to the school, which I did. After another two weeks, however, I again escaped by bus back to Kandahar. When the military school sent letters to my parents ordering them to send me back, my father and uncles once more asked me to go back to Kabul.

My Third Escape

On my third return to the military school I was beaten. That night, when I walked into the dining hall, a lieutenant stood in the shadows watching us. We waited in a line, walking past a server who poured soup into our bowls from a huge pot. I stood behind a student who said something nice about the school. I still remember his name and his face as if it were yesterday. He was Sahar gul. From the rear I flipped his cap off his head and it fell forward into the big pot of soup. The lieutenant rushed out from the shadows, called everyone to attention, marched all of us out of the hall, and ordered us to low crawl on our knees and elbows in the gravel. My classmates were angry at me for causing them the punishment. This was not the first time, though, that we had to low crawl. For small infractions we were often forced to march and then low crawl through the rocks. I had bruises on my forearms from previous low crawls. But this time the punishment got worse.

The lieutenant stopped everyone and yelled at us to stand up and form a line. He ordered me to step forward in front of him. Then he repeatedly slapped me hard on the face. It was late at night in

November and in Kabul it was freezing. At the military school, when ordered to march, you must continue until told to stop. The lieutenant marched me into a canal. I was forced to step and sink into the ice-cold water. Another higher ranking officer, a major, was on night duty and saw what was happening to me. He was a medical doctor and called me out of the water. He ordered the lieutenant to stand at attention. Nose to nose he yelled, "Are you killing him? He is a boy! Are you human?"

I was confined to the barracks for an indefinite time and was not permitted to leave the camp. Everyone in the camp knew what had happened to me. I was treated very badly and I hated it. I wanted to get an education. The military school was a dead end for all the students and me.

There were 900 students at the military school. My class had 60 remaining students. A classmate said, "Let's escape!" Another said to me, "You will never escape again." I defiantly replied, "I will escape but you will not." Determined to show him, I walked over to the officer on duty and said, "I want to use the latrine." He called a common soldier to accompany me to the building containing the latrines. It backed up to a large wall. The trench under the latrines was filled with dung and pee. It extended under the wall and to the outside of the military compound. Today this military school is used by the US military to train the Afghan military.

Inside the building individual stalls were separated by brick partitions. I walked into a stall and looked down into the big hole. I closed my eyes, held my breath, jumped into the smelly trench, slid through the dung, and felt my way out to the other side of the wall.

After emerging from the dark trench, I stood shivering in the freezing winter wind. I took off my stinky uniform and boots and ran in my long underwear and bare feet toward the bazaar in Kabul to my uncle Ka Ko Jan's shop where he sold pomegranates and other fruit. It was about a mile and a half away.

My older brother, Wahid, and several cousins were also visiting at the shop. My cousins were in Kabul attending a regular military school to become officers. It was a Thursday. Our family members in Kabul usually gathered on Thursday and Friday evenings. I smelled and looked terrible. Surprised, my uncle asked, "What are you doing here?" I explained. Still shivering, I took off my long underwear, washed, and put on clean civilian clothes that previously I had stored in a trunk in his shop. As usual my cousins made fun of me. My brother scolded them and ordered them to stop.

I did not realize then that it was regarded as an offense to disrespect one's military uniform. It was also a crime to escape from the military compound. A year later I had to pay for the stinky uniform and boots left outside the camp latrine.

Back to School

My brother bought me a bus ticket and I returned to Kandahar. My parents were happy to see me. I gradually explained the story of my escape. The Army sent letters each week to my parents asking them to send me back to the school. This time they ignored the letters.

Instead I started working for a German power company in Kandahar which produced electricity. It was within walking distance from my home--about two and a half kilometers. I worked very hard cleaning old machine parts and was paid very well. When I was in the fourth grade, I had started learning German from my brother, Wahid. So I was able to communicate with the Germans…a little bit.

A month later, in December, although it was three months after the school year had begun, I unofficially started attending the seventh grade in Kandahar. It was at the Ahmad Shah Baba High School, a civilian school. After school hours, Syed Ahmad Shah volunteered to be my tutor and teach me English for the next four years. He told my father that if I did not make effort to learn, he would not waste his time to teach me. I got good grades (except for drawing) and was determined to do well. When the seventh grade final exam was ready, I was desperate to take it. Syed took me to the superintendent of schools and requested that I be allowed to take the exams. At first the superintendent did not agree and argued that I was under the authority of the Minister of Defense. Syed convinced him, however, to unofficially allow me to take the exams. He agreed and I scored very high on the tests.

During the summer vacation, my cousin, Ghulam Nabi, came home from training at a military school. He later rose to the rank of general and now lives in London. He saw me lying on the floor and we started talking. In frustration he said, "I want to delay two weeks before returning to school." "Don't do that," I replied. My mom heard it and scolded me, "How can you give that advice? You are a loser. You escaped from the military school." Frustrated and without thinking, I threw a spoon over my head and accidentally hit her on the forehead. In no way did I think that the spoon would hit my mother. I felt very bad. I was both embarrassed and scared; so I ran away.

I hurried to the German power company. On the way there I made up my mind to go to the Minister of Defense to clear up the trouble caused by my escape from the military school. I didn't know what would happen. He could send me back to the military school. I knew he could also send me to prison. However, I wanted to tell my story. I earned good grades in school and wanted to accomplish something with my life. I explained to the German manager in charge, Mr. Bullock, that I was going to Kabul that day and asked for my salary.

It was almost at the end of the school summer vacation. I was so determined that I just left my home without telling my parents that I was leaving. I took no clothes and bought a bus ticket to Kabul. When I arrived in Kabul, I bought some clothes and rented a room for five Afghanis a day; it had no furniture or bed. I spent three Afghanis a day for food which was enough for tea and bread. At that time in 1960, 60 Afghanis was about one US dollar. Although I had the equivalent of 1000 US dollars earned from working, I conserved my money. I knew how hard it was to earn it.

Standing Before the General

I searched and located civilian legal advisors. They wanted money paid up front for their services. I paid them and explained my story while one advisor wrote it down. I emphasized that I was misled: when in the sixth grade, I was told that I would become a pilot, but was drafted into an anti-aircraft school. I stressed that I wanted to continue my education. Of course, I did not mention my stinky escape. The legal office prepared a document with my explanation and I delivered it in the morning to the office of the Minister of Defense, General Khan Mohammed Khan.

"…Just Came Out of My Mouth"

My appointment was for 2 p.m. I first met the general's aide-de-camp. He asked me whether I had submitted my legal document earlier in the morning; I said, "Yes." Escorting me through tall doors into the three-star general's office, the aid said, "Go, General Khan wants to talk to you." Usually the general would not speak directly to an underage boy. I was just 14 years old and scared. After I walked in and stopped in front of his desk, General Khan looked at me, pointed to a paper on his desk and asked, "Is that your paper?" I could see that it was and replied, "Yes. If I could have told you in person myself, I would not have brought it to you in writing." Those words just came out of my mouth. General Khan was surprised by what I said and so was I. He was the top general in the country!

His face was a little friendly. I said, "I want to go to regular military school," thinking that it would lead to graduation as an officer. General Khan was aware that I had escaped from the anti-aircraft school. He responded, "Why don't you raise dogs for fighting?" Dog fighting is what gangsters did in Afghanistan. I quickly replied, "If I wanted to do that, I would not come here to see you." General Khan liked that answer and became more friendly. He knew my parents in Kandahar since he had formerly been the Governor of Kandahar as well as the Army Corps General in Kandahar. A few years ago he passed away in San Diego, California.

I explained my entire story and reasons for my escape. General Khan then agreed to help me and referred my appeal to the Military

Department of Education. I started walking out of his office when General Khan called me back and said, "If you run into difficulty again, return to my office."

Next I was assigned to a regular military school. There the official in charge wanted to put me back into the sixth grade. However, I was already in the eighth grade. So I returned to General Khan and protested, "But I am 14 years old, too old for the sixth grade." He replied that it was the law that I go to the sixth grade. General Khan asked whether I would like to attend a civilian school. "Yes," I answered. He asked, "Will you pay for all the expenses that you incurred while at the military school?" "Yes, I will." That week I was informed of the amount that I had to pay. It was 1300 Afghanis for everything: from transportation to Kabul, uniforms, boots, and meals. I paid it immediately with money earned at the German company.

General Khan, in his position as the Minister of Defense, called the civilian Minister of Education and explained, "This young boy is highly motivated for education. He is already in the eighth grade. Currently he is stuck in the military system which requires him to be in the sixth grade. Can you accept him back into the civilian system?" The Minister of Education requested General Khan to send me to his office. When he arranged for me to be discharged from the military school system and assigned me to the civilian system, I was very happy.

They Both Closed Their Eyes

I had good luck because both the civilian and military Ministers of Education could have denied my request and fired the Kandahar Provincial School District Superintendent for allowing me to take the seventh grade tests. I had escaped from the military school and was in legal trouble. Fortunately, they recognized that I was highly motivated and my desire to get an education was very strong. So they both closed their eyes and allowed me to go forward with my life.

When I think about it, I was very brave, which surprised both government ministers. I lived in a culture where younger people were to remain silent, take orders, and talk only when asked to talk. To do otherwise was to receive severe punishment.

My experience with the Ministers of Defense and Education taught me that I could accomplish a great deal if I didn't give up. Even if I failed, I could still be successful in building my character. It prepared me for hardships ahead and taught me how to talk to high-level officials.

In the Western culture it is okay to talk to anyone. In an Eastern culture like Afghanistan, though, a highly sensitized respect for position restrains open and spontaneous talking. It would be impolite and disrespectful to do so. Any question must be carefully crafted. The same applies with family members or elders. Regardless of your rank, when giving speeches, you must respect the age, social and family position of others. When you teach someone older than yourself, especially someone who has higher authority, you must learn the best way to be respectful. A few years later, as a student at Kabul University, when I first began to tutor King Mohammad Zahir Shah in English, every time he moved, I would stand. Recognizing that the strictness of my respect for his position interfered with my teaching and his learning, he put me at ease and said, "I am your student. You are my teacher."

So on with my story: The civilian Minister of Education wrote a letter that assigned me to a school in my hometown of Kandahar. I returned there after one month of absence. My mother was so relieved. She thought that either I was lost or had killed myself. In the eyes of my classmates, I had returned as a hero. The superintendent greeted me and advised me that I was behind in attendance and needed to catch up on much homework. My school was supported by Americans from the seventh to twelfth grades.

Before and after my return, I always had perfect attendance. I was not one minute late. For the next six years I ate no lunch. Although I had money, I had no time since I also taught Pashto and Afghan culture to my Peace Corps friends. They paid me 40 Afghanis per hour. The principal of my school was paid 1200 Afghanis per month.

Minimum wage in the workplace was 300 Afghanis per month.

I had some good teachers. One of them was Ghulam Nabi Affendi, my high school teacher in the Ahmad Shah Baba High School in Kandahar. He motivated my classmates and me to be honest, respect all human beings, and to value freedom and democracy.

"You Could Be Sent to Jail"

One year later, while on summer vacation, I was contacted by a military lawyer to come to Kabul to appear before a board of military officers. By then the anti-aircraft school had been dissolved. When I stood before them, I explained my entire story and showed them the orders from the Minister of Defense to prove that I had been released from the military. Also shown was a receipt for payment of all my military expenses. They said, "You are very lucky since you are underage. You could be sent to jail for many years." Fortunately, I was not prosecuted.

I had a strong desire to learn and educate myself and I studied hard. When doing my chores, I would lead my uncle's cow to an area near a canal to eat grass. With one hand I would hold a rope connected to the cow's neck, and in my other hand I would read an English book. My uncle saw me doing that and encouraged other family members to make similar efforts to study and learn English. In the early Sixties, there were few Afghans in Afghanistan who could read, write, and speak English. In junior high and high school I started teaching English to Afghans and continued tutoring Westerners about Pashto and Afghan culture.

US Cold War Competition

Those events occurred during the Cold War when many Americans visited and worked in Afghanistan. After WWII the US had begun strategic, economic investments in Afghanistan which continued until the Soviet invasion in 1979. Afghanistan was a non-aligned nation where the US competed against the Soviet Union's "economic offensive" for influence. The US desired to maintain land-locked Afghanistan as a buffer state in South Asia, and prevent it from becoming a proxy of the Soviet Union to attack Pakistan, a US ally. Pakistan was targeted by the Soviets as a bridge to achieve its longstanding ambition to control the oil routes in the Persian Gulf.

President John F. Kennedy supported the strategic vision of his two predecessors that linked alleviating poverty and improving education globally with lessening the chances of war. As part of that vision, Peace Corps volunteers were sent to Helmand and Kandahar Provinces in southern Afghanistan. They were well received by ordinary Afghans. Peace Corps volunteers served as lab technicians, nurses, advisors to farmers, and English teachers in high schools. The volunteers were young, energetic, respectful, and very friendly with me and other young Afghans. They lived among the people. Although their housing was much better in comparison to how common Afghans lived, it was modest compared to the accommodations of US Embassy and the United States Agency for International Development (USAID) workers. If those individuals were to return to Afghanistan or any country like it in a similar capacity, they would be very successful because they had grassroots experience and were humble enough to respect and serve the people.

Many of the Peace Corps volunteers became my friends and I began tutoring them in the Afghan languages and culture. As I increased my proficiency in English and gained more experience tutoring them, it was necessary to increase my knowledge and skills for both Western and Afghan culture and languages.

Intercultural Challenges

In the tenth grade I interpreted for Peace Corps nurses who were serving in both the men's hospital and women's hospital in Kandahar. Here is a story that shows the intercultural challenges that I faced. I was interpreting for Mary, a nurse from California. She requested that I ask an Afghan patient who was very skinny to lie down on his stomach on a table. I interpreted what she said into Pashto. He wore pants and a hospital sheet over his upper body.

Other Afghan nurses being trained stood around in the room watching. Suddenly, without telling me what she was going to do, she gently pulled down the patient's pants just enough to show a bit of his butt where she gave him an injection of medicine. The Afghan man became outraged and the nurses were also visibly offended and upset. So was I. Exposing a portion of a man's butt and touching it after he is seven years old, especially before other women, was regarded as sexual harassment in the Afghan culture. I asked Mary, "Why did you do that?" Shaken by the man's outrage and the other nurses' disapproval, she nervously replied, "I was helping him. When a person is as skinny as he is, the butt is the fleshy part to make an injection."

The incident was reported to the director of the hospital who was an Afghan. He politely explained to her, "I understand what you did, but unfortunately, the other Afghans do not." I was blamed as too young and immature to interpret for the nurse even though Mary defended me saying that she had not told me what she was going to do. No one else could be found to replace me. Therefore, I continued to interpret, translate, and tutor Westerners during my high school and college years, which were intense and difficult periods of learning. I was forced to ask more questions about my own Afghan culture and history, and about the American culture and language.

Being more cautious and culturally sensitive, when the American nurses would ask me questions, I would do additional research to determine the best answers. My family warned me, "Why are you going to people asking all those questions? People will get mad at you and beat you up." In my earlier years I looked only through the lens of Afghan culture and disapproved of many things those Western doctors and nurses did. However later, when I learned the value of what they did, I changed my mind about many things. My high school teacher, Ghulam Nabi Affendi, also encouraged my classmates and me to think globally beyond the borders of

Afghanistan, and to be concerned with building a better world. He was truly an inspiration to us.

Good Intentions--Not Good Enough

Interpreting and tutoring for other languages and cultures require serious study and experience. You must know what is regarded as good and bad in a culture, whether you agree with it or not. When dealing with sensitive human issues such as religion, health, family, and legal and tribal affairs, proper interpreting is more than just repeating words. Interpreters must understand the cultural context and even anticipate attitudes and actions. Today there are not enough experienced and skilled interpreters to serve the US military, US Government foreign affairs and civic action programs, or NATO. The wars in Afghanistan and Iraq are prime examples. Unqualified interpreters can cause tragic misunderstandings. Qualified interpreters, at the same time, can also be scapegoats for the mistakes of others.

Prime Minister Daoud

My escape from the anti-aircraft military school took place in 1960. Sardar Mohammad Daoud Khan, a member of the royal family, was Prime Minister at that time. His policies caused national crises, which led me and many other young teenage boys to be drafted into the military.

While holding the office of Prime Minister from 1953 to 1963, Daoud also controlled the military. He sought to modernize it and retake the territory along the Afghanistan-Pakistan border inhabited by indigenous Pashtuns to form an independent, sovereign "Pashtunistan." The word means "land of Pashtuns." That led Afghanistan on a collision course with Pakistan and increasing dependence on the Soviet Union.

Daoud attempted to extract aid, development and military assistance from the two superpowers, the US and the Soviet Union. He felt increasingly pressured to turn toward the Soviets for aid and believed that he could do so without losing US assistance. Through 1954 and 1955, Afghanistan's requests for military aid had been rejected by the US. Although the US was willing to give economic aid in exchange for an air base in Shindand District, it was not willing to give military aid. The US did not want to arm Afghanistan and aggravate relations between Pakistan and Afghanistan.

At that time General Muhammed Omar was a colonel in the Ministry of Defense and worked closely with Prime Minister Daoud. Later he would become my brother-in-law. According to General Omar, when Daoud discovered that US officials had shown Pakistan officials his aid requests, he became furious.

Daoud told King Mohammad Zahir Shah that he would ask the Soviet Union for the aid. The King initially opposed the idea and wanted to consider all options. Daoud forcefully pushed ahead and the King did not stop him. I heard from one source that the King said his confrontation with Daoud was the only time anyone had ever shown great anger toward him. Daoud was part of the royal family. He was the cousin and brother-in-law of the King, married to the King's sister.

Daoud went to the Soviet Union and requested aid. Premier Nikita Khrushchev happily agreed to provide both economic and military aid without any conditions—in contrast to the US. He immediately poured military hardware into Afghanistan such as jet planes, tanks, heavy and light artillery, in addition to economic aid.

The Soviets knew that if they provided arms to Afghanistan, the country's young men would need training to operate them. Through the training they could be influenced to be pro-Soviet. By the end of the 1950s, Daoud had converted the Afghan military from the Turkish system to the Soviet system.

The first treaty with the Soviets was a Non-Interference Treaty in which both Afghanistan and the Soviet Union agreed not to interfere with one another. The second treaty was to provide arms at a much discounted rate, and to expand trade, for instance, for wool and fruits.

In 1960, Prime Minister Daoud, desiring to establish Pashtunistan along the Afghanistan-Pakistan border, sent troops across the

Durand Line into Bajaur to retake an area regarded as Afghan territory. The Durand Line is an artificial border line created by the British in 1893 to separate then India from Afghanistan. The incursion was a critical threat to the Pakistan Government whose policy was to keep Afghanistan weak and prevent it from claiming territory along the Durand Line. Afghan military forces were badly defeated by local Bajaur Pashtun tribesmen. Those events were likely reasons that caused teenagers like me to be drafted into the anti-aircraft course.

The Pakistan Government was angered by the attack, and in 1961 closed its borders to Afghanistan, thereby creating an economic crisis in Afghanistan. That forced Afghanistan more toward the Soviet Union which provided alternative routes to transport Afghanistan's agricultural products to India.

Closing the borders prevented the movement of food back and forth between the two countries. That hurt people on both sides of the Durand Line. Half of my extended family lives on the Afghanistan side and the other half on the Pakistan side. Both suffered from the closure of the borders. For many years the father-in-law of my aunt on my mother's side had a large fruit export business. He transported raisins from his vineyards in Kandahar to the port in Karachi, Pakistan. When the Afghanistan-Pakistan border was closed, he was prevented from shipping his raisins to India, which then rotted in the port. That bankrupted him as well as many other Afghan and Pakistan merchants. On the Pakistan side, food prices suddenly rose as fruit supplies decreased.

Daoud's policies were causing mounting economic emergencies and confrontations with Pakistan. At the same time, King Mohammad Zahir Shah wanted his government to be a constitutional monarchy similar to that of Britain. One of its provisions was that the King and the Prime Minister could not be from the same family. For more than one reason, therefore, the King in March 1963 requested Daoud's resignation as Prime Minister. Daoud agreed and was replaced by Dr. Mohammed Yousuf, a dynamic member of the

Cabinet who was very effective, improving relations with other countries such as Egypt, India, and Germany. He was also a strong advocate for freedom of speech.

3
LESSONS FORGOTTEN OR DISREGARDED

During those turbulent times, America invested heavily in Afghanistan to maintain a strategic position in South Asia. Most Americans have little or no knowledge or memory of that, and of the "Little America" that was built in Lashkar Gah, Helmand Province. It was the Cold War era during the formative years of my life when I grew into a young man.

From Law to Agronomy

Since the fourth grade I had always scored well in history and geography and had hoped to make improvements in society. At the same time, life was hard as a farmer, especially in a poor country like Afghanistan. I did not want to continue with that impoverished way of life. Upon completing high school, I had planned to study law. My college placement test scores were high and qualified me to enter the law school at Kabul University. I had to wait nine months, though, for the law school to reopen because it was closed in winter. You see, the school years in Afghanistan were organized by the seasons. In Kandahar, due to the extreme heat, schools were closed during the summer months, June to September. In Kabul all schools were closed during the winter, due to the severe cold and snowfall. So it was that I entered Kabul University in the spring of 1969.

I Knew What Hunger Felt Like

While law was my original choice of study, I changed my mind and pursued a degree in agronomy. Here is why:

Dedicated USAID workers inspired my change of career. While waiting to begin my studies at Kabul University, I continued to interpret for the USAID, the US Bureau of Reclamation and US Geological Survey (USGS) engineers and specialists. They were working in Helmand and Kandahar Provinces and I taught them about Afghan culture. Many of them brought their families to live in Afghanistan during their tours of employment.

Sanford Caudill was among the first American engineers that I met, a person whom I admired and would work with for seven years. He headed a team of USAID specialists that helped Afghan farmers improve their irrigation systems and crop development. Sanford was a veteran of both World War II and the Korean War, and a dedicated, honest, and hard-working humanitarian who represented

the best of American ideals. At the time I thought that all Americans were like him. In this September 1969 photo I was traveling with Sanford and his wife Mildred as their interpreter and we had paused at the

Ma He Per Pass in Jalalabad.

Sanford and other Americans inspired me to believe that agronomists could enable Afghanistan to become agriculturally self-sufficient. I knew what hunger felt like and helping my people raise enough food was important to me. At the same time, the *Green Revolution* and the global movement to support sustainable farming were being promoted.

Those factors motivated me to change my studies from law to agronomy, which was not as prestigious as law. When I told a close friend that I was switching from law to agronomy, he joked, "So you want to become a dog washer?" Dogs were considered the lowliest creatures and were not allowed inside homes in Afghanistan. In spite of agronomy's lower prestige, the Department of Agronomy required higher test scores than the law school because its professors were Americans.

Cold War Nation-Building Lessons
Permit me to digress here to provide a larger historical context

for this stage of my life and for Afghanistan's development during the Cold War. It will better explain the challenges that Sanford was up against, and the lessons that US policy makers, the military, and the USAID *could* have learned to guide their policies and programs in Afghanistan after 9/11. They were ignored or forgotten.

Mistakes of the past are often repeated. America's previous Cold War foreign aid efforts in Afghanistan provide lessons and shed light on a question many Americans ask today, "Why is there so little result from our billions of dollars invested in Afghanistan's development?" The lessons are also useful for Afghan officials who are genuinely dedicated to advance their country's best interests.

Immediately after WWII and before the Soviet invasion of Afghanistan in 1979, Sanford Caudill was part of an almost three-decades-long period of US foreign aid investment in Afghanistan. Its purpose was to further the Truman Doctrine of containing Soviet expansion. The doctrine's basic idea was that totalitarian regimes like the Soviet Union would gain control over independent nations that were impoverished and weakened by internal conflict. Therefore, the US had the moral obligation to help those nations and prevent them from falling into the Soviet orbit and "going Communist." In Afghanistan, US foreign aid was primarily directed through the Helmand-Arghandab Valley Authority (HAVA).

King Mohammad Zahir Shah and his Royal Government of Afghanistan (RGA), especially Prime Minister Daoud, wanted to stabilize and strengthen Afghanistan's economy and political control by modernizing its agricultural, industrial, and military sectors. Modernization in the twentieth-century, though, had been resisted by Afghanistan's traditional agrarian society divided by many ethnic and tribal rivalries. While attempting to modernize Afghanistan, the RGA sought to maintain the country's neutrality and not become dependent upon the Soviet Union or any Western nation. Daoud, though, moved Afghanistan closer to the Soviet Union to offset what he viewed as the King tilting the country toward the West.

Make a Desert Bloom

In 1946, with accumulated cash reserves from selling food products to the Allies in India and karakul (high-quality lamb's skin) on the New York and London markets, the RGA hired Morrison Knudsen Afghanistan (MKA). It was a subsidiary of Morrison Knudsen Company (MKC), which was an engineering and construction firm from Boise, Idaho. Afghan officials in Kabul were confident that they could buy needed foreign technology and hire engineers to irrigate publicly-owned desert lands in the Helmand-Arghandab Valley and make them bloom for nomads (Kuchis) and landless farmers to farm.

The irrigation project was intended to expand agricultural areas, improve crop yields and the standard of living for farmers, and reduce the import of food, which would also preserve foreign exchange. It was an overly ambitious technological undertaking. Later USAID studies would conclude that both Afghan officials and MKA made major technical errors and cross-cultural miscalculations. They overestimated the project's benefits and underestimated its negative ecological and human impact, and its costs.

The RGA's objective was to persuade fiercely independent nomads, who were herders by tradition, to move into the Helmand Valley and there change their way of life and resettle the newly irrigated desert as farmers. Moving some of the one to two million nomads from along the Pakistan (India before 1947) borders was intended to integrate them into a national economy and minimize their skirmishes with Pakistan. That shifted the irrigation project into a rural development program.

The first contract assignments were to build two diversion dams, and renovate and extend the Boghra Canal into the areas designated to be irrigated for farming: Nad-i-Ali and Marja terrace tracts and the Shamalan floodplains. Tragically, half-way through the project the areas were observed to be unsuitable for farming.

A Top-Down Plan

From the beginning, the Helmand Valley Project was a top-down plan by government officials in Kabul who did not understand the ecological impact that building two dams and renovating the canal and other changes would have. They also had little consideration for the villagers who would be forced to manage new water flows from the dams on a wide range of soil qualities. A USAID report concluded that both Afghan officials and MKA technicians ignored the human problems. American anthropologist, Louis Dupree, observed that they were unable to adequately answer how "will the old villagers [who had lived along the river system for generations] be prepared to use the extra, off-season water? Who will tell them?" The reply of officials was that the farmers have known for centuries how to manage water. In reality, villagers could not even imagine the magnitude of the water coming from the massive dams which would eventually flood their villages.

MKA expected that the Afghan officials would inform the farmers. When asked how they would attract and settle nomads, the officials vaguely responded that it was only necessary to offer land to the nomads and that they would come because land was their most important desire. That was far from reality. Economic incentives and social support services would further be required that were not on the central government's drawing boards.

Beginning in 1954, 5500 nomads and existing farmers were resettled on the lands. Under protest, many were forced onto the land by military escort. Once there, intense ethnic rivalries among the nomads eventually pressured a large number of them to leave the valley. Prior to beginning settlement, the nomads and existing valley farmers were not trained in water management and irrigation methods to control the large, new water flows. There was also no plan in place for land distribution and title transfers.

MKA was directed to begin the Boghra Canal renovation project without extensive groundwater and soil surveys. Reluctantly MKA agreed. Midway through the project in 1948, when costs had exceeded original estimates, MKA workers observed that the areas targeted for irrigation had fundamental soil problems: they were shallow, poorly drained, were saline in various places, or had waterlogging and high water tables. Waterlogging occurs when soil is so wet it chokes off needed oxygen for plants to grow. It destroys crops and leads to desertification. To make matters worse, the half-renovated main canal was wrongly located for proper gravity water flow and drainage.

The Minister of National Economy and other Afghan officials and MKA were faced with a critical dilemma. If the project was ended at that point, their mistakes would have been exposed and it would have been a loss of face and prestige for all of them. At the same time, continuing with the irrigation plan would aggravate the already degraded soil conditions in the project areas and undermine future efforts to develop the valley and successfully resettle families.

Afghan officials and MKA decided to proceed; MKA further recommended that to make the best use of the renovated canal, another storage dam and reservoir were needed to achieve the irrigation objectives. Initially MKA was reluctant to again proceed without a complete field survey of the valley to assess whether there was enough water to irrigate the targeted areas. Nonetheless, again MKA agreed with its boss, Afghan officials in the RGA, to continue without a survey. They all decided to push ahead even if there was "a 20 percent margin of error in estimating the acreage or water supply."

The building of another dam and reservoir expanded the original project and pushed the RGA beyond its financial capacity and administrative abilities. Those decisions and degraded soil conditions proved to be fatal weaknesses that compromised the Helmand Valley Project, which would evolve to become the cornerstone of US development and nation-building efforts in Afghanistan for the next three decades. It would be a "rocky and soggy" history.

As a for-profit company, MKA's overriding priority was profit for its shareholders and not the long-term benefits for the people of Afghanistan. MKA could not make a profit unless the RGA received a development loan because it had just about depleted its foreign exchange reserves paying MKA for its services. This is where the US came into the picture and tied its prestige to salvaging the efforts of

MKA, a private contractor.

US foreign policy interests overshadowed the serious soil, engineering, economic and social planning defects of the Helmand Valley Project. It was the Cold War era and the US feared that Afghanistan would become economically dependent upon the Soviet Union. In northern Afghanistan the Soviets were engaged in Premier Nikita Khrushchev's "economic offensive" competing against the US by providing the RGA in 1955 with a US $100 million development loan to build hydroelectric, storage and diversion dams, irrigation systems, and roads to improve agricultural yields and distribution. Both the Soviet Union and the US held the unquestioned belief that they had the modern "know-how" and the ideology to make life better for underdeveloped countries like Afghanistan. President Harry S. Truman and the US presidents who followed him believed that they must compete with and contain Soviet expansionism. That prompted the US State Department to indirectly support the Helmand Valley Project in southern Afghanistan with US Export-Import Bank loans.

During 1949 to 1950, although the US Export-Import Bank initially approved a $21 million agricultural development loan to fund the proposed expanded capital improvements, funds to pay for important groundwater and soil surveys recommended by MKA and the RGA were deleted by the bank from the loan request. That would leave the project's defects to be further aggravated and fester.

HAVA Provided Social Benefits

As a loan condition, the RGA created the multipurpose Helmand Valley Authority (HVA) in 1952, which was modeled after the Tennessee Valley Authority (TVA) in America. Later it would expand to become the Helmand-Arghandab Valley Authority (HAVA). American engineers led the building of the 200-foot-high Arghandab (Dahla) Dam and 320-foot-high Kajaki Dam. At the same time, the HAVA gradually delivered rural social services to the resettled nomads and existing farmers, which was also a condition of the development loan. By the mid-1960s the HAVA became an agency that attempted to integrate the development of schools, hospitals and health care, housing and utilities, communications, agricultural research and extension. It even helped build Ariana Airlines, the national airlines of Afghanistan, and Kandahar Airport.

The US continued to fund and expand the HAVA projects to keep alive its political relationship with the RGA and its strategic position in South Asia. A 1983 USAID study reported that approximately $111.5 million from the USAID and the US Export-Import Bank were poured into the HAVA from 1949 to 1979.

Progress was weighed down with the project's original engineering problems: the main canal was in the wrong location for proper water flows, there was inadequate drainage and waterlogging, and salinization in the soils was advancing. Floods fractured dams and spread salinating soils that destroyed crops. Water temperatures also fell in the reservoirs which caused the water to be unsuitable for certain crops such as vineyards.

The human side of the HAVA project continued to be neglected. The resettled nomads and traditional farmers in the valley were the end users of the monuments of modern technology--the dams and reservoirs. They were not educated, though, to understand their value and not trained to manage the massive amounts of waters that would come their way. It was similarly so for the use of high-yield seeds and fertilizers. It is fair to say that, at the time, those mistakes were not unique to Afghanistan and could be observed in other countries such as Egypt.

The Green Revolution

The problems became too big to ignore. During the Sixties and Seventies, the US took more direct involvement in Afghanistan. The Kennedy and Johnson Administrations renewed funding for the HAVA projects which included a new Green Revolution initiative to develop education and support systems for individual farmers. The US Bureau of Reclamation replaced MKA in 1960 to correct the fundamental irrigation and drainage problems that existed from the beginning of the Helmand Valley Project. I interpreted for the specialists at the US Bureau of Reclamation as they attempted to settle the nomads on the lands.

Progress Yes, But Unsustained

Sanford and other specialists from US agencies did the best that they could, considering the earlier engineering and political mistakes made by Afghan officials and MKA, the advancing soil degradation, and inherent cross-cultural communication problems. I interpreted for them while I attended high school and college and during my school vacations. During those years I saw progress being made on the farms and I was hopeful.

In late July, 1970, while I was working for the USAID and a US Geological Survey (USGS) team as their interpreter/transl ator in Helmand and Kandahar Provinces, I took them on hunting trips looking for mountain goats.  This photo was taken by a USGS engineer traveling with us on one of those hunts.

Drainage Systems Improved

USAID engineers worked to build over 24 miles of large irrigation drainage systems with spurs that led to the Turnak River, which in turn connected to the Helmand River. It was an important advancement for the Afghan people. Before drainage systems had been laid, villages were usually flooded during the rainy seasons, and the water tables were very high causing salt to be forced to the surface and ruin crops. Now the rains would become a constructive force rather than a destructive force. The drainage systems made it possible for farmers to cultivate thousands of acres of land and expand their production of crops. Many farmlands became fertile and received a rating of grade one. Serviceable roads were also built on each side of the large drains.

A 1973 USAID analysis reported that by then a basic infrastructure had been established to maintain "water command" of the dams and reservoirs in the Helmand-Arghandab Valley. Also the "region's farmers have taken the critical first step required to move from subsistence farming to management of modern inputs" by using fertilizers, improved seeds, and tractors.

High-Yield Seeds and Fertilizers

Irrigated areas in the Helmand Valley were expanded. New high-yield seeds and fertilizers were distributed and gradually used by farmers. Wheat crop yields and farm net incomes had generally multiplied, although they varied widely. There was the expectation that a new phase of crop yields would "take off." Unfortunately, the 1971 El Niño drought destroyed many of those crops, and diminished monsoon rains blocked progress for the following two years.

When the HAVA project funding was scheduled to end in 1974, USAID officials recommended that it not be renewed. Again, though, the foreign policy priority of containing Soviet expansionism led Secretary of State Kissinger to override their recommendation and the HAVA's funding was continued.

Stagnation

By 1975 crop yields had stagnated in the newly settled areas of Marja, Nad-i-Ali, and Shamalan because of the poor soil quality resulting from salinity, drainage problems and waterlogging. They limited the net incomes of even the most experienced farmers. The resettled nomads' lack of experience and farming knowledge and inequitable government credit policies locked many nomads into poverty and forced them to move away and return to their nomadic lands. When the Soviets invaded in 1979, the HAVA project was terminated.

Important Lessons from US Cold War Foreign Aid

Inadequate and Top-Down Planning

Afghan government officials imposed a top-down agricultural program which was not adequately planned nor did it factor in the needs of the ultimate users of the dams and irrigation systems, seeds and fertilizers. The officials also did not understand the ecology and soils in Helmand and Kandahar Provinces since they repeatedly declined to conduct soil surveys to save monies. The US had no real partnership with the Afghan Government that required it to make changes necessary for agrarian and social reform. There was "no agreed overall plan defining exactly the concrete results [HAVA] intended to gain, and how they [were] to be gotten." The US was primarily concerned with maintaining a strategic geopolitical relationship with Afghanistan and other issues took a back seat to that priority.

Saving Face, Making a Profit, Corruption

In 1949, Afghan officials sought to cover up their mistakes. Both they and MKA gave priority to saving face rather than to the needs of the nomads and farmers and success of future development.

The 1973 USAID analysis stated that MKA had general development responsibilities because its decisions would impact 40% of Afghanistan. MKA's engineering and construction was criticized for being "a classic example of the backward approach to irrigation development." It was basically *fire, aim, ready*. Dams were built first, lands were then prepared for irrigation, then soils tested, then settlers were taught how to irrigate. MKA did what was immediately expedient without concern for the long-term impact on the Afghan people. Specifically, MKA was regarded as responsible for the decision to build the Kajakai Dam, continuing land development without completing adequate soil surveys, and underestimating the gypsum deposits and dumps which occurred beneath and beside the canals. Therefore, MKA decisions contributed to the failures in the Helmand Valley that occurred after it left Afghanistan.

The US, through the US Bureau of Reclamation and the USAID, was saddled with making the best of MKA's compromising decisions.

Attempts to correct the improperly positioned main canal and realignment of farming plots did not occur until MKA was replaced with the US Bureau of Reclamation. Genuine attention to assessing the needs of farmers was not given until the 1970s.

A 1983 USAID study reported that "[c]orruption on the part of Afghan officials is a frequently voiced complaint. 'They will agree to anything to get a project approved and get the equipment they want, and then they won't make good on those agreements.'" The study added, "Corruption, often, is a matter of cultural definition." In Chapter 7 I explain how I was assaulted by the Minister of Agriculture after disclosing the corruption of his cousin in a USAID sponsored fertilizer distribution program.

Lack of Genuine Communication

Language and cultural differences created barriers to understanding and cooperation. In hindsight the USAID recognized that few American advisers at the HAVA spoke an Afghan language and few Afghans spoke English. It was no surprise that Americans and their Afghan counterparts at the HAVA worked and lived separately. The HAVA headquarters, located in Lashkar Gah, the capital of Helmand Province, was an isolated oasis in the desert for American employees working there and became what Afghans would call "Little America." The BBC has provided a collage of photos and film from the 1950s recorded by Glenn Foster, a former employee of MKA, which captures the lives of ordinary Afghans and Americans working in Helmand and Kandahar Provinces. It was regarded as a "Golden Age" in those two provinces.

You might expect that Afghan officials at the HAVA would have regularly communicated with the Afghan farmers. Not so. A USAID study noted that "[n]ot only was communication between H[A]VA and the Americans a problem, but there was also a long-standing, tacit H[A]VA policy not to communicate with farmers." The Afghan staffs at the HAVA were, like the Americans, regarded as outsiders by the nomads and farmers. Without adequate communication between all parties, a project will likely fail on some fundamental level.

Overreliance on Technology

USAID workers discovered that modern technology did not always produce better sustainable yields. Agricultural technology must be adapted to the unique physical and cultural environments of a region. USAID specialists personally experienced that in the HAVA project.

I interpreted for Dr. Pillsbury from the USAID. He was a nice man and an agronomy professor at Kabul University where he regularly encouraged me to become one of his students. He was so insistent that one day a Peace Corps volunteer with us lightheartedly joked, "Don't brainwash him!"

Dr. Pillsbury knew that Afghan farmers traditionally let grape vines hang in ditches. At first he had advised them to hang grape vines on trellises presuming that suspending the vines above the ground could potentially result in a 50 percent increase in yield. He was unaware, though, that those dirt-poor farmers could not afford the posts and wires needed to construct the trellises. More importantly, Dr. Pillsbury was not aware of the danger posed by wasps and bees in the region. The trellises would expose the upright, hanging grapes to the bees and wasps, which could destroy the entire crop. Later, when he discovered those facts, he realized that his advice could actually lead to greater crop destruction.

Village Development:

Learn and Support from the Bottom Up

If USAID advisors did not generally speak directly with farmers, as the 1983 USAID study reports, Sanford Caudill was an exception. For many years, while in high school and at Kabul University, I worked for him part-time and full-time during my summer vacations. He followed my advice for how to respect the Afghan people and earn their trust. I interpreted for him when he traveled to the villages, taught him about the Afghan culture and to speak Pashto. Americans don't realize how different the Afghan culture is from the American culture. The pace of life is different. In the US things are done quickly. In Afghanistan quickness could be regarded as rudeness and be offensive. Sanford learned, for example, that Afghans are very sensitive to how the words *elder* and *leader* are used. Why? It is a religious reason: only God is the leader.

Genuinely Make Efforts to Help the People

Sanford further earned the trust of Afghans by his tireless dedication to help villagers in the most remote and inaccessible parts of Helmand and Kandahar Provinces. He routinely went to places no one else would go. We were amazed by how fearlessly Sanford drove his pickup through rocky areas.

Study the Village Social Network

It is important to work with people at the grassroots level in developing countries, and to respect people in their different social positions in a village. Sanford recognized that and the value of seeking the best advice from local Afghan cultural experts.

My father advised him about the fundamentals of earning the trust of local villagers from farmers to village chiefs and elders. He recommended that Sanford first go to the mullah in the village: "But don't go inside the mosque. Greet the mullah, explain to him that you are an engineer studying canals and ask, 'Who should I talk to?' He will tell you. There are other people above him in the local social network. There is the chief of the village and the tribal elder. It is very important to speak with them. Then cross-check and ask the farmers about the condition of the soil and water. Since farmers rarely own the land, then talk to the landlords to get their support." In this photo Sanford, on the left, bought  raisins from a farmer while I interpreted for him on the right.

Cross-Reference and Verify

Because Sanford respected all the people and asked good questions through the entire network of a village, he could cross-reference villagers' statements and determine who was telling the truth and who was not. In this way he learned to accurately understand the villagers' and farmers' basic needs. That enabled him to more effectively adapt modern agricultural technology to the unique physical environments in Kandahar and Helmand Provinces. In the end, Sanford was better able to support the villagers' capacity for self-reliance.

Eventually, the USAID recognized the importance of its specialists collaborating directly with farmers: "Although the American 'specialists' did not always fully understand the complex environment, when they did communicate with the Afghans, particularly the Afghan farmers, useful compromises could be found."

Sanford followed the advice of my father to gradually help poor farmers at the village level. That provided greater assurance that US dollars would be effectively used. Verification at the village level is a major part of the solution to countering corruption in US foreign aid programs whether in Afghanistan or in other countries.

Why is it important for Westerners in developed countries to wisely work with poor farmers and villagers in countries like Afghanistan? Self-interest, at least! The danger of expanding extremism is alarming. Impoverished countries can become incubators for terrorism; or they can become non-threatening members of the international community of nations and stable trading partners. The fundamental fight against extremism and terrorists taking control of underdeveloped countries occurs at the village level. Bottom-up support of villagers to be self-sufficient is also a solution for preventing poor countries from becoming safe havens for violent militant extremists to export terrorism.

Development Priorities

There are three basic capacity-building areas at the village level in developing countries that international development agencies should support: 1) teach villagers how to produce *food* to satisfy their essential nutritional needs; 2) instruct them about basic sanitation and *health care*; and 3) develop their literacy and basic *education*. Why? When you help people fill their stomachs and become healthy, they are less likely to feel resentment against you. Basic education enables villagers to make better critical, political, economic and social decisions. Satisfying those three needs at the village level are the foundations for democracy and positive foreign relations. Western developed countries can reap many benefits by supporting those efforts.

Building Cultural Bridges

Since I was the son of a farmer and reared on a farm, I taught Sanford and his USAID team how to work with Afghan farmers. I was learning, in turn, how to build cultural bridges between the East and West. Those types of experiences prepared me for my future role as the interpreter and Senior Cultural Advisor for US and NATO commanding generals in Afghanistan, in Europe, and in the US after 9/11.

Failure to Learn from History

Cultural intelligence plays an important role in winning the hearts and minds of people. In the nineteenth century, the Russians and British held a naïve belief that their military power was invincible in almost any circumstance. Repeatedly they would ignore decades of failed military intervention in Afghanistan. Lack of understanding and respect for tribal cultures contributed to those historic mistakes.

Since 9/11 US policy makers and officials, military leaders, and defense contractors have said, "We know it is important to understand cultural things and history." But how clearly do they know, and in Afghanistan, have they effectively applied those lessons from the past?

Would you be surprised if the same mistakes made during the Cold War through the HAVA were repeated after 9/11 in Afghanistan: that

- the US did not establish a genuine partnership with the Afghan Government that required it to make changes necessary for agrarian and social reform;
- top-down, inadequate control and administration from the Kabul central government was detached from the real needs of villagers;
- the overriding priorities of Afghan government officials and US private contractors were saving face and making a profit;
- corruption was widespread;
- the use of development dollars as agreed was not usually verified;
- there was an overreliance on technology; and
- a lack of genuine communication and cultural understanding at most operational levels undermined progress?

4

INTERPRETING FOR THE LAST KING OF
AFGHANISTAN

It was February 1969 when I met King Mohammad Zahir Shah in

Kandahar. He was visiting to thank USAID engineers for developing the canal drainage systems. In this photo courtesy of Sanford Caudill I am second from the right shown running to greet the King (in the middle). During the course of interpreting for him and the American engineers, the King asked me, "Where did you learn English...in America?" I replied, "No, I was tutored and learned it here in Kandahar." He was surprised. For some reason the King liked my interpreting. Asking whether I was going to Kabul, I answered, "Yes, I am enrolling at the University in the next few weeks." He continued, "Have you translated documents?" "Yes, I have." "Will you translate for me?" he asked. "Yes!" I happily replied. The King told his aide to arrange for me to begin translation work at the palace when I arrived in Kabul. There he had a cadre of translators, writers, and researchers for many languages working on various projects in the palace.

During the next four years I was among that group from which he selected to translate foreign magazines such as Time, Scala, Newsweek, Readers Digest, and National Geographic—his favorite magazine. When visiting ambassadors and other officials came to the palace, be it from the US, Europe, Australia, or Eastern Bloc countries, who spoke English, I also interpreted for the King.

Kabul University, when I entered it in 1969, was very international. Different countries provided educational materials and teachers for various disciplines. The schools of education, agronomy, and engineering were taught in English by Americans. French and Afghan professors taught at the Law School. Economics and science were taught by Germans. Students declared their major course of study upon entering Kabul University, although they could later change it. There were 180 students in my freshman class which was divided into sections of 30 students. I was in Section C and my student number was 1019.

The Demand to Teach English

My roommates and I lived in the dormitories with students from other schools within the university. Mir Rajan was one of my roommates and a family friend from Kandahar. Remember that name! Years later he would threaten my life as an agent of the new communist government.

The dormitories for the freshmen were at the Polytechnic School built and operated by the Soviets. Since all the textbooks were written in English and published in the US, my first year classmates in agronomy often came to my room asking me to translate their homework into Pashto or Farsi. It made sense to start holding English classes in my room. That, however, became so disruptive for my roommates that they urged me to find a different location for the classes. The only room available and close to my dormitory was in the Polytechnic School.

Reluctantly I went with my roommates to the Dean of that school requesting a room. He asked, "Why do you want one?" I replied, "My roommates complain that they cannot study with many students constantly asking me for help with English. It is for everyone's benefit." The Dean understood and gave me two rooms. From 9 to 11 p.m. at night I taught two one-hour classes each with about 40 students. They would ask me to translate homework questions from English to Pashto and Farsi. I wrote the translated questions on the blackboard and required the students to share them with other students in the school. We all helped one another regardless of our political or ethnic differences—and those differences were very strong. There was no need to motivate the students in my classes. They wanted to be there.

"Why Do You Charge Us More?"

Soviet professors noticed that the lights were on in my classrooms late at night and they were curious. The classrooms were on the third floor which they could see from where they lived in the adjacent building. The professors asked the Dean what was going on. He explained that a student was teaching English. They came to me at the end of a class and asked to attend. I said, "I charge the students 30 Afghanis per month." The exchange rate was 60 Afghanis per dollar then. I was willing to teach my classmates for free; however, my roommates said that I should charge something. I told the Soviet professors that my fee for them was 300 Afghanis per month. They tried to bargain with me saying, "Why do you charge us more money; we will sit in the same class?" I replied, "You have income, but the students do not." With the Dean's permission, 15 Soviets joined my class. Some were professors but most were their wives and they were very courteous.

Working with the King

One day while working in the King's palace library, the head librarian complained to me, "You are very impolite laughing around the King." Surprised I responded, "The King likes it when I laugh. I know when to laugh and not to laugh around the King." In the Afghan culture it is not polite to laugh in public gatherings and I respected that.

I could tell that the King liked me. He was not an arrogant man wanting people to bow down to him wherever he walked. The King by nature was serious and would rarely laugh; but sometimes he would smile. On several occasions in his spare time he would invite me to his farm and say, "Sher, would you like to come with me?" He would drive us without any security. On the farm the King would dress in ordinary clothes and together we would clip grape vines. You could not tell that he was a king. He was very humble and always polite to the workers on his farm. Since I had grown up on a farm and was a student of agronomy, he would ask me questions. When I did not have immediate answers for his questions dealing with the soil, I would research the question and confer with my professors. Other students were jealous of me. But I did not think that I was a more important person.

Three times per week I translated and interpreted for the King. I also worked part-time teaching languages and culture for the USAID, Peace Corps, and for other Western workers. I was exhausted studying and working 18 or more hours per day. My life was very different from my friends'. They had a leisurely schedule that allowed them time to socialize, play chess, go to the movies, and play cards. A few of them smoked hashish and drank. I did not and stayed healthy. When I did have a rare moment to relax and go to the movies with my friends, as soon as I would sit down, I would fall asleep.

The Motorbike and the Basketball Game

As a college student I earned a good income from my different jobs. One of my part-time jobs while attending Kabul University was to look after the children of Western workers who lived in Kabul. Sanford Caudill's teenage son, Bob, was on of them. I had rented an apartment in my name for Bob while he attended the American International School (AISK), a high school in Kabul. The apartment had three bedrooms. Sometimes I would stay overnight in one of them. I was not only Bob's big brother but also a big brother for many other American teenage boys and girls attending that school.

Previously I had worked for the USAID and their parents in Kandahar and Helmand Provinces as an interpreter. Privately the parents hired me to supervise and teach their kids local languages while they worked on the Kajakai Dam in Helmand Province and in other projects in Kandahar. They were mostly worried about keeping their kids out of trouble. One evening I was visiting Bob in his room when three Japanese girls came to the door. I turned them away and told him that no girls were allowed in his room. He didn't like that. Bob now lives in Washington State and we still joke about that.

The parents trusted me and I felt responsible to be a good role model for their children. They asked me to report whether their sons and daughters were having wild parties, consumed alcohol or smoked cigarettes. I tried to guide their teenagers as best I could. They had no interest in Afghan culture or languages and their high school was solely American and not intercultural. Since there was no TV available or Internet, social events were most important to them. Twice a week I would take them to a place where they could play their guitars and sing folk music. Other Afghans would join them.

It was the beginning of the Seventies. Kabul was a very different place then. It was known as the "Paris of Central Asia." It attracted tourists, hippies, and adventurers who delighted in the scenic beauty of the city's gardens and surrounding mountains. It may be hard to believe, but women working in offices and attending Kabul University dressed stylishly in knee-level skirts and even in miniskirts. In the City of Kabul, head scarves and burqas were optional. Women were also professors who taught at Kabul University and in high schools.

The Booming Motorcycle Upstairs

Bob Caudill was an independent and adventurous teenager. There is one special memory that I have of him. One day he bought an old, broken, disassembled 750 cc motorcycle. We carried its individual parts up the stairs and into the third, empty bedroom of his apartment for him to repair and reassemble. After a few months of tinkering, one evening about midnight, during a traditional Afghan celebration, there were fireworks. At the exact moment that the fireworks began, Bob had completed reassembling the motorcycle and kicked the starter. It caused a powerful boom. Exhaust and smoke filled the apartment. The engine roared and shook the entire building. People ran out thinking there had been an earthquake or an explosion. I yelled, "Turn it off," but Bob could not turn it off. The motorcycle continued to howl.

The next morning it was apparent that the huge motorcycle was too big to carry down the stairs. It was like trying to push an elephant through a narrow hallway. The solution was to lower it with ropes over the balcony and down to the ground. Six of us lowered the motorcycle, while another nine on the ground received it. It was not very safe, but it was funny. Onlookers pointing to Bob joked, "Look at that crazy American. He didn't think about getting the motorcycle down while he was assembling it." His motorcycle was the only one of its type throughout Kabul.

On several occasions Bob rode it to the dormitory where I lived. Some of my college roommates were famous basketball players. They and Bob arranged a basketball match between the American International School (AISK) and the sons of the Soviet professors. Employees from the US and Soviet Embassies, the USAID, and the teachers and students from AISK came to see the big game.

The gymnasium was packed with Americans on one side and Soviets on the other side, with Afghans mixed amongst both sides. Again, this was during the Cold War. I was not happy that the competition was being held, fearing that I would be blamed if anything went wrong. I don't remember who won; however, everyone was orderly and respectful. The players shook hands at the beginning and at the end. Later, when I was at the palace interpreting for the King, I told him about the game and he laughed.

5

AN OFFER I COULD NOT REFUSE

I was matched to Bibigula to be my wife when I was 26 years old. For three months I was unaware of it.

In the very cold winter of 1972, during my winter break, waiting to begin my last year at Kabul University, I was in Kabul working for the USAID. Bibigula's nephew, Abdul Qadir, was a close friend of mine and a medical student. He had just returned from Helmand Province. Today he is a doctor at the Lashkar Gah Hospital in that province. Upon arrival in Kabul he came to me and said, "Congratulations!" Surprised, I asked, "Why the congratulations?" "You are engaged," he answered. Thinking that he was joking, I replied, "Which donkey?" At 26 years old I had no thought of getting married, nor did I feel ready to get married. "Don't make fun of my aunt," he shouted. I was shocked. When Abdul said, "My aunt," I knew that he was not joking. Our families were close friends and I was aware that he had aunts, but I thought that they were all married and lived in Kabul or in Switzerland. So I asked Abdul who she was. He said, "She is my aunt from my father's side of the family."

In this way I came to discover that I was matched to Bibigula, who was then living in Helmand Province. Her family was from an upper class in the Afghan Government. Bibigula's father had once been the First Deputy Minister of Defense. One of her brothers was General Muhammed Omar. He was then the Chief of Staff for King Mohammad Zahir Shah. From time to time when I translated for the King, I met General Omar at public meetings. Bibigula's family was well known throughout Afghanistan and internationally. But I was not ready to get married.

Many thoughts raced through my mind: "Why should I take on this kind of responsibility? If I say 'no' to the engagement, no one will ever marry her, thinking that something is wrong with her. Plus we are from two different tribes that are not friendly with one another. Her future is in my hands. If I refuse, her family will be offended and anything is possible: they could take revenge on my family." I did not want to make my parents unhappy and an arranged marriage was the tradition in my country.

I said good-bye to Abdul, walked a long way and went on to my tutoring job. After work I continued to walk and contemplate, "This could be the brightest or the darkest day of my life. I trust my parents. They really love me and would not do anything to hurt me."

I was against forced marriages, though. My friends and colleagues knew this and I felt sad that I could not live by that ideal. I continued to walk and finally decided that I would agree to unconditionally accept her.

Matchmaking

Later I discovered how I had been matched to Bibigula. Our two families were close friends, often visiting one another. The ladies would meet and matchmaking was always a very interesting subject for them. In Kandahar City, Bibigula's sister-in-law had asked my mother whether she thought Bibigula and I would be a good match. Both Bibigula's parents had passed away and she was the youngest child of her father. Bibigula was living with her brothers and their families in Kandahar City, in Lashkar Gah--the capital of Helmand Province, and in Kabul. My mother knew her, but my father did not; so my mother took the lead and discussed the possibility of the match with him. They agreed and thought that it was a good idea.

My mother returned to Bibigula's sister-in-law and informed her that she and my father felt that it was a good match. She informed her husband, Bibigula's brother, Hajji Mohammed Hashim. They discussed the possibility of the match and finally agreed to it even though there were strong resentments between the tribes of our two families and resentments against me by members of Bibigula's family. Hajji Mohammed Hashim and Bibigula's nephew were strong advocates for me because they personally knew me for many years. Hajji Mohammed Hashim and his wife asked Bibigula for her permission for the match. She agreed.

In previous years my mother had recommended and sought my approval for three or four different girls as a match. I had declined each one because I was not ready to get married. My parents did not ask for my permission this time. They wanted to prevent me from again saying "no."

Hajji Mohammed Hashim sent one of his sons to my parents and informed them of their agreement and asked them to travel to Helmand where an engagement ceremony would be held according to Afghan tradition. That meant that neither Bibigula nor I were present. Up until the engagement ceremony everything was kept secret. No one knew of the match except for the family members. After the ceremony, though, the news was publicized widely. Everyone knew even before I did.

Our Wedding

A few months later, in March of 1973, I met Bibigula on the day of our wedding. It was held in Helmand Province in the huge villa of Bibigula's brother, Hajji Mohammed Hashim. Over a thousand people attended including my international friends like Sanford Caudill. Bibigula and I were separated in different rooms, one for the men and another for the women. Before the main religious ceremony, separate rituals were conducted for each of us. One of the rituals was for the mullah to place a cape over my shoulders. Bibigula and I then sent our representatives to stand before the mullah to confirm our commitment to our marriage. She sent her brother, Hajji Mohammed Hashim, and I sent my father, Hajji Mahmood. It is the custom that I would also stand beside them and Bibigula would remain in a different room. The mullah provided sacred words and final commitments were made. In our tradition, until the moment of the final marriage agreement, I was called a "boy;" afterward I was called a "man." Likewise, Bibigula was called a "girl" until the final marriage commitment, and then she was called a "woman."

The Silhouette

Before the wedding I was warned about a practical joke that

might be played on me. A long time ago, one of Bibigula's brothers-in-law married one of the ladies in our tribe. Tradition calls for the bride's family on the wedding night to set aside a special room for the bride and groom. My tribal people wanted to play a joke on him and directed him to a dark room with a small kerosene lamp. When he walked into the room, he saw a silhouette that he thought was his bride wearing a burqa. He sat on a mattress and *she* was still standing without saying anything. The tradition was for her to say, "As-Salaam-Alaikum," or some other friendly greeting. There was no response, though. He thought, "God help me in my future. These tribal people are very disrespectful." Then he heard some kids outside the door laughing. He knew then that something was wrong. Looking outside he saw other adults laughing who told him, "You are in the wrong room." A burqa had been put on a broomstick to appear as a woman in the dimly lit room.

When I was invited to go to a special room in the villa for our wedding night, I refused to go, thinking that the same joke would be played on me. Even my friends tried to pull me into the room. But I would not go. I said, "I want to go to my own hometown for our wedding night." They gave up on the joke and Sanford Caudill drove Bibigula and me to my home in Kandahar City.

"Hey, Boss!"

I began to learn how to be a husband and we began to learn how to love one another. It is the Afghan custom for newlyweds to give one another nicknames. Affectionately I called Bibigula "Boss," not because she tended to boss me. Not at all! She was very nice. Bibigula called me "My Heart." When we traveled together in a bus or walked together through the bazaar, she sometimes wore her burqa. I would often look to her and say, "Hey, Boss,..." We would get the strangest looks from people. In the past 40 years we have never been bitter toward one another.

Forced Marriage and Dowry

Let me say more about marriage in Afghanistan. First of all, there is a difference between the Islamic religion and Afghan

49

tradition. The Islamic faith requires a free-willed decision to marry. There are different ways that can occur: A man and woman can face one another and verbally agree in front of witnesses to form a marriage; or they could write to one another and state that they agree to marry one another, or have a representative agree on their behalf. On the other hand, for many centuries, as a matter of Afghan tradition, families would decide who would marry whom. The man and woman gave no independent agreement to marry. The boy's family was required to pay a dowry to the girl's family. If a father had five or six sons, it was difficult to pay a dowry for each one. When their families could not pay a dowry, many young Afghan boys were prevented from marrying.

Dowry is a bad practice because it undermines marriage and sets up women to be treated as slaves and become a basis for feuds between families. The boy's family could be resentful for paying a high dowry. Often his family would mistreat the girl and prevent her from visiting her family for several years. Those were causes for terrible feuds.

My friends and I were against forced marriages and dowries because women were treated as property until they became mothers. In the Afghan tradition, the mother is the boss inside her home and controls the finances. Sometimes a daughter-in-law lives in the same house with her mother-in-law, husband and children, and sometimes in a separate house with her husband and children. In both living arrangements the mother-in-law's influence and control over the daughter-in-law becomes less and less over time as the daughter-in-law gets older.

Historically there was another method of forming a marriage in Afghanistan referred to as a *calling marriage*. It was very rare, though. In the Afghan culture, if a man and woman decided to marry independent of their parents' selection, the woman would stand in the corner of a public square where people were passing by, and shout three times, "He (the name of the man) is my husband." The man did not need to be present. If two people heard her, that would satisfy the witness requirement for forming a marriage in Islamic law. This is an example where Afghan culture and Islamic law coincided and were not contradictory. If the woman lied and the man had not agreed to marry her, he could merely say one word—divorce—or publicly dispute her claim to end the marriage.

The calling marriage required great courage because, if the couple's parents did not support their marriage, it would be in defiance of their parental position to recommend a spouse. There could also be opposition from their communities due to religious and ethnic differences. Traditional Afghan communities would at best tolerate the marriage; but there would still be risks. The woman would have a bad reputation. Even among her grandchildren she would be known as the woman who *called*. The man, though, would not incur a bad reputation. The community would accept the calling marriage as long as the couple's relationship was in the open. If it was a hidden relationship, the community would not tolerate it.

While honor killings were not part of the Afghan tradition, when extremism gained influence within the villages and districts during the past few centuries, tolerance was often abandoned and honor killings occurred.

A typical arranged marriage in Afghan culture is one in which the parents recommend a spouse for their son or daughter, who then in turn freely agree to the recommendation. The decision to agree is motivated greatly by a sense of cultural honor. That was the tradition in villages. Both forced marriages and arranged marriages can be found in rural areas and they vary from region to region.

During the late 60s and 70s, westernization was expanding in the big cities of Afghanistan such as Kabul, Herat, and Mazar-i-Sharif. Primarily among the intellectuals, Afghan girls chose a husband based on whether he was educated, had a good job, and owned a house and a car. At that time, it was presumed that if he met those qualifications, he would likely become a reliable husband. Those were some of the expectations for marriage in our community of students at Kabul University.

While attending Kabul University, fellow students and myself didn't think that we were being westernized by associating with hippies and tourists. There were many of them throughout Afghanistan, not only in Kabul.

In my high school days during the tenth to twelfth grades, among my close Afghan friends, we privately discussed how to improve our culture. We opposed forced marriages, dowry, and marriages between first cousins. My friends and I also advocated for women's rights. When I entered Kabul University, however, there was little discussion among my classmates about human rights. They were concerned only with their professional studies. At the same time, communists and Islamic extremists were mobilizing on the campus. Among the 15,000 students at Kabul University, only about 2000 organized into political groups. A minority of them were extremists. They did not study much and most students did not like them because they were disrupting their classes.

6

THE 1973 BLOODLESS COUP

Four years had passed at Kabul University and I was married. Suddenly, during my last semester, in the summer of 1973, my life was turned upside down.

Before the King Left to London

While serving as the English interpreter and translator for King Mohammad Zahir Shah, people often asked me to do a favor for them by putting in a good word, or request the King to do something for them. I agreed to do so only once.

Some of my Pashto students were Christian missionaries. They asked me for help to prevent their church from being demolished. It was located near the Soviet Embassy in Kabul. Soviet officials had accused both Christian missionaries and Western governments of using the church to spy on their embassy. Mohammad Musa Shafiq was the Prime Minister at the time. He was a fundamentalist and a member of the Muslim Brotherhood.

When I conveyed the missionaries' appeal directly to the King, he said that it was a touchy subject and that he would decide the issue after his return from Italy. I also asked my brother-in-law, the King's Chief of Staff, General Omar, to do what he could to prevent the church from being destroyed. He told me, "The King discussed it in a meeting. He said he does not understand why a house of worship would be destroyed." Although the King was a Muslim, he respected other people's beliefs. No decision was made about the church at that time. In June 1973, King Mohammad Zahir Shah traveled to London for eye medical treatment and then to Italy for a short period of recovery.

Even before the church was built, I had advised Gordon Stinson, Executive Secretary of the International Assistance Mission (IAM) in Kabul, that the design and odd shape of the new church building would draw opposition in this Muslim country. As a member of the

Muslim Brotherhood, Shafiq did not want the Christian presence in Afghanistan. Although he was very anti-communist, Shafiq used the Soviets' accusation of spying as an excuse to destroy the church. There was no justification for destroying the church since religious freedom was guaranteed in the Afghan constitution. Therefore, Shafiq ordered a search for listening devices in the church but none were found.

In spite of that, two months later, while the King was still in Italy and without the King's agreement, Shafiq had the church demolished under the pretext that it was being used for spying. He, like others, underestimated the treachery of the Afghan communists. Later, during the initial stages of the communist Afghan coup in April 1978, he was assassinated by them. They also killed another prime minister, Noor Ahmad Etimadi, formerly a pro-Western Afghan Ambassador to the US.

The Coup

Shafiq's decision to override the King foreshadowed the end of the King's reign. On July 27, 1973, the King's cousin, Sardar Mohammad Daoud Khan, who ten years earlier had been dismissed as Prime Minister for reasons already explained, led several hundred supporters in the Afghan Army to carry out a bloodless coup and took control of the government.

The coup happened during the middle of our final examinations. On the first day of the coup, some of my classmates remembered the many times when the palace car had picked me up to do my translation work in the palace. Unexpectedly they turned against me and threatened, "You will never again set foot in the palace." I was shocked how suddenly they had changed. I had never bragged to them about translating for the King. I had talked more about my work with the Peace Corps volunteers. It is sad how people can pretend to be your friend and then turn against you.

My brother-in-law, General Omar, was the King's Chief of Staff. He had resisted the young Afghan communists who had taken over his office in the palace. I was told that he had been shot dead. Just four months earlier, in March, I had married his youngest sister, Bibigula. My brain became blank and I could not focus to take the exams. I rushed to his home.

Gathered there were his military assistants and General Omar's wife who said that he had left in the morning as usual and had taken his pistol with him. Normally he would not carry it. She explained that at 3 a.m. he had been awakened by a phone call and was informed that a coup had begun and Daoud was in control. She heard reports about the coup on the radio and was worried that those carrying out the coup would hurt her family. "Please stay with us. We don't feel safe," she pleaded. Of course I remained with her and her family. I missed taking my exams which delayed my graduation.

On the third day of the coup we were surprised and so relieved when we received a note from General Omar requesting clothes and toiletries. He had not been killed; instead he had been confined to the guest quarters of the Prime Minister's office. Later he was taken to the Deh Mazing Prison.

Daoud declared himself President of Afghanistan. He was not a communist and was unaware that the young Afghans who had supported him in the coup were communists. Many of them were part of the anti-aircraft class that I had escaped from when I was 13 years old. After completing that six-month class, the remaining students had been sent to the Soviet Union where they had been further indoctrinated. If I had remained in that class, I might have been swept up by the same circumstances that led to their participation in the coup.

When King Mohammad Zahir Shah was deposed in 1973, he was the last King of Afghanistan. He had reigned for 40 years. In 2002 the King returned to Afghanistan and was given the honorary title of "Father of the Nation." In 2006 I met him in the Kabul palace and asked, "How different are things now?" He answered, "The friends are not here now." In 2007 he was buried in Kabul with full state honors.

My Family Caught in Political Storms

The political history of Afghanistan since its independence has had many storms and my family has been caught up in them. My mother never liked the King's family and was not happy when I began interpreting and translating for him because the King's father had persecuted her father, General Sator Khan Achackzai, and her family. She was very outspoken about that. There is a longer history behind this; so let's go back in time to 1919 when Amanullah Khan led Afghanistan to attack British forces and declare its independence, a struggle known as the Third Anglo-Afghan War.

Britain was recovering from WWI and soon relented to the independence declaration. It negotiated a treaty with Afghanistan to prevent it from falling into the hands of the Soviets who had earlier launched their revolution in 1917. Amanullah Khan first took the title of Emir; and then in 1926, after solidifying Afghanistan's independence from Britain, he declared himself *King Amanullah*. My grandfather, Sator Khan Achackzai, was one of King Amanullah's commanding generals for the armed forces in Kandahar Province, and fought alongside Sadar Abdul Qudos Khan, another famous general.

King Amanullah went on to become the first Afghan ruler to *attempt* modernization of Afghanistan based on Western standards. That included a constitution that abolished slavery, recognized women's rights and individual freedoms. His wife, Queen Soraya, was very influential in promoting those reforms. They campaigned to end polygamy and strict dress codes for women, and to establish modern schools for boys and girls.

King Amanullah developed friendly relations with the new Soviet Union since it was the first nation to recognize Afghanistan as an independent country. As a non-aligned nation he also maintained cordial relations with Britain and attempted to manage the Britain-Soviet Union rivalry to Afghanistan's advantage. The formation of a small Afghan Air Force supplied with donated Soviet planes was one of those advantages. King Amanullah toured Europe and continued a close relationship with Germany that had existed since the nineteenth century. He also expanded trade with other parts of Europe and Asia.

The British were very concerned about Amanullahs's close ties with the Germans and the Soviets and covertly disrupted economic and social progress among the Afghan tribes. The writings of King Amanullah's grandfather, Emir Abdur Rahman, warned him against trusting either the Russians or the British, and between them the Russians were regarded as the least trustworthy.

Unfortunately, King Amanullah's reforms to modernize Afghanistan were too quick and did not have a broad base of support among the tribes and religious leaders to succeed. The tribal people were not ready for it. In 1929, Habibullah Kalakani, supported by the British, with extremists led a popular uprising to overthrow King Amanullah. Habibullah is commonly known by Afghans as Bacha Saqao meaning "son of a water carrier." King Amanullah fled the country to prevent a civil war and bloodshed among his people. Upon leaving, he said to the Afghan people, "You will regret allowing these extremists to take control of your country."

During the nine months of civil war that followed, extremists abolished all the reforms and the new constitution, reinstated strict dress codes, shut down the schools, and disbanded the army. That was not the first or last time that the British would support extremists in Afghanistan if it furthered their foreign policy interests. Although the British realized that the extremists could become a threat to them, they still aided them.

It is an interesting story how Mohammad Nader Khan (the father of King Mohammad Zahir Shah) regained control of the government from the extremists and restored order. He was a prominent leader in the 1919 Third Anglo-Afghan War for independence. Nader Khan had been a commanding general in the Afghan military under King Amanullah and was later his Minister of Defense and ambassador to France. At the time of King Amanullah's removal from power, Nader Khan was in France serving in his ambassadorial role and was sick. In spite of his sickness he started his return to Afghanistan through British-controlled India to retake Afghanistan. His reentry into

Afghanistan was a dilemma for the British. Knowing that they had supported the extremists to overthrow King Amanullah, Nader Khan was not friendly to them. Nevertheless, the British decided that Nader Khan was less of a threat to them than Bacha Saqao and the extremists. Therefore, the British gave a green light enabling Nader Khan to return to Afghanistan through India.

Nader Khan and his brothers mobilized the support of tribes in southern Afghanistan. Marching with those tribes to Kabul, they launched attacks, uprooted the extremists from their positions, and hanged their leader, Bacha Saqao. The Afghan public expected that Nader Khan would reinstate King Amunullah. His tribal army, though, insisted that he become king and Nader Khan agreed. He called a *Loya Jirga* (a Grand Assembly) of countrywide tribal representatives to legitimize his ascension to the throne. It voted and affirmed him as the King (*Shah*) of Afghanistan. *Khan* was dropped from his name and he was called King Mohammed Nader Shah.

The tribal leaders who helped Nader Khan regain control asked for compensation. He had no money and the national treasury was empty. They responded by looting government buildings and the homes of the wealthy in Kabul, as well as the properties of the extremists and their supporters. The new king could do nothing to stop them. He was deeply saddened by the looting. The tribes' loyalties were to themselves and not to his position as King of Afghanistan. It was the darkest time of his public life.

Solidifying his control as king required him to rebuild an army with volunteers from the tribes and to increase their pay as an incentive to join. Later the ranks of the military were filled through a national draft. The army became strong. With an iron fist King Mohammed Nader Shah brutally suppressed opposition from the extremists and from anyone. With the help of his brothers who were stationed in the provinces, he capably exerted influence and control over the religious and tribal leaders without fighting. Prioritizing stable and peaceful relations with them, King Mohammed Nader Shah did not reinstate social and political reforms such as relaxed dress codes and equal rights for women.

That was how the father of King Mohammad Zahir Shah, King Mohammad Nadir Shah, took power from King Amanullah. As a young girl my mother had visited King Amanullah on several occasions and had grown very fond of his family, especially his wife, Queen Soraya, who was very pretty and an outspoken activist for women's rights. When King Amanullah was not reinstated by Nadir Khan, my mother was deeply disappointed. Her distress turned into hatred for King Mohammad Nadir Shah and his family after he persecuted her father, General Sator Khan Achackzai, and her other relatives for attempting to bring back King Amanullah into power.

King Mohammad Nader Shah and his brothers established an extensive intelligence network, and skillfully managed foreign relations with the British and the Soviets to maximize Afghanistan's position as a buffer country between British India and the Soviet Union.

King Mohammad Nader Shah reigned from 1929 until 1933 when, while visiting the Najat High School in Kabul, he was assassinated by a student named Abdul Khaliq. Upon his death his son, Mohammad Zahir Shah, then 19 years old, was proclaimed King. He would reign for the next 40 years. Let's examine those years which many Afghans regard as a *golden age* of peace in Afghanistan's history.

King Zahir Shah's 40-Year Reign

As a teenager Mohammad Zahir Shah was educated in France when his father was stationed there as an ambassador. He became fluent in French and came to believe in democracy even though his father's reign was an oligarchy with power concentrated in a small group. The influence of his European education would be seen decades later in 1964 when, as the King, he voluntarily formed a constitutional monarchy.

The King was a courageous man and genuinely believed in human rights. There was a time, when one of his sons who was flirting with a girl, got into a fight with her brother. His son's eye was badly injured requiring him to travel overseas to a hospital for treatment. The Afghan police arrested the other boy, beat him up, put him in chains, and threw him into jail. When the King discovered that his son had been flirting with the imprisoned boy's sister, he immediately ordered the boy to be released. The King was not power hungry and was straight forward with both Afghans and foreigners. He also followed the same policies of his father in attempting to balance foreign relations between the Soviets and the British.

Foreign Policy as a Non-Aligned Nation

At least since the nineteenth century, Afghanistan has resisted Britain's long history of attempting to exert influence and control over it. Afghanistan asserted its non-aligned status during WWI. Therefore, Afghanistan did not do everything that Britain wanted it to do. Immediately after WWI, Afghanistan fought and gained its independence from Britain. During WWII it remained a non-aligned and neutral country. When the war was finished, the Allies were not happy with Afghanistan because during the war, German and Italian engineers working in the country were not handed over to them as requested. A Loya Jirga had decided not to hand them over to the Allies because of Afghanistan's centuries-old code of hospitality to protect guests.

After WWII, when Britain decided to leave India, it supported the formation of Pakistan, thinking it would further its efforts to influence Afghanistan in the region. The US also recognized Pakistan as its proxy in the region.

Daoud Not a Communist

Now back to the 1973 coup: Daoud declared himself president and not king. He was not a communist; in fact, he was even more religious than King Mohammad Zahir Shah. Those who were communists and supported him at that time did not say they were communists. Nur Mohammad Taraki, Hafizullah Amin, Babrak Karmal, and Najibullah each said that they were "revolutionaries" and denied being communists.

Daoud made efforts to improve life in Afghanistan. He did not change social policy, though. Women continued to enjoy the right to work in public places, and they could choose their husbands. As under the King, the tribes did not oppose those social policies.

Afghanistan is a small country, and it became common knowledge that while Daoud included pro-Soviet Afghans in his Cabinet, he did so merely to appease the Soviets who had dramatically increased economic and military aid. That would become a deadly miscalculation for Daoud who was politically less cautious than King Mohammad Zahir Shah. The King had excluded both communists and Islamic extremists from his government.

The Afghan Communist Party, known as the *People's Democratic Party of Afghanistan (PDPA)*, was formed in 1965 after the new 1964 constitution allowed political parties to be formed as an expression of free speech. In 1967, it split into several factions. The two largest were the *Parcham (Banner)* headed by Babrak Karmal, and *Khalq (Masses)* headed by Nur Muhammad Taraki. They differed in their strategies, but tended to divide along traditional tribal and ethnic loyalties. Blood and culture were stronger among Afghans than Marxist ideology. They were careful not to call themselves communists. Marxism provided a convenient anti-government platform. The Khalq members were mainly Pashtuns from the countryside. The Parchams were non-Pashtuns largely from the cities and were intellectuals.

Daoud had made other miscalculations a decade earlier. His policies had created military confrontations with Pakistan and an economic crisis. That had led to his resignation in 1963. His 1973 coup was bloodless. Six deaths occurred; however, they were the result of a tank accidentally running into the Kabul River. Daoud, unfortunately, was not as lucky when he was removed from office five years later. His removal was not bloodless. It was full of blood— his and his family's. He had gravely underestimated the treachery of the Soviets and Afghan communists.

7

KISSINGER OF THE AFGHAN FERTILIZER COMPANY

Six months after the coup I was able to take my final exams and graduate from Kabul University. I continued working for the Afghan Fertilizer Company (AFC) and was promoted to be a deputy manager. During my years at the university, I had worked at the AFC on a part-time basis as an interpreter. The company was a project of the USAID, a cooperative between Afghanistan and the US, that provided cutting edge agricultural and organizational technology and materials. My deputy manager position was usually held by a man much older than me—at least in his forties. It was a prestigious position and difficult for many people to accept me since I looked very young and was skinny. There is a funny story about that.

My office was on the second floor in the former USAID compound in Kabul. Outside my office there was an information desk staffed by a person called a custodian. One day a businessman, Hajji Ali Akbar Shah, came to the desk and asked if the deputy manager was in. "Yes, go inside," the custodian said. Hajji Shah was a Hazara and well respected as a wise person from Maidan-Wardak Province. He lived within one of the 11 provinces that I supervised. Provinces are like states in the US.

"That Kid?"

When Hajji Shah walked in, he saw me in a big, spacious office sitting behind my desk writing some papers. I wore a tie and a nice jacket in an attempt to offset my young looking appearance. "Is the deputy manager in?" he asked. I laughed to myself. "Yes, you can sit over there on the couch. He will be available in about ten minutes," I said. After a few minutes Hajji Shah walked out and asked the custodian, "When will the deputy manager come?" "He is inside," the custodian replied. "That kid?" Hajji Shah shouted.

He walked back in and I pretended that I did not hear him shout, "That kid!" I walked from behind my desk to a conference table in the middle of the office. He sat across the table from me while for the next hour I thoroughly reviewed his application and asked him questions. After the first five minutes the custodian knew to come in and deliver Afghan tea and pistachios. I explained to Hajji Shah that while I could authorize three retail shops in his District of Jillraiz, as a condition he would be required to set up and operate two shops in the bordering district of Behsud. He complained, "Behsud is not my headache and I am not interested in it."

Since I was in charge of granting licenses to sell fertilizer to farmers through retail stores in the provinces, he and other businessmen submitted their applications to me for approval. Within my 11 provinces there are districts comparable to our counties in the US. Some districts were better farming areas (in terms of soil, water, climate, and roads for transportation) than others. The higher profit retail stores, for those reasons, were located in those areas. I wanted to encourage development in all districts, especially those less fortunate to have good soil and climate. Therefore, I required less profitable districts to be combined with more profitable areas as a condition for granting licenses to sell fertilizer.

Pulling out three other thick files of applications for retail shops, I said, "These are applications from other qualified people. I can give them the licenses for the shops under the same conditions. It is up to you whether you want to agree or not." Hajji Shah tried to reduce my conditions and argued, "Okay, give me the shops in Jillraiz and if I make enough profit, then I will set up shops in Behsud." I countered, "No."

Thinking he could override my decision, he went to my boss, Dr. Zarif Salam, the president of AFC, and appealed my decision. He was formerly my professor and Dean of the School of Agronomy. In Afghanistan, a student will more likely defer to the opinion of the professor. Dr. Salam told him, "He is my student, but this is his area of responsibility and he knows very well what to do."

The next day Hajji Shah returned to my office and agreed to my terms. "You are a very tough negotiator," he said. I replied, "Yes, I am a bad kid," which revealed that I had heard him call me a kid. He made a big laugh and was obviously embarrassed. "For the next year you will be dealing with this bad kid," I said. "Tell me, how did you reach this position being so young?" he asked. I told him, "Go to my professor and ask him how this kid got this position." Hajji Shah became one of our most successful retail shop owners. In this photo I am fourth from the right  wearing a suit and tie sitting with my colleagues.

I learned from my Peace Corps and USAID friends how to respectfully say "no" and maintain the integrity of my position. It was difficult to do in the Afghan culture that stresses obedience and loyalty to elders. This was another stepping stone experience that prepared me to later work as the Assistant Coordinator of the Inter Aid Committee (IAC) in Baluchistan, Pakistan, where powerful mujahideen commanders would attempt to manipulate medical and other supplies away from me.

In 1974 I traveled extensively throughout my assigned 11 provinces providing training to farmers, observing the effectiveness of different fertilizers, and overseeing distribution of fertilizer from the retail shops.

The provinces had very difficult terrains to travel. In Kunar Province, for instance, the roadways carved into the edge of the mountains were dangerously narrow. Our Toyota pickup would hug the mountain walls and its tires were literally on the edge of cliffs. We could have fallen off into the river below.

Around this time, US Secretary of State Henry Kissinger was traveling extensively conducting shuttle diplomacy to ease the tensions in the Middle East. I was compared to him and became jokingly known as the "Kissinger of the Afghan Fertilizer Company." Kissinger also visited Kabul in 1974 where President Daoud urged renewal of US investment in the Helmand Arghandab Valley Authority (HAVA) project, which was scheduled to expire in July.

Farmers' Resistance

The traditional practice of fertilizing crops in Afghanistan was to prepare piles of compost, a mixture of cow dung, leaves, and soil. It yielded low levels of production and limited what farmers could harvest for themselves and sell for Afghanis to others so they could buy necessary goods for their families. When chemical fertilizers of diammonium phosphate and nitrogen were first introduced to the farmers, the substances were totally foreign to the farmers and they would not use them.

Farmers needed to be educated and recognize the value of fertilizers and learn how to use them. We did this by bringing farmers to government experimental farms to show them the results of using fertilizers. My staff and I negotiated with farmers to set aside selected plots of their land to use the fertilizers. They were called observation plots. When the farmers saw that the yields more than doubled, they began to buy and use the fertilizers. Production improved for wheat, alfalfa, and fruits such as pomegranates, nuts, beans, and corn. That in turn enabled the farmers to buy more clothes for their children, motor bikes, and tractors to replace the oxen. The tractors could also be rented to other farmers.

Initially farmers resisted the use of fertilizers. Here is one story that illustrates that: One day I was returning to Kabul from Paktia Province in a Toyota pickup with two technicians and my driver. Another pickup with technicians followed us. When we arrived at an intersection in a rural area, I told my driver to stop. I saw in one quadrant a wheat field that appeared healthy. On the other side was a very poor-looking wheat field. It was gently raining and a good time to apply fertilizer to the crops. I looked around for the farmer of the wheat field but didn't see him. I got out of my pickup and strapped a fertilizer spreader on my chest and began to fan the fertilizer on his crop. I did this even though I did not get the farmer's written permission. I was taking initiative and wanted to help the farmer. My technicians in the pickups, whose jobs were to spread fertilizer, did not want to do it, even though the best time to spread fertilizer is when there is moisture in the air. They were reluctant because when it rains, wet fertilizer on the ground smells very bad--like urine.

I was careful not to step on any plant. We were all trained by the Americans how to properly apply the fertilizer: when and how to either step forward or backward while turning the fertilizer spreader wheel.

The farmer suddenly appeared and started shouting the worst obscenities at me. It was unusual that he was so angry. I tried to explain to him the value of the fertilizer, but he would not listen. I was warned beforehand, "The farmers would curse you, beat you up. But don't retaliate."

I was angry but I didn't react. My staff sitting in the Toyota pickups must have thought that I was crazy. They did not criticize me because I was their boss. On the way back to Kabul I didn't say a word. Since the highway system was good during President Daoud's rule, it took us only a few hours to get back to Kabul.

Immediately I reported to my boss, Dr. Salam, the results of the day and the incident with the farmer. He listened intently, and then asked, "What is the difference between you as an educated farmer and an uneducated, traditional farmer?" I understood him to say that I should not complain that I have the responsibility to educate the farmers.

The story does not end here. Staff from our office later applied two more spreadings of fertilizer on the same angry farmer's field when he was not there. They were applied selectively in different sections, so he could see the difference that fertilizer makes. Just before his harvest, photographs were taken. Dramatic improvements were seen.

In my own family I saw the difference that fertilizers could make. My uncle was a landowner. At first I could not convince him to use fertilizer. Using my own money I bought fertilizer and spread it in his vineyards. When he saw the doubling of the yield, he changed his mind and purchased fertilizer. It was a good feeling to see progress.

My assistants were my friends, but they did not like my schedule of hard work. My drivers told me, "You are pleasant to work with but you kill us with too many hours." Although I was paid a set salary, they were paid overtime for their extra hours. Long hours are needed to help farmers. I talked with them in their fields, in their homes, and in the mosques. During the mornings I gathered information, asking tax collectors what taxes the farmers paid so I could estimate their yields. In the afternoons and evenings I spoke with the tribal leaders, chiefs of villages, and mullahs seeking their opinions about the local water needs.

Today the Afghan Fertilizer Company continues to operate and there is no need to convince farmers that fertilizers can improve their yields. Billboards in Afghanistan show successful farmers using fertilizer. Fertilizers are both imported and exported to Pakistan through the black market. District by district I can explain the agricultural developments since the 1970s in most of the provinces in Afghanistan.

Have Patience and Faith

When introducing new technologies to improve crop yields, initial opposition from local farmers is likely. Patience is required to find acceptable ways to work with them. Simple ways can be initiated for them to see the genuine benefits of the technologies. Improved agricultural production enables families to better their way of life. Local people desire to be independent and improve their standard of living for their families. Have faith that your good efforts can help farmers.

Burqas Not Worn Everywhere

As a side note to farming, there is a widespread stereotype that all women in Afghanistan in the past and today were/are pressured to wear burqas. In the villages, when I was growing up and even today, women did not wear burqas. They are not practical to wear when working on farms. In my hometown of Kandahar my mother would not wear a burqa. Burqas are worn mainly in the urban areas. I mentioned earlier about Bibigula wearing a burqa in a bazaar. Some days she chose to wear a burqa, other days she wore Western pants and skirts in public. For women it was just a matter of wearing different fashions. Even when the Taliban came to power after 1996, they could not force women to wear burqas in the villages, particularly among the nomads. It was mainly in the cities and surrounding villages that the Taliban enforced the wearing of the burqa.

"Kicked Out"

Two years after the coup, in 1975, the Minister of Agriculture, Ghulam Jalani Bakhtari, a communist, came to the Afghan Fertilizer Company (AFC) to finalize the conversion of the company. Control was transferred from the USAID to the Afghan Government. The company was a project funded by the USAID. The agreement between the two countries was that initially it would be managed by Americans who would train Afghans to take over their positions. After a period of time, Afghans would become the managers and the Americans would become their advisors.

Bakhtari was also the head of the board of directors of the AFC. Since I was a deputy manager, I was being groomed for leadership and, therefore, I expected to become one of the new managers. One day, at a company meeting, Bakhtari suddenly pointed to me and three other Afghans and declared, "You, you, you and you are no longer with the company. You are American spies." I was kicked out of the company. As long as Bakhtari was Minister of Agriculture, I was blacklisted. Opportunities to work in my profession were severely limited. That is the reason I was forced to leave my profession of agronomy.

Looking back, it was actually for the best because if I would have continued working for the fertilizer company, I would have been more vulnerable to being killed by the Afghan communists when they overthrew President Daoud in 1978.

Discovery of Corruption

There is more behind this story of me being kicked out of the AFC. Bakhtari, the Minister of Agriculture, had a cousin, Hajji Osman, who was a retailer for the AFC. I had discovered that Hajji Osman had skimmed off 5000 bags of fertilizer from the AFC and was selling them under the table at his shop in Kabul Province. I did not know at the time that Bakhtari was his cousin.

When newly assigned to oversee the Kabul region where his cousin was operating, part of my job was to review invoices of the fertilizer retail shops. While visiting a retail shop in a district of Kabul Province, a shopkeeper nearby told me that another retailer (Hajji Osman) had illegally put bags of fertilizer in a nearby warehouse. He pointed to where it was located. Hajji Osman would submit an invoice that noted "X" numbers of bags of fertilizer had been distributed to farmers, and AFC would give him "Y" amount of money. He conspired with the farmers to lie that they had received "X" numbers of bags of fertilizer. The shopkeeper asked me not to disclose his name.

Sure enough, when I went to the warehouse, although it was locked with a padlock, I could see through an opening that inside there were bags of fertilizer. Only certain warehouses were authorized to store fertilizer bags. That warehouse was not one of them.

When I reported the violation to my boss, Francis Hicks, he advised me that we must be very certain before making accusations against Hajji Osman and arresting him. I informed the local police to seal the warehouse and guard it. When we arrived at the warehouse, there was no padlock on its door. We opened the door and counted 5000 bags of fertilizer and took pictures of them. A full report was sent to the board of directors of AFC.

When Hajji Osman learned that we had discovered the

warehouse, he came and knocked on my apartment door. I invited him inside. Hajji Osman was much older than me. "You are from Kandahar," he said. I knew he recognized that from my accent. "I am from Parwan," he went on to say. "Our tribes do not get on very well. Look, we don't want bad things to happen between our people. Here is money to pay for the 5000 bags of fertilizer. Write a paper saying that you have transferred the bags to me in exchange for the money." "I cannot do that," I replied. He insisted, "The money is not much but it will be bad for my credibility. You know how our tribal systems work. My reputation will be damaged. Take the money." He left the money on a table as he started walking out. I pushed the money out the door saying, "I won't take the money." Hajji Osman was later arrested.

A few days later Minister Bakhtari called me into his office and asked me to tell him the story about the 5000 fertilizer bags. When I did, he called me a liar, and insulted me with the worst possible profanity. "I know you are an American puppet," he yelled. I protested, "Mr. Minister, in your position you are not acting as a good example." Enraged he kicked me in my back and pushed me out the door.

Called into President Daoud's Office

The next day the AFC President, Dr. Salam, called me into his office. As my former professor at Kabul University he expressed alarm: "You put yourself in danger." "Why?" I asked, "I am just doing my job." Then he said that President Daoud wanted to see me. "Take one of the company cars to the palace." I got very worried. President Daoud was quick-tempered. It appeared that things would get worse for me. I debated with myself, "Go, don't go, go, don't go." Then I went.

The palace was a familiar place where I had served King Mohammad Zahir Shah. I was escorted into President Daoud's office. His physical appearance was very different from his cousin's, the King. He was chubby-faced while the King was lean. I was so nervous that I was shaking. President Daoud could see that. He asked, "Where are you from?" "Kandahar," I said. I knew that he was once the Governor of Kandahar. "Which high school did you attend?" he continued. After I answered with the name, he asked in a cheerful voice, "Do you know who built it?" "No," I replied. "I built it!" He was trying to calm me and I began to relax. "Who is your father?" he asked. I responded that he was Hajji Mahmood and a city councilman. "I know him very well," he explained.

Then President Daoud inquired, "Son, tell me about the fertilizer story." I told him everything. After a pause he said to my surprise, "Our country needs young men like you. I am proud of you." So I added, "Your Minister of Agriculture kicked me in the back." I showed him the black and blue and green marks in my back. He appeared to be shocked and said, "He did that?!"

I was told three or four months later that Minister Bakhtari had been relieved of his position in the government and at the AFC. At that time I still did not know that Bakhtari was related to Hajji Osman.

There Is Ultimate Accountability

Another lesson that I have learned along the way in this life is that everyone will eventually die and there is ultimate accountability. It is important to act according to one's conscience. I could have stolen millions of dollars from the Afghan Fertilizer Company. I was in powerful positions while there and never abused them. At the AFC I managed 140 staff members in 11 provinces.

I put the interests of others first. When traveling long distances to the provinces, we had little food to carry with us. Retailers in the districts regarded me as an important person and invited me to eat with them, but I would not eat unless my drivers and other employees had eaten. My Afghan counterparts and colleagues criticized me for doing that. They complained that by being too close to my employees I was not affirming the dignity of my manager position. My belief was that my employees and I were a team; we are all human beings and have the same stomach. Treat everyone with dignity. I had no regrets.

After being fired, I did not attempt to return to the AFC or seek employment in any part of the Afghan Government, even though corruption was not then institutionalized. President Daoud opposed corruption. The next step in my life was clear. I was being drafted into the military. Nonetheless, even if I had not been drafted at the time, I still would not have pursued employment in the AFC. Even though Bakhtari was fired, his friends within the AFC would have continued to persecute me and effectively ended my opportunities there for advancement.

Also, when Bakhtari fired me, it was an attack on my reputation. I had helped build the company from the ground up and had been the AFC's first employee serving as its interpreter. It had been a part-time position while I continued my studies in my junior year at Kabul University. During that time I interfaced with the USAID and Afghan officials who were establishing the AFC organization and implemented its programs with the farmers. When the company was formed according to the American system, I was assigned as a trainer and later promoted to be a deputy manager and trainer. Working for the AFC was very prestigious at the time. Everyone there was paid about six times more money than a comparable Afghan Government job.

Drafted into the Afghan Army

I was drafted into the Afghan military in March 1975. Ironically, I was again assigned into an anti-aircraft unit under the command of Lt. Col. Raz Mohammed. When I was first drafted into the Afghan Army at 13 years old, he was a lieutenant and an instructor and administrative officer in the six-month anti-aircraft class. He was not the lieutenant who abused me. When I was initially processed into the unit, I mentioned to him that I had been his student in 1960, and that I had escaped from the school. In the same breath I said in a humorous way, "Sir, I promise that this time I will not escape from you." He did not recognize me and with a surprised look asked, "How did you get to college?" I did not say much and moved forward through the processing line. For sure I did not mention that

I low crawled in my uniform through the dung in the latrine to escape. My brother Baz still remembers that time and jokes with me. After that escape, whenever I meet Baz, he puts his hand over his nose and says that I still smell.

There was an Indian who taught English to young Afghan officers preparing for further study in India. He became very sick and returned to India. During the induction process, when it was noticed in my application that I had taught English, I was assigned to replace him and teach English to the officers. Since I was a college graduate, I was also assigned to be the secretary for the general of the entire camp. I wrote all his letters and he just signed them. I was a good soldier and conscientiously completed my required military service.

8

THE DARKEST DAY

While I was serving in the Afghan Army in Kabul, our first child, Pashtana, was born at our family compound in Kandahar in the month of December 1975. A few months later I was permitted a short leave to visit Bibigula and our baby girl. After I completed my one-year military obligation in March 1976, I returned home to Kandahar. Six months later we moved back to Kabul.

From the Farm to the Hospital

In Kabul I went to see my friend, Gordon Stinson, for advice and asked, "Where should I work?" He recommended that I consider working for CARE-MEDICO (Cooperative Assistance for Relief Everywhere-Medical International Cooperation Organization), a Western NGO (non-governmental organization) operating in Kabul. I took his advice and Gordon introduced me to Fred Davis who interviewed me. He was the Country Director of CARE-MEDICO. Dr. John Mowbray was the head of the MEDICO branch of CARE. He became our very good friend who two years later would manage the care needed to save Bibigula's life.

Dr. Mowbray was a very dedicated humanitarian. Since 1966 he had rotated between serving at the Kabul hospitals and teaching at the University of Saskatchewan in Canada. Dr. Mowbray was tall, good-looking, had brown, curly hair, blue eyes, a reddish complexion, and wore glasses. He was calm, quiet, and very well-liked by young Afghan resident doctors who were his students. He also supervised visiting volunteer medical specialists, doctors, professors, and lab technicians from the US, Canada, and Europe.

I was hired at CARE-MEDICO in May 1976. For the next three and a half years, until immediately after the Soviet invasion, I served there as its medical stock officer and senior interpreter. The MEDICO branch relieved doctors of many management and administrative duties that allowed them to focus on caring for patients. In my position I ordered and distributed each year more than a million US dollars in medicines, hospital supplies, equipment, and books to various hospitals.

As a side job I taught Pashto, Dari, and cultural awareness to Western doctors, nurses, and staff. They were members of the USAID, International Assistance Mission (IAM), and United Nations organizations.

My job as a medical stock officer in a hospital was a new profession for me. I experienced the change from farming to a hospital environment as depressing. The hospital with its confined spaces felt like a different world, not a happy place, and I missed the outdoors. I also missed seeing the improvements in people's lives when we introduced the smart use of fertilizers, better seeds, and reclamation of the land. But I threw myself into my work and did the best that I could.

On occasion, however, my work did take me outdoors. This

September 1976 photo shows me when I traveled with a CARE-MEDICO team to Band Amir in Bamyan Province, Afghanistan, to set up a temporary clinic. I was their interpreter.

At home Pashtana was growing and becoming cuter and sweeter every month. She was the joy of our lives. During a Christmas party she was chosen as the happiest child.

Before the Coup

About two years passed and darker days were approaching. Since overthrowing King Mohammad Zahir Shah in 1973, President Daoud's relations with the Afghan communists and the Soviet Union got worse. At the same time, he angered Islamic fundamentalists and tribal leaders who objected to his involvement with the Soviet Union. Daoud came down hard on any resistance. Tensions were rising as there were economic problems and unemployment was high.

In April 1977 President Daoud flew to Moscow for an official meeting with General Secretary Leonid Brezhnev. I heard from a staff member accompanying Daoud that during the second day of the meeting, out of the blue and not on the agenda, Brezhnev angrily told Daoud, "I am hearing these days that Western spies by the name of *experts* come to the northern part of Afghanistan and work there. This is not acceptable to the Soviet Union." Brezhnev wanted Daoud to break Afghanistan's ties with Western countries. Daoud angrily objected, "Afghanistan is an independent country and will not take directions how to run the country from anyone. It will send any foreign expert to anywhere it desires." Daoud then abruptly stood up and started walking out of the meeting. Daoud's delegate did the same. When he was in the middle of the room, Dr. Wahid Abdullah, his Deputy Minister of Foreign Affairs, advised Daoud to wait for Brezhnev, and as a matter of protocol, to shake his hand. Foreign Minister Andrei Gromyko helped Brezhnev stand up and they walked toward Daoud. Brezhnev put his hand on Daoud's shoulder and said, "You have asked for a private meeting with me. I am at your disposal at any time." Daoud responded, "I don't need a meeting with you," and immediately left.

When Daoud returned to Kabul, right away he flew to Cairo, Egypt, seeking the advice and assistance of President Muhammad Anwar al-Sadat who urged Daoud to without delay first remove all Soviet military advisors from Afghanistan. Sadat promised him assistance. Immediately Daoud flew to Saudi Arabia and other Arab countries. The Emir of Kuwait assured him that he would support his separation from the Soviet Union and write a blank check to pay for Afghanistan's existing debts and for future development.

Daoud set out on a path to distance Afghanistan from the Soviet Union. He sent Afghan military officers to train in Egypt, India, and

Turkey. Economic aid agreements were negotiated with the US and Saudi Arabia, each for $500 million. Meetings with the Shah of Iran and President Jimmy Carter were scheduled in mid year. Daoud continued discussions with General Zia in Pakistan to resolve their countries' longstanding disputes. Zia's military regime was pro-West and had deposed pro-Soviet Prime Minister Zulfikar Ali Bhutto. All those actions threatened to weaken the Soviet Union's power and influence in the region.

Mohammed Khan Jalallar had accompanied President Daoud as his interpreter during those very sensitive diplomatic visits to Arab countries. He was also Daoud's Minister of Commerce and previously had been the Minister of Finance under King Mohammad Zahir Shah. After Daoud's assassination and the Soviets had occupied Afghanistan, many thought it was very suspicious that Jalallar continued as the Minister of Commerce for the next almost ten years under the Soviet-backed and brutal Afghan communist regime. He was the son of an immigrant from Uzbekistan, a country occupied by the Russians in the early 1900s.

In mid April 1978, Mir Akbar Khyber, leader of the Parcham faction of the Afghan Communist Party (PDPA), was assassinated outside his home. The Parcham and Khalq factions blamed Daoud's government officials who denied the murder. Previously, Daoud had removed most of the communists in his Cabinet and the new one-party constitution had outlawed the PDPA and its two factions. The assassination of Khyber appeared to be part of Daoud's plan to remove all communist leadership from the government. That fear united the two communist factions.

There are different theories as to who was responsible for the assassination. Some Parchamis believed that the rival Khalq party led by Hafizullah Amin was the culprit. It is plausible, though, that the KGB murdered Khyber, thinking that it would unite the Parcham and Khalq factions.

After the assassination and during the funeral of Khyber, the two communist factions held a massive demonstration of thousands, threatening revenge upon President Daoud and his government. Daoud ordered a crackdown and arrested the major Afghan communist leaders: Babrak Karmal, Nur Mohammad Taraki, Hafizullah Amin, Dr. Shawali, and a few others. When that happened, Karmal's wife walked into our home next door and took Bibigula's burqa to conceal her identity. To this day she has not returned it.

Fears on all sides escalated. Under house arrest, Hafizullah Amin, leader of the Khalquist faction of the communist party, reportedly used his freedom to order Khalqi communists, who were also Afghan Army and Air Force officers trained in the Soviet Union, to launch a coup and overthrow President Daoud. The Afghan communists called it the Saur Revolution.

Descent into Darkness

After President Daoud was assassinated in the communist coup on April 27, 1978, Taraki was appointed as the President of the new Afghan communist government, the *People's Republic of Afghanistan (PRA)*. Karmal was appointed as Prime Minister, and Amin as the Secretary of Foreign Affairs. Again, it is important to note that none of those men openly declared themselves as communists or that their government was communist, for fear that traditional Afghans would revolt against them. They called themselves "revolutionaries."

On the first day of the coup, I was in Kabul working in the Jamhuriat Hospital for CARE-MEDICO. Bibigula was pregnant. During the initial stages of the coup, by around 3 p.m., the Afghan communist soldiers were losing and being pushed back; thousands of soldiers were killed during the first day and night of the coup--most were Afghan communists fighting to overthrow President Daoud.

After a heavy rain shower ended, however, Soviet fighter planes manned by both Soviet and Afghan communist pilots bombed the palace and surrounding areas. That was the turning point in the battle. Fierce fighting continued through the night. My small daughter Pashtana asked me, "What is that noise and shooting?" I said, "It is a wedding." It was customary to hear gunfire at Afghan weddings. "Oh, why don't we go there?" she said. I had no answer.

Two more days passed before it became clear that the Afghan communists had taken control. President Daoud and most of his family were murdered. April 27, 1978, was the darkest day of Afghanistan and its resulting problems continue today. Nur Muhammad Taraki became President and Babrak Karmal assumed the position of Deputy Prime Minister of the new government.

My family and I lived next door to Karmal. He was living rent-free in one of the homes of his father-in-law who was wealthy--it was the Afghan way. Although Karmal was the son of a general, he did not have wealth. Karmal rented his own home to others for income, while his wife continued to work as a teacher. Karmal's security guards set up a guard post which blocked the front door of my rented house. It forced us to enter our home through a hole that we had carved out in our neighbor's side wall.

Under Suspicion

We were under surveillance by the communist Afghan Government because my wife's family was associated with the royal family. Her father had been a First Deputy Minister of Defense for King Mohammad Zahir Shah, and her brother, General Omar, had been the King's Chief of Staff. My father also had been a high official with the Kandahar City Council for many years, and I myself was working for the Americans at CARE-MEDICO. Karmal could see big American cars come to my home. Therefore, I was considered a public enemy number one.

Most of the mid-level communist officials at that time were my former classmates from Kabul University. They were aware that I had been a student of agronomy and had taught Pashto and Afghan culture to Westerners. One of the communist officials was Dr. Mohammad Najibullah. He had been a medical student and head of the student communist party at the university. He was anti-American. Later Najibullah became head of the KHAD, equivalent to the Soviet KGB, and in 1986 he replaced Karmal as President. Najibullah was the most hated man.

Bibigula Almost Died

During the aftermath of the coup, our staff at the Jamhuriat Hospital in Kabul was struggling to attend to the wounded. Headed by Dr. John Mowbray, the hospital had provided a residency program for Afghan doctors graduating from Kabul University. We were all stretched beyond our fullest capacities.

At the same time, Bibigula was nine months pregnant, her blood pressure was high. Dr. Mowbray asked me to take her urine samples to the hospital for analysis every day. Her albumin level was rising and she was in danger of developing toxemia (eclampsia). In those days, 99% of Afghan women who got toxemia, died from it.

On May 11, 1978, I received a note in my hospital mailbox from Dr. Mowbray: "You must admit Bibigula to the hospital immediately." I met him while rushing through the hospital corridors. We then jumped into his car and drove to my home. While in his car, I was thinking, "How can I take care of Pashtana while Bibigula is in the hospital?" I asked Dr. Mowbray, "What shall I do with our daughter, Pashtana?" She was then about two-and-half-years-old. It had been less than two weeks since the communist coup on April 27 and there was an 11 p.m. curfew. Dr. Mowbray knew that my parents who lived in Kandahar could not travel to be with us to help. It was too dangerous at that time. Bibigula's parents and brothers were prevented from even contacting us due to their past working relationships with King Mohammad Zahir Shah. Their safety and our safety would be compromised.

Dr. Mowbray replied with a solution, "My wife, Kay, will take care of her." Pashtana was familiar with Kay Mowbray because our families were close friends. Kay was very kind, pleasant, and we enjoyed being together. She taught English at the American School. Dr. Mowbray dropped me off at my home and continued on. Another friend would take Bibigula and me back to the hospital.

As usual I entered my home through the hole in my neighbors' wall. When inside, I saw neighbor women standing around Bibigula who was lying unconscious on the floor. I was shocked and thought she was dead. Death was so common then. Mr. Saleh Razai, another neighbor, said, "Let's take her to the hospital!" He was the Personnel Director at Kabul University and a close friend of ours. Heart-broken I responded, "Why? She is gone." "Let's do it anyway," he encouraged. I was so distraught.

The neighbors immediately helped to carry Bibigula into Razai's car. I left Pashtana at home with the neighbors. He drove and I told him to stop on the way to the hospital at Dr. Mowbray's home. It was just a few blocks away. When we arrived there, his gardener explained that he had not yet come home. The gardener knew me and I told him to ask Dr. Mowbray to come to the hospital.

Halfway to the hospital and near the Kabul Zoo, Bibigula had a seizure which was a symptom of toxemia. I knew then that she was still alive, but likely was dying. Upon arrival at the Jamhuriat Hospital, Bibigula was immediately rushed to the emergency room. Dr. Osman Omary, a resident doctor and head of the emergency unit on duty at that time, started working on her. He now lives in Germany. Dr. Sadiq, who now practices in Orange County, California, and Dr. Toryali Amiry, who is now a doctor in Boston, continued to oversee Bibigula's care. Each doctor was very dedicated to their patients and was also a friend of mine.

A nurse administered oxygen and IVs. I walked to the administrative office in the hospital and ran into Dr. Mowbray who was rushing to see Bibigula. "I received your message. That is why I am here," he said. Walking into the emergency room, he first observed Bibigula. Then Dr. Omary explained his diagnosis of her condition. Dr. Mowbray assigned him to care for Bibigula and to report directly to him.

By 9 p.m. the emergency room informed him and then me that there were signs that Bibigula was in labor; she was also still unconscious. Jamhuriat Hospital was not equipped to support the delivery of babies. Therefore, Bibigula was put into an ambulance and taken to the maternity hospital two blocks away. Dr. Mowbray, his wife Kay, and I followed the ambulance.

Upon arrival she was rushed to the emergency room. Kay remained with her. The doctor on duty told us to get blood for her from the blood bank so they could start the delivery. Dr. Mowbray drove me to the nearby blood bank and we returned with the blood.

Kay said that Bibigula had started natural delivery and extra blood was not needed. After our baby was delivered, Dr. Mowbray asked whether the nurses from the Jamhuriat Hospital could remain with her. The maternity hospital nurse said, "No, it is not the policy of this hospital." We were forced to take Bibigula back to the Jamhuriat Hospital. Our baby was left behind in the maternity hospital.

Dr. Mowbray assigned Ms. Anna Claire to attend Bibigula. She was a nurse at MEDICO and a personal friend of Bibigula. Anna was a Canadian, always smiling and very kind. She was well liked by the other Afghan nurses. Anna said, "I will sit with her till tomorrow morning." Dr. Mowbray told Anna and the other doctors, "I am going home because the curfew begins at 11 p.m. I will have the telephone by my bed if I am needed."

Kay asked me, "Where is Pashtana?" I replied, "I don't know!" Kay said that she would drive to my house, pick up and take Pashtana to her home. Soon afterwards Kay called me from her home saying, "I went to your house, the doors were open and there was no sign of Pashtana." It was after the curfew and I was forced to wait till the next day to look for her.

During the night Anna remained with Bibigula in the intensive care unit (ICU), patiently draining her stomach of toxins with special tubes. I waited nervously at the door of the ICU. Fortunately our medical team of Afghans, Canadians, and Americans was so nice to her.

Early in the morning a nurse from the maternity hospital called me to pick up our baby boy. At a loss I replied, "I don't know where to take him. I am with my wife in the ICU." She only said, "We can't keep him here." Then about 25 minutes later, someone from the maternity hospital called to tell me that our boy had died. It was such a shock and my heart sank. That feeling was indescribable.

I still did not know where Pashtana was. I walked to the home of Bibigula's brother and told him of our baby's death. He asked a few people to come and help dig a grave for our baby. I pleaded with him, "Don't come with me because of the security problems." Again, it was only two weeks after the communist coup. Horrifying fear and bloodshed stained the city.

I returned to the maternity hospital and received my baby boy. When a baby has died, it is the Afghan custom for a parent to extend his arms forward and hold the baby in his hands. You can only imagine how difficult it was for me. As I was walking to a car through the front door of the hospital and holding my son, the poorest of the poor stood inside the gate of the hospital begging, "Sweets, sweets." It is another Afghan custom for the relatives or parents of newborn babies to give tasty sweets to people who say, "Sweets, sweets." The reply of those who receive the sweets is, "God bless you!" I had no sweets and the beggars did not realize that my boy had died. I did not say a word. Only God understood my grief.

In spite of the tragedies that fell upon us, I had to return to the hospital to work, which was overwhelmed with people wounded by the continued fighting in the bloody aftershocks of the communist coup.

Afterward I went home and searched for Pashtana at several neighbors' homes. Finally, one of the families said that Pashtana was with them. Relieved, I brought her to the home of Bibigula's sister and returned to the ICU to be with Bibigula. Dr. Tor Amiry was at the ICU. He was a close friend of mine from high school. I asked him, "How is she doing?" He replied, "Her output is much less than her input." That meant that whatever was put into her through the IV was more than she discharged through her urine. Bibigula was still unconscious.

After 48 hours the examining doctor rubbed a bar on the bottom of her foot and she responded. Gradually Bibigula became more conscious. However, she could not talk or move or recognize anyone. Bibigula lost sight in one eye and her brain was partially damaged. She remembers everything up to the time she became unconscious. Bibigula now has difficulty remembering and learning new things; nevertheless, she is still a great wife, mother, friend, a wonderful cook and partner who cares for our home so nicely.

Bibigula's sister and younger brother, Lt. Col. Daoud, insisted on visiting her in the hospital even though I warned that doing so would put their lives and our lives in danger. The communists were tightening their grip of control on the country and Bibigula's high profile family was more closely watched. Even so, Bibigula's sister and younger brother came to see her. When she saw Bibigula, she fainted and was admitted to the hospital as a patient.

A week later I brought Pashtana to see her mother in the hospital. Bibigula did not recognize her and Pashtana did not recognize her mother. By that time, though, Bibigula did recognize me. I said to her, "This is your daughter." She did not say anything. Her condition gradually improved and she was transferred from the ICU to a regular room in the hospital.

Down the hall from her room were many communist Afghan soldiers guarding the rooms of injured relatives of former President Daoud. Only three weeks earlier Daoud had been assassinated in the communist coup. Those relatives were the lucky ones, since 17 other family members of Daoud had been murdered with him during the coup. We did not know at the time where they had been buried. It was only a few years ago that their unmarked mass grave was discovered.

After 18 days Bibigula was discharged from the hospital. I told her, "Don't cry. You had a baby." "Where is the baby?" she asked. "He died," I said. "Was he a boy?" "Yes."

A Surprise Visit

A few days later in the afternoon, as I was entering my home, I was startled to see our next door neighbors about to leave. They were Babrak Karmal, the new communist Deputy Prime Minister, and his wife. Later Karmal was appointed President by the Soviets in 1980 after they had invaded Afghanistan. He said to me, "We wish good health for Bibigula. If there is anything we can do for her, let us know." I answered, "Your security guards have taken away access to our front door." He replied, "Come with me." We walked to his guard post in front of my home and he ordered the guards to shift it onto his property. Later, when Karmal became President, he moved into the palace.

My mother eventually traveled to Kabul from Kandahar and stayed with us for many months. Also, I was able to hire a home care provider to help Bibigula. Dr. Mowbray, Kay, and other Afghan and American doctors and nurses would often visit to check on Bibigula. They were our friends and were very nice to us. Bibigula was well-liked by them. They had come to parties in our home and she had volunteered to cook for parties held at their homes.

She Will Be My Only Wife

In our Afghan tradition men can marry up to four wives. Some of Bibigula's own family members told me that although it was sad what had happened to her, "You are young and should marry another wife." I would not answer. But within my heart I replied, "That will never happen. Whether Bibigula is sick or dead, she will be my only wife. We are best friends."

9

UNDER CONSTANT SURVEILLANCE

After the initial bloodshed of the April communist coup in 1978, for the next three months everything became quiet and stable in Kabul. The two Afghan communist parties (Khalq and Parcham) were cooperating with one another and with the Soviets. That would not last for long, though.

There were several factors that initially strengthened the communists' control of the country. One was that they ruthlessly eliminated any potential opposition. They assassinated President Daoud and his extended family, and continued to murder high-level officials and their families. Branded as counter-revolutionaries, key intellectuals, government, military and religious leaders throughout the country were also eliminated. At first we thought that they had been imprisoned.

Photographs had saved the life of General Omar, my brother-in-law. In 1978 General Omar had no military, government or social position. When his home was searched by Afghan communist officials, they saw many pictures of him with Brezhnev and other world leaders including President Eisenhower. Since Afghanistan had been a non-aligned country, he had attended all high-level meetings when King Mohammad Zahir Shah met with Western and communist world leaders. The photos showing General Omar standing with Brezhnev saved him from being assassinated by the communists in power.

Another contributing factor that initially strengthened the communists' control was that huge floods had swept through different parts of Afghanistan, especially the northern part of the country. The new Afghan communist government immediately provided aid to the flood victims. Even though the villagers were helped, they were still suspicious of the communist government because, at the same time, they knew that people were being taken away. The villagers presumed that they were put into prison. Later, though, they would discover the mass killings.

Before the coup, with the help of Japan, President Daoud had built transmitters and TV stations so that TV would be available in various parts of Afghanistan. After the coup, the stations were completed and used to publicize the government aid. It became a major propaganda victory. The communist government subsidized television sets so the military and other government officials could buy them at a cheap price and use them for their continued propaganda.

Stability did not last long. Spontaneous uprisings throughout Afghanistan began in mid-year. Taraki's communist government's efforts to implement socialist land reforms made life worse for the poor, and social reforms such as forced mixed-gender classes in schools offended religious leaders.

A "Friend's" Threat

One day a former friend from my hometown, Mir Rajan, came to my home in Kabul with three other mutual friends. Do you remember him? He was my roommate at Kabul University. Mir Rajan had attended medical school and was a communist. Two of the other three friends were also communists. While we were having tea and joking, I said to Mir Rajan, "At least your regime did one good thing to reach out and help the victims of the floods." He replied, "Sher, do you know why we are here? We are here to warn you that this is a time of revolution. It is like a flood. It takes away any small rock or piece of wood in its path. It is up to you how to interpret this. We are warning you as of today, do not visit your brother-in-law and his family; do not go to your American friends' homes. You can work for them, but we can give you a better job if you want. Don't allow them to come to your home. If you paint yourself from head to toe with red blood, you cannot change who you are. Your cells are still made from imperialist American dollars [meaning I could not become a communist revolutionary]. We don't want you to become dead. But we cannot save you."

I got mad and replied, "Men die only once in their lives. I will be your regime's enemy as of this moment even if you shoot me right now. You can do it." Bibigula had brought tea and heard what we both had said. Shocked, she stood frozen like a statue. Mir Rajan and I continued to argue. I was outraged.

At that moment, our neighbor Hussein, who was Director of the Treasury in the Afghan Government, walked into our backyard. We could see and hear him from our living room but he could not see us. Bibigula went to see him. Hussein asked her, "Who are the people with Sher in the living room?" She told him their names. Hussein was very anti-communist and knew who they were. He got mad and shouted, "Sher is also an atheist and communist to allow those communists into your home."

Mir Rajan heard that and said, "Hussein deserves revolutionary action." That meant to shoot him on the spot. Mir Rajan and the three others each wore a pistol but not a military uniform. Hussein rushed toward the living room. I went out to prevent him from entering our room and pleaded, "Please don't come in. Go to the other room." Hussein continued, "They are communists and you are the same." I was getting accused from both sides. Hussein finally left and returned home. The other three friends urged Mir Rajan and me to also calm down.

We all quieted down and the others changed the topic. Mir Rajan and I just remained silent. After a while they left. When I went to Hussein's home, he was still angry at me. I explained to his wife and his mother what had happened. They shouted at him, "Please shut up! Be careful, you will be killed."

Our Nicknames

Hussein and I were very close friends and gave one another nicknames. Since I was working for the Americans, he called me "Carter," referring to President Jimmy Carter, then the US President. Hussein was a Shia from Kandahar. Therefore, I nicknamed him "Khomeini" for Ayatollah Khomeini who was leading the Iranian Revolution which eventually deposed the Shah of Iran in early 1979.

At that time both names were considered enemies by the Afghan communists. Occasionally we would see one another in the street. Once, while I was walking with others, he shouted out to me, "Hey, Carter! Where are you going?" I replied, "Khomeini, I am going to Khomeini's home."

Concealed under His Shawl

A few weeks later Hussein came to our front door which was only a few feet away from the communist guards who stood in front of Babrak Karmal's front door. Hussein was wearing a large shawl around his neck. Stepping inside he asked, "Do you want to do something very important for Afghanistan?" "Like what?" I replied. "To save Afghanistan from the communists!" he answered. I asked, "How?" He pulled a concealed rifle from under his large shawl. "Just allow me to get on your roof to shoot Karmal." Only a common mud wall separated our homes. From our roof you could see the rooms where Karmal was living. "If you want to do that, first let us both send our families to Kandahar. Then if you shoot Karmal, our wives and children will not see us in blood and can be protected by our families there," I replied, hoping he would realize that it was a reckless idea.

Actually I was very scared seeing his gun. If anyone from the government would have seen him with it, they would have shot him on the spot with his own gun. They would have also shot me since he was inside my home. Hussein had lost self-control. My maternal uncle was caught carrying a gun in Kandahar and the communists shot him on the spot with his own gun in front of everyone.

The communists threatened people to obey and showed that they had zero tolerance. Certain communists were authorized to carry a gun and to kill anyone they felt was a threat to the regime without any investigation. Mira Jan was one of them. Today the Taliban has the same policy. The communists justified their authority under Lenin, and the Taliban argue that God justifies their actions.

Hussein's blind hatred for the communists was jeopardizing his safety and the safety of his family. There was another occasion, when the newly appointed Minister of Borders and Tribal Affairs, Sahib Jan Sarayi, knocked on Hussein's front door. They had been college and family friends. Sarayi was also a hard-core communist. He left his guards outside and walked to the rear terrace where I was sitting with Hussein's mother. Dressed in a western business suit and tie, he extended his hands to greet Hussein and embrace him as a friend. Hussein walked toward him and instead of extending his hands, spat in his face. Hussein hated anyone even his former friend, Sarayi, who was a communist.

I was not surprised that Hussein did that, but I was afraid that Sarayi would do something extreme like shoot him. Although Sarayi was a communist, he still respected his friendships. He knew that Hussein was anti-communist when he came to visit. Sarayi said to Hussein's mother, "He is crazy, let him be." We all had tea together But Hussein just sat there and would not say a word. Sarayi continued to be humble and friendly to everyone and jokingly said to Hussein, "Son, come over here," even though they were the same age. Hussein's behavior was embarrassing for me and I left.

The next day I advised Hussein, "What you did yesterday was stupid." He and I were very trusting and open to one another and he said, "You think that I am just like you to sit and have tea with communists in your home?" I replied, "But they are our friends in spite of being communists."

Hussein eventually escaped from Afghanistan, leaving his expensive home and beautiful carpets. First he fled to Iran and then to Germany where he lives today.

An Unexpected Visit

My cousin's husband, Ainuddin Alakozai, unexpectedly came to visit me in Kabul and stayed for one week. He was a well-known anti-communist and tribal leader in Kandahar, so it was dangerous for him to be in Kabul. Ainuddin was in his early 40s, tall and good-looking; he had a big, white, bushy beard, red face, and blue eyes. Without hearing him talk you might think that he was British.

Ainuddin was a wealthy landlord, well-educated with a degree in theology, and very open-minded. On several occasions he had invited Sanford Caudill and other American engineers to speak at a gathering of tribal elders in Kandahar, to discuss water tables and drainage systems.

Ainuddin came to encourage me to move to Pakistan and form a resistance movement with him against the Soviets and the Afghan communist government. When his tribe, the Alakozai, and my tribe, the Achackzai, are combined, there are over one million Pashtuns on the Pakistan side of the border that our families could mobilize. Similarly, on the Afghan side of the Afghanistan-Pakistan border there are over one million Pashtuns.

Ainuddin said, "You know many Americans who could help to start the resistance movement." I answered, "I don't know the American's policy on this. My friends are engineers...they are not politicians." "You know how to work with Americans and can contact them in Pakistan," he persisted. I respectfully declined his proposal because my wife was still recovering from toxemia.

On the day that Ainuddin had arrived at my home, while I was working at the hospital, Mira Rajan came to my home. When he knocked, my little daughter, Pashtana, opened the front door. He asked her, "Who has come to your home?" She was then about three years old. "Uncle from Kandahar has come," she answered.

When I returned home, Pashtana informed me, "Daddy, Mira Rajan came and asked me if we have guests." "What did you say?" I asked. "Uncle is here," she said. I immediately became suspicious. I told Ainuddin that things were very dangerous in Kabul. "If anyone knocks at the door at night after the 11 p.m. curfew, they come to take you to prison. The slightest criticism of the communist government could lead to your death."

While there are no official records, from the April 1978 communist coup to the Soviet invasion in December 1979, it is estimated that many tens of thousands of Afghans were executed in jail with or without a trial, or killed indiscriminately in bombings, raids into villages and under torture. During that time period, in my extended family alone, we lost 39 members who were murdered by the communists.

Informers Were Everywhere

At the CARE-MEDICO medical facilities the Afghan Government had planted informers who reported anyone who expressed criticism against it. Within the circle of my close European and North American friends, I could freely express my opinions. However, among the Afghan doctors and nurses, and increasingly among some Afghan "friends," there were informers.

The KGB trained the Afghan Secret Police, the KHAD, who came to the hospital and took accused people away. I knew that one of the nurses, Sadique, was planted to trick me into saying something critical against the government. She baited me saying, "They are atheists, communists." I wore a surgical mask during my work--it was one of the hospital rules. While looking at her, although I nodded my head in agreement, I said nothing. Once, as I was counting pills and putting them into bottles, she cynically said, "Look, he can move his big head, but he cannot move his small tongue." My surgical mask saved my life. It discouraged Afghans from talking to me and I would not give any of them the opportunity to talk to me.

In the medical stock room I routinely counted thousands of multi-vitamin capsules and put them into bottles. They were transported to various hospitals. The contents smelled good, like melon. Sometimes the capsules would break and spill onto my clothes. When I traveled in a city bus, people would sniff and look around for the source of the scent because it was so strong. It was funny. Even the chickens at my home were attracted to the fragrance and would chase me.

Our neighbors had agreed to help one another escape if they received a knock on their doors at night. I warned Ainuddin and rehearsed with him how to rush through the back wall and hide with our neighbor if there was a knock at our door after curfew. The neighbor was also our landlord.

A Knock at 2 A.M.

Mira Rajan rang our door bell at 2 a.m. Hours earlier little Pashtana had told him that "uncle had come." The bell was loud and could be heard by our neighbors. Ainuddin ran to our backyard neighbor. Awakened, I walked to the front door and looked through the peep hole and saw him. Mira Rajan was accompanied by armed guards in a Soviet jeep. At that time I still regarded him as a friend even though he was a communist and I did not think that he had come to get me. When I opened the door he slyly said, "Look, we are patrolling the area and protecting you while you sleep." I replied, "Before you communists took over, who protected us? No one needed to protect us." "Okay, let's have some tea," he insisted as he walked in.

When we got to the living room, he said, "Don't wake Bibigula to make tea." Mira Rajan pretended to be concerned about her, asking how she was recovering and how I was doing. Then he said, "Let me use the toilet and I will leave." It was understood that the toilet for guests was in the backyard. He knew where it was because he had visited my home many times before. Mira Rajan walked the contour of the property and fanned his hand along the roses as he walked. It was obvious that he was looking for someone. Then he left. I went through the back gate and warned Ainuddin, "Wait! Mira Rajan might come back in a few hours."

About five years later I discovered that Mira Rajan had been assigned to spy on me. If he had discovered Ainuddin, it would have been a feather in his cap. Ainuddin was a well-known anti-communist. If he were in Kandahar, Mira Rajan would not have been able to arrest him because of his political and military strength there. But in Kabul, Mira Rajan would have gone to the jeep and ordered other soldiers to arrest Ainuddin and me. Mira Rajan had been my long-time family friend and roommate for four years at Kabul University. It is a shame how ideology and politics can turn friends into enemies.

"What Happens If I Get Caught?"

In November of 1978 I went home to Kandahar with my family for a vacation. It was cold in Kabul while in Kandahar the weather was pleasant. I discussed with my father Ainuddin's proposal to form a resistance movement against the Afghan communists from a base in Pakistan where a house and all my financial needs would be provided.

My father argued that fighting the communists from Pakistan was not effective. He said, "Now you must fight the communists. But you don't need to use a gun. You can encourage the Afghans in your home country to stand against the communists. Since you have worked throughout Afghanistan with the fertilizer company, the USAID and the Peace Corps, you know a lot of Afghans. You should go underground and encourage our people in our country to resist." "What happens if I am caught?" I asked. "That is your luck. This is war. Those things happen. I have been in war and it is not fun," he said. My father had fought the British for Afghan independence in 1919. I knew that my grandfather, Hajji Rawouf, had also fought the British at the Battle of Maiwand in 1880.

Failure to Learn from the Past

Historical resentment runs deep. After 9/11, when British troops were sent to Helmand Province, the villagers believed that they were there to get revenge for losing the Battle of Maiwand in 1880. When Prince Harry came as the "Warrior Prince" to Helmand, the villagers were outraged. Certainly that was not the intention of the British. However, it was a strategic mistake to send British troops to Helmand or Kandahar Provinces. It would have been far better to send them to other provinces in Afghanistan. Americans would have been welcomed at the beginning of the war in 2001 in Helmand and Kandahar because of their past service projects providing health care, education, and agricultural assistance through the Peace Corps, the USAID, and other development agencies.

10

THE SOVIET INVASION

After our winter vacation in Kandahar, we returned to Kabul where I continued working as a medical stock officer for CARE-MEDICO. The Soviet invasion would soon come like a tsunami and our family and millions of other Afghans would be caught up as pawns in the struggle between regional and world superpowers.

Kabul was under the iron grip of President Nur Muhammad Taraki's communist regime. Uprisings against its land and social reforms erupted and spread through most of the provinces. Taraki ruthlessly countered the revolts and solidified his control of the communist party (PDPA) by purging government offices of key rival (Parcham) communist members, sending some of them out of the country as ambassadors. Babrak Karmal was one of them.

After the bloody overthrow of President Daoud, Taraki and Hafizullah Amin had a close working relationship. In meetings, Amin praised Taraki as "The Great Leader" and Taraki returned the compliment calling Amin "The True Disciple and Student." Their relationship soured as they competed for control of the Afghan Army. A failed assassination attempt against Amin by generals loyal to Taraki alienated Amin and led him to order Taraki's murder--he was suffocated with a pillow.

Taraki's assassination occurred on September 14, 1979. The reason that I remember the date so clearly is that our son Mirwais was born on September 12, at 9:15 p.m., two days prior to the assassination. While I was at work, Bibigula was rushed to the maternity hospital. Our neighbor, affectionately known as "Aunt," her brother, and his wife drove Bibigula there. Aunt remained in the hospital during the delivery.

When I returned home from the Jamhuriat Hospital, I was informed of what had happened. About 9:30 p.m. Aunt called me to congratulate me on the birth of our new son, Mirwais. I was very happy. My wife and baby were both healthy! Mirwais was a light-skinned and handsome baby. His character has become like his father's: very determined, strong, and polite.

I told Aunt that her brother and I would pick her up from the hospital and bring her home. Half-way to the hospital we were stopped by a grouping of tanks at Deh Mazang, a big traffic circle where two mountains converge at Kabul Gorge. We were forced to return home and Aunt was required to remain at the hospital until the following day. There was no bed or chair for her to sit in that night, only a cold concrete floor.

That morning a public announcement reported that Taraki was very sick; a second announcement, only a short time later, stated that he had died; no mention was made of murder.

Hafizullah Amin assumed the presidency of the communist government. However, it would be short-lived as it had been for Taraki. Amin launched a reign of terror and mass murder to solidify his control. He had anyone executed who disagreed with him whether they were in the communist party, the military or elsewhere. Estimates are that Amin's purges reached 50,000 people. Death was everywhere. Three months later Kabul was jolted by the Soviet invasion.

The Soviets' Decision to Invade

There is a long history behind the Soviet Union's interest in Afghanistan. At least since the nineteenth century the Russians have attempted to gain control of the oil routes in the Persian Gulf and Arabian Sea partly by creating a 1000-mile bridge from Turkmenistan through Afghanistan and Pakistan. An Afghan communist government in Afghanistan would provide a major platform toward that end.

However, the two warring Afghan communist factions, Parcham and Khalq, forming the government were threatening Brezhnev's bridge to the oil resources, or "final thrust to the South." They were fighting and killing one another, and brutalizing and committing massacres against the Afghan people which led to revolts. Their infighting and repression were so destabilizing that they were the major reasons the Soviets invaded and occupied Afghanistan with ground troops.

The Politburo feared that the Muslim resistance led by Gulbuddin Hekmatyar would topple the two communist factions and spread extremism to the Soviet bloc countries along Afghanistan's northern border. Senior Soviet politicians argued that if Afghanistan turned away from the Soviet Union, they would lose face in the Third World, and influence in Central Asia and the Middle East. At the same time, Soviet Army leaders and the head of the KGB, Yuri Andropov, argued against intervention: tanks could not solve a fundamentally political problem, and Soviet troops would look like aggressors to the Afghan people.

The Iranian Revolution earlier in 1979 also encouraged Soviet leadership to invade Afghanistan, because the anti-US Government in Iran would not provide a base for the US to oppose the Soviet invasion. Madeleine Albright, former Secretary of State in the Clinton Administration, uses the Iranian Revolution as a case study for what happens when the departments of the US Government are deeply divided by different sources of information, views about what is happening, and what to do about it.

US Government officials were caught off guard by the Ayatollah Khomeini seizing power. They did not understand the extent of the Iranian people's hatred for the Shah—Mohammad Reza Shah Pahlavi—or the ability of the Muslim clerics to mobilize support. Efforts of Khomeini's aides to communicate with US officials had even been rejected. The new Iranian political structure was not based on democracy or communism but on a religious worldview and a narrow interpretation of the Quran. As former Secretary Albright concluded, the US undervalued the role of religion in Iran.

Zbigniew Brzezinski, former President Jimmy Carter's National Security Adviser, disclosed in a 1998 interview that President Carter was aware that his July 1979 approval of covert aid for opponents of the pro-Soviet regime in Kabul would increase the likelihood that the

Soviets would send troops into Afghanistan. Brzezinski explained that the strategy was to draw the Soviets into an Afghan quagmire, drain the Soviet Union of economic and military resources, and take Soviet pressure off Poland and other Eastern Bloc countries, which in fact it did.

Brezhnev eventually ordered Soviet troops to occupy Afghanistan and stabilize the communist Afghan Government. He and other senior Soviet officials failed to consult with their many cultural experts. Instant experts with little or no experience appeared in Kabul to replace them when the invasion began. As a result, few in the Politburo understood what would be involved after occupying Afghanistan. The US would make the same mistake after 9/11. In the end, the decision to invade was made because there appeared to be no better alternative.

The Invasion

On the cold winter afternoon of December 26, 1979, we returned from a short vacation in Kandahar on a 45-minute flight from Kandahar to Kabul. While landing, I saw small tanks and artillery surrounding the airport. I had never seen them before.

After a short taxi ride, we arrived home about 2 p.m. At 10 or 11 p.m., while watching then President Hafizullah Amin giving a speech on television, the screen went blank. I switched on the radio and heard Babrak Karmal. He condemned Amin as brutal, a CIA agent, and reported that he had been killed. Karmal declared, "We are in a new era of our revolution." Then he announced the formation of a new government under his leadership.

Soviet troops had launched their invasion and Operation Storm 333. Kabul was in lockdown. About 10 miles from the center of Kabul were the Darul Aman Palace and Tajbeg Palace, the residences of President Amin. They were within one kilometer of one another, under siege and on fire. We could see them from our veranda since we lived within one kilometer of them on Aliabad Road. There was gunfire outside our window and showers of bullets filled the sky like fireworks.

Elite Soviet troops dressed in Afghan uniforms had stormed and occupied Darul Aman Palace and assassinated President Amin. Brezhnev feared that Amin might ally with the West or the fundamentalists in Pakistan, and concluded that he could no longer be trusted and should be eliminated.

After the siege, everyone in Kabul was talking about the story of a Soviet commander and his troops who had occupied the palace. He had ordered the palace to be in lockdown with the order to shoot anyone seen leaving it. Ironically, when he stuck his head out of a window, he was mistaken as a palace guard and shot dead by another Soviet soldier. The real details of the siege are cloudy. This story points, however, to one probability: in the darkness, fury, and confusion of the battle, at least one Soviet soldier dressed in an Afghan uniform was inadvertently killed by another Soviet soldier. That is known as "friendly fire." It also foreshadowed the unintended consequences of occupying Afghanistan when blind to its culture and history.

With Taraki and Amin assassinated, Babrak Karmal was, as you might say, the last man standing and was installed as the new President of Afghanistan. The Soviets thought Karmal was "their guy" who would not turn to the West. Later, Mikhail Gorbachev would replace him with Mohammad Najibullah. Karmal was fortunate to leave with his life.

Escape to Kandahar

On February 14th, 1980, CARE-MEDICO suspended its operations in Afghanistan due to the violence caused by the Soviet invasion. It was time for us to leave. Bibigula and I flew by Ariana Airlines to our home in the city of Kandahar with our young daughter, Pashtana, and our son Mirwais, who was only about three-months-old. We were not suspected by the Afghan communists or Soviets of escaping Afghanistan because we were native Kandaharis.

Women's Uprising in Kabul

Shortly after we arrived in Kandahar, the first uprising against the Soviets occurred in Kabul in March 1980. It is known as the "Third of Hoot." For Afghans it is similar to D-Day of World War II. It was initiated by a protest march of university women at Kabul University and led by Nahid Saaid. Those educated, secular Muslim women wearing western skirts were the first to lead an uprising against the Soviets and were not mujahideen Islamic fundamentalists or extremists. They burned the Afghan communist flag and the Soviet flag shouting, "Down with the Soviets and down with the Afghan communists." Nahid and about a dozen other young women leading the march were shot dead by the Soviets at point blank range.

Immediately, within an hour, the residents of Kabul erupted into rioting. At night the people climbed on the rooftops and shouted "Allah Akbar," "God is Great," which demonstrated unity, defiance and encouragement to resist the communists. That was a shock to Brezhnev and the Soviet officials. It was a shock to the Western world, too. An uprising led by secular, Muslim women was beyond any expectation. Babrak Karmal's leadership also came into question. Nahid Saaid's father, Yousaf Saaid, later moved to Fremont, California.

The Soviets ordered a lockdown of Kabul, declaring that if anyone attempted to leave their home or office, they would be shot. Do you remember the previous story about Mir Rajan who warned me against working for Americans? During the lockdown he stepped outside the door of his home to see what was happening. At the end of his street was a small Soviet tank. According to his wife, the Soviet soldiers in the tank saw him and shot a projectile that blew off his head.

In Kandahar when we heard the news of his death, a friend and I visited his mother to express our condolences. Mir Rajan was her only son. We were crying with her because she had no other relatives to care for her. She had been a good friend of ours. After the birth of Mirwais, she had stayed in our home for 10 days to help Bibigula. At the same time, I had mixed feelings about Mir Rajan. He was a hard-core communist who had participated in killing other innocent people and had threatened me in my home in Kabul in 1978. As we left her home, my friend and I expressed what a strange world we lived in. Our mixed feelings about Mir Rajan's death are an example of a Pashto proverb, "One eye cries and the other eye laughs."

Escape to Pakistan

In Kandahar I planned the future of my family. Since my mid-twenties I had worked for European and US agencies. It made sense that I would go to the US or Europe and later arrange for my wife and children to join me. Although the separation would be difficult for all of us, they would be safe with my family in Kandahar.

In March I departed from Kandahar to Pakistan. I did it without telling my parents because my father was against me leaving Afghanistan. Even my wife didn't know that I planned to leave the country. My life was in real danger. I was widely known as an anti-communist and had worked all my life for Americans and other Westerners; therefore, I was suspected of being an agent of the CIA. It was wartime.

Although I did not say where I was going, Bibigula presumed that I had left to look for a new job. It was customary for Afghan wives not to question where their husbands went even when they were gone for several weeks. I did not tell her fearing that if the Afghan communist government officials or Soviets questioned my family, she and other family members honestly would not know where I was and were less vulnerable to intimidation.

It was a comfortable life for Bibigula and my children living in the family compound. They resided in a large home with nearby pomegranate and apricot orchards, and vegetable gardens. We had a large extended family and I was confident that my brothers and parents would take good care of them. The only thing missing was me. It was very difficult to leave my disabled wife and two children. I believed, though, that it was the best option for my family's future.

The journey ahead was uncertain and dangerous. Disguising myself in ordinary villager clothing, I traveled with five Afghan businessmen by bus. We lifted and stacked our bicycles on the top of a bus and journeyed about 70 miles to Spin Buldak where we got off the bus and rode our bicycles on a side road that weaved through villages for the remaining 12 miles. Undetected we crossed the Afghanistan-Pakistan border and arrived in Chaman, Pakistan. We spent the night there at a friend's home. Chaman is at the base of a huge mountain range called Kozak Mountain and Kozak Pass. It is similar to the Sierra Nevada Mountains except there are few trees.

The following morning we left our bicycles at that home and rode another bus almost 85 miles to Quetta, the capital of Baluchistan, Pakistan. It was a 10-hour drive climbing and winding through narrow roads. It took much longer than from Kandahar to Spin Buldak.

The other Afghan businessmen with me were continuing a many centuries-old trade of smuggling and transporting tea pots and herbs to Pakistan and returning back to Afghanistan with medicines and medical supplies. They evaded government officials to avoid paying a tax. They regarded me as a fellow smuggler, only one of them knew who I was.

Stuck in a Box

When we arrived in Quetta, I was filthy. My fellow travelers took us to a shopkeeper they knew whose shop was located on Lytton Road. He was a wholesaler of tea.

When we entered his shop and extended our greetings, the shopkeeper invited us to sit down. There were only two chairs and one huge, empty cardboard tea box in front of the shop on the sidewalk. I was asked to sit on the box. I sat down on it and the shopkeeper offered each of us hot tea to drink. When I extended my hand to grab a tea cup, the top of the box ripped open and I collapsed into it. My knees hit my chin. I tried to get out of the box but I was completely stuck. The shopkeeper and two of my companions all attempted to pull me out without success. I was a funny sight and it created quite a scene. The street became blocked with people who rushed to see the man stuck in the box. The shopkeeper finally fetched a pair of pliers and tore open the box at its seams. I crawled out of the box. A friend of the shopkeeper passing by the tea shop joked with him, "I thought you were selling only tea. But it looks like you are selling people, too. What is the price of this tea box including the man?" The shopkeeper was embarrassed and didn't reply.

After this humbling experience, I thought to myself, "Now you are a refugee. Here is your life, embrace it! You have no freedom. You are countryless, homeless, and jobless." That was my definition of a refugee and my first such experience as a refugee. I remembered the Palestinian refugee family in 1952 that came to our classroom begging for money.

With my companions I left Quetta. We traveled by train to Karachi, Pakistan—a distance of about 430 miles. They had traveled this route for many years. It was my first experience on a train, since there were no trains in Afghanistan. We sat in economy class and were packed like sardines. The weather was hot and dry. The windows were open and the air was filled with dust. The train ticket cost about three dollars in today's money.

At that time Afghans fleeing from Afghanistan were not officially recognized as refugees by the Pakistan Government. In Karachi my companions and I walked to an open-air building that served as a hostel for travelers, a place to sleep, eat, and acquire visas for those traveling to Europe, Hong Kong, and other destinations. It was also an export center selling carpets.

"You Are Like My Own Blood"

I remained quiet during the first two days and pretended to be illiterate to maintain a low profile. The owner of the building was Hajji Masho. He was named "Hajji" because he had been on a Hajj, a pilgrimage to Mecca. We didn't know one another. But after two days he became curious, wondering "who is that quiet young man over there?" He walked over to me and we started talking. We discovered that we were from the same tribe and he knew my parents very well. Hajji Masho became upset that he had not been told that we were related. "You are like my own blood. You are the grandson of Hajji Rawouf," he said. He knew that my grandfather was a very well-known Islamic scholar and freedom fighter during the Second Anglo-Afghan War.

Later that day two Americans came looking for carpets. Delighted to hear English spoken, I walked over and informed them about how carpets were made and that the ones they were eyeing were of poor quality. They were surprised and said, "You are someone. Who are you? Your appearance and American accent don't match." I explained that I had worked for CARE-MEDICO, the Peace Corps, the USAID, and other Western NGOs and was escaping from Afghanistan. They said, "You can work here for the US Consulate." Hajji Masho and others watching us were amazed and excited to see my ability to speak English. They saw the possibilities of me selling carpets to Europeans, Australians, and Americans.

I confided to Hajji Masho that my parents didn't know where I was. He advised me to return to Kandahar and tell my parents that I would work with him. I agreed and he provided security for my return to Kandahar.

Back to Kandahar and Kabul

When I returned home to Kandahar and explained to my father the job opportunity with Hajji Masho, he strongly encouraged me not to live and work in Pakistan. My father advised me to stay in Afghanistan, but not to work for a foreign agency or the Afghan Government while the Soviets occupied the country. I considered his advice.

I changed my mind about going to the US or Europe. It seemed likely that if my family moved there, we would live in a big city like New York where I could be hired by a humanitarian aid organization. We would likely live in a high-rise apartment which would be very difficult for my disabled wife. Toxemia had impaired her ability to read numbers and find her way to places near home. At the same time, I did not want to live in Kandahar which was a battleground between the mujahideen, Afghan communists and Soviet troops. Life in Kandahar as a subsistence farmer would be more than frustrating for me. In the midst of the Soviet occupation and civil war around us, as odd as it may appear, Kabul still offered better possibilities.

My wife, children, and I left Kandahar and returned to Kabul where we met some friends and relatives of Bibigula. I was unemployed and needed to earn a living for my family. While we initially looked to buy a grocery store, I ended up buying a small stationary store.

At the same time I ran into Frances Illif. She was a nurse from Britain working for the International Assistance Mission (IAM), a Christian NGO operating in Afghanistan since 1966. Frances and I had been friends since I was in high school in Kandahar. Back then, while interpreting and translating for the USAID, the agency had loaned me to IAM's mobile clinic for a few weeks to interpret and translate. Since then, on and off through the years, I had taught the Afghan languages and culture to Frances and other American, European, and Australian members of IAM.

When I ran into Frances in Kabul, she encouraged me to work for IAM at its NOOR (National Organisation for Ophthalmic Rehabilitation) eye hospital in Kabul. The political situation was expected to change for the better. I was offered double salary and early in May 1980 I started working for IAM as a translator for medical teaching materials and books for nurses in its Kabul headquarters. It would be a safer, low-profile environment for me. We kept the stationary store and hired another person to operate it until my brother Zeke arrived to manage it.

The Herat Hospital Staff Rescue

Three months later, in August 1980, we were informed that 15 IAM staff members who were operating another eye hospital (the NOOR Hospital) in the outskirts of the city of Herat were in trouble. They were Europeans, Australians, and Americans whose spouses and children lived with them. Herat City is within Herat Province located in the western region of Afghanistan, bordering Iran and Turkmenistan (then part of the Soviet Union).

George Terry, who was the Executive Secretary of IAM in Kabul, came to me and asked for help. He explained that Herat had come into the hands of rebels. At that time they were not called freedom fighters or mujahideen by the Afghan people. For one month, communication with the Herat hospital had been cut off. It was presumed that the IAM medical staff had run out of money to pay for food, fuel, the salaries of local employees, and rents for the hospital and the compound where they lived. Mail was also stacking up, waiting to be sent to them.

During the previous year there had been a major revolt in Herat against the Afghan Government. Other smaller revolts throughout Afghanistan had preceded it. The revolts protested against the government's socialist land reforms that made life worse for the poor, and social reforms that challenged traditional Afghan values and local tribal power structures. Marxist propaganda, for example, was mixed into the literacy programs' teaching materials, and males and females were taught in the same classrooms, and forced marriages were declared illegal.

Herat had come under the control of local insurgents--soldiers of the Afghan Army who had mutinied. Anarchy had broken out and mobs killed communist government officials and Soviet advisors. It was a major threat and crisis for the Afghan Government, which responded ruthlessly with aerial bombardments and tank assaults to regain control. Many thousands of civilians were killed. It was a major threat that seriously worried the Soviets.

Herat was again in the hands of the rebels and the Afghan Government could respond as it did before—with overwhelming force and destruction. George pleaded, "I know your uncle has buses; you are from Kandahar." My uncle's buses were like greyhound buses in the US, traveling a circuit from Kabul to Kandahar to Herat and back. Sometimes they traveled to Mazar-i Sharif.

George continued, "Can you take a bus to Herat for us? We can't ask any of the other employees from our local office to help because they would inform the communist officials." I replied, "How can I go to the rebels and ask for help? They don't know who I am. The bus would be stopped at security checkpoints and I would be asked by communist soldiers, 'How can you go through the rebel territory if you don't have connections with the rebels?'" They would presume that I was a rebel. But George and the medical staff were my colleagues asking for help. I had to do something.

I went to see one of my uncle's drivers and asked whether he could take me to Herat. He answered, "Only to some point along the way, but not all the way; it's not safe. This is no time to go to Herat." I told George that my uncle's bus company was unable to take me to Herat.

The next day George asked, "If we provide you a plane ride to Shindand Airport, and from there a bus to the hospital, would you go to check on the condition of the staff at the hospital?" I said, "Yes." Then I went home and told my wife, Bibigula, and Baz, my brother, that I would go to Herat.

They pleaded with me not to go. I responded that I must go. "How can you make our children fatherless," Bibigula cried. "I have promised them," I said. Baz argued that it was not my responsibility: "There are other human relations people in IAM who are responsible for the staff members. You are only a translator there." He knew that the level of danger was very high. I asked Baz, "Do you remember the Peace Corps people who helped us in Kandahar many years ago?" "Yes I remember," he replied. "They have their children with them in Herat," I said. "But you have children, too!" he disputed. "It is my ethics and they are my friends," I said. "It's their problem," Bibigula repeated. It was hard for me.

I thought of Dr. John Mowbray, his wife Kay, and other doctors and nurses like Anna Clare who had cared for Bibigula when she almost died. Afghanistan is a very traditional society with a low level of health care and education. There is about one doctor for every twenty-five thousand people.

I remembered my experiences in the 60s and 70s with Peace Corps nurses who shoulder-to-shoulder showed Afghan nurses how to raise the standard of health care by doing simple things such as cleaning the mouths and teeth of Afghan patients. Afghan nurses did not realize the importance of sanitation and prevention and would not have otherwise given attention to a patient's cleanliness. They thought health care was just about injecting drugs and giving pills. Ordinary people presumed that doctors could perform miracles. It is difficult for a Westerner to understand the stubbornness of people in a country like Afghanistan. There was immediate improvement in the health of patients from the treatments of Peace Corps nurses and the Afghan people saw it.

I remember in the Kandahar Hospital there was an American nurse returning to the US saying her good-byes. An old lady weeping grasped her arm in gratitude and would not let her go for half an hour. This is an example of how genuine grassroots service is the best way of earning friendly relations with developing countries.

Even though I estimated that the chances of me getting killed were 90 percent, I felt gratitude and an obligation to those who had helped my family and fellow Afghans. I had to go. George did not understand the level of danger that he had asked me to face. He was obliged, though, to do whatever he could to save the lives of his staff, their wives, and children.

George arranged for me to travel on Ariana Airlines and land in Shindand Airport about 70 miles from Herat. At the Kabul Airport I loaded into the plane two trunks containing medicines. One of the trunks had a box of money inside to give to the director of the hospital. The supplies and monies would help to stabilize the Herat team's mission, at least temporarily. When the plane ascended into the sky, I thought of my family. But I had to go. When the plane landed safely, I thanked God. I transferred the trunks onto the bus that took me to the hospital near the city of Herat.

In August it was sweltering hot. The bus ride along the Kandahar-Herat Highway was dusty and dangerous. Bandits were common. I told the bus driver, "When you get to the NOOR

Hospital, stop for me." The hospital was famous and everyone knew where it was. Fortunately, I arrived at the hospital without incident.

The bus stopped in front of the entrance gate to the hospital compound. It was such a relief. The bus conductor and I unloaded the trunks from the bus. Custodians from the hospital came to the bus and carried them into the compound. I asked to see Dr. Fred Fredrickson, an American and head of the hospital team. After I was led into his office with the two trunks, and was alone with him, I opened one of the trunks and pulled out the box of money. "I have brought two trunks of medicines and here is a box of money. Also, this is your mail," I announced.

He welcomed me warmly. The nurses rushed in and organized the mail for distribution. Then I gave Dr. Fredrickson two letters from George Terry. One of them stated that I was to stay in their hospital and remain there for three days until the next Ariana flight would depart from Shindand Airport. I did not know the contents of the other letter. He and another British doctor, an optometrist, discussed the letters and then said, "We will take you to the town." I was surprised, but didn't say anything.

We drove to a large compound where all the Western staff members were living with their spouses and children. Their situation was critical. Everyone was so excited to read their mail. Then I took a shower and ate a quick meal.

Next, Dr. Fredrickson said, "I am going to take you to the Mofaq Hotel. It belongs to one of our employees." Again I was surprised. At the hotel I saw about 10 to 12 people from the Afghan Government and heard them bragging about how they were strong communists. The hotel owner escorted me to a small storage room by the kitchen with a tiny window high up the wall. He brought me a mat to sleep on. That was my room for the night!

During the night it was extremely hot and the mosquitoes were not friendly. I couldn't sleep. In my mind I asked, "Why do they put me in this storage room with mosquitoes and insects? It's filthy." Suddenly the hotel was attacked and the air exploded with gunfire.

For the next two hours a firefight raged. Then I realized that I was put in the small room for my own protection.

In the morning the hotel owner opened the door and apologized: "I am sorry! I had to put you here. I was told that the hotel would be attacked last night and I could not tell Dr. Fredrickson about it. I could not take you to my home because it is packed with people."

Later I had dinner with Dr. Fredrickson and then relaxed for the next two days in a nice room at the hotel. On the second day I borrowed a bicycle from a hotel employee to explore the town. Dressed as a common Afghan I rode invisibly through the government held areas and rebel held areas. I did not get off the bicycle.

On the third day I was ready to go home. Dr. Fredrickson drove me into the compound where the Ariana Bus Line was located. The compound had huge, thick mud walls. We said our farewells, I walked into the bus terminal and waited for a bus to take me to the Shindand Airport.

A few minutes later the bus arrived and I boarded it. When it had inched halfway out the compound gate, a rocket whizzed by and exploded. Our bus driver quickly reversed back into the compound. We all ran into the bus terminal and dove onto the floor. After a while the gunfire and explosions ended. We boarded the bus again and cautiously headed along the dangerous Kandahar-Herat Highway.

This time we were not so lucky. We were stopped by bandits. "Give us your money," they shouted. Standing up I said, "Look, I have nothing," showing them my empty pockets. Others were robbed of their watches and other small valuables. The bandits left. We continued on and finally arrived at Shindand Airport. Boarding the plane I thanked God that I was able to return home to my family.

Upon landing at the Kabul Airport, I was picked up by an IAM vehicle and brought to our headquarters. There I handed George Terry a letter from Dr. Fredrickson. I thought that my mission was over. George, though, turned to me and again pleaded, "Now we need your help to find a small airplane that can land in the Herat Airport." The letter stated that the staff asked to be evacuated.

It was too dangerous for them to remain in Herat. The airport was about 10 miles from the hospital. At that time Herat Airport was not fit to receive large planes like those from Ariana Airlines. Bakhter Airlines had smaller planes, though, and could land at Herat Airport. After explaining to Bakhter officials the need to rescue the entire staff of doctors and nurses and their families, they agreed to cooperate with us.

Originally the plan was for me to go on the flight and, when on the ground, guide the staff and families to the plane. However, since every seat in the small plane was needed for the Herat hospital members, I was not able to go. The airline officials sent a flight attendant from the plane to escort the Herat staff and families to the chartered plane for their escape. Happily the rescue mission was successful!

Risks for Humanitarian Aid Workers

The entire Herat staff was very appreciative that I had risked my life to save them. It may be difficult for you to imagine that the level of danger traveling to Herat was extreme. I was not a US citizen then. It is worth noting that many Americans do not realize the risks that citizens in war-torn countries like Afghanistan and Iraq take working for US and other Western humanitarian aid agencies. Why did I take such risks? Dedicated, idealistic, energetic Americans who worked in the Peace Corps and USAID in the 60s and 70s had made a strong impression on me. They and other aid workers from Canada, Europe, and Australia had inspired in me gratitude and a desire to be like them.

Life was and continues to be hazardous for international humanitarian workers in war zones. They are often viewed as foreign agents serving political purposes and are attacked.

George Terry was a nice man. I remember his son Don. When Don married, he continued to work as an aid worker in Afghanistan. Tragically, in August 2010, he and other colleagues were killed by the

Taliban. His wife is now living in Chicago. More recently, in September 2014, British aid worker David Haines was beheaded by the Islamic State group.

Escape Again to Pakistan

The political situation in Kabul got worse. In the last days of 1980, after Christmas, two IAM international workers were killed in their homes—a nurse and her husband who was a pharmacist. In mid January 1981, the Kabul IAM headquarters decided to suspend its operations and all international workers were directed to leave the country. George asked me to take charge of the local staff of Afghan workers. I declined and returned to Kandahar with my family. There I informed my father that I would go to Karachi to work with Hajji Masho, and that Bibigula and our children would remain in our family compound.

In Kandahar I contacted Hajji Masho's family who knew about the previous plan for me to sell carpets to foreigners with him in Karachi, Pakistan. I traveled to Chaman where they provided security for me to join him in Karachi. After arriving there, I worked at night selling carpets. During the day, I began assisting the Inter Aid Committee (IAC). It was a US-European humanitarian organization in the initial stage of expanding refugee camps for Afghans. That was just before millions of Afghan refugees flooded into Northwest Province (Peshawar is the capital) and Baluchistan Province (Quetta is the capital) in Pakistan.

Daily I visited Afghans who were staying at Hajji Masho's hostel and were in transit to Europe and Hong Kong. One day I was asked by James Dobbie, the Director of the Inter Aid Committee (IAC), to fly to Peshawar for an interview with Mr. Dean, the regional director of the IAC. He needed a deputy assistant. There I could decide whether to work in Peshawar more permanently or rotate between Karachi, Peshawar, and Quetta.

11
HOSTAGE FOR 13 DAYS

Before arriving at the Karachi Airport terminal, my gut instinct told me that something would happen to me. It was early Monday afternoon, March 2, 1981. I was preparing to fly on Pakistan International Airlines (PIA) flight number PK 326 from Karachi to Peshawar, Pakistan. This flight would come very close to being my last.

I insisted that Hajji Masho take me to the airport, even though he was very busy. He agreed, but reminded me that he would not be permitted to go with me inside the terminal because of the Pakistani policy which allowed only ticketed passengers to enter. Perhaps my feelings of foreboding came from the fact that this was my first flight inside Pakistan and my first flight to Peshawar, the headquarters of the Afghan mujahideen.

After arriving early at the airport, I started to write a report about the newly arrived Afghan refugees whom I had interviewed, and the war conditions inside Afghanistan that they had described. The report was a last minute request of Mr. Dobbie. The plan was for me to hand my report to the PIA office in the Peshawar terminal upon my arrival. Later that day, an IAC office custodian would pick up the report.

I was the first person in the terminal boarding area. While sitting and thinking about the report, I saw five men walk into the boarding area and sit down. They wore baggy pants except for one who was in western pants and a shirt. They kept changing their positions from one corner to another. Their movements were so distracting that I decided to write the report on the plane. When the announcement to board the plane was made, three of the men rushed forward. I was right behind them. The other two men followed. As we walked to the plane, I was surprised to see no security checkpoint. There was no one to check for weapons or bombs. Accustomed to the Soviet-

Afghan security system at airports, I expected a thorough physical search, even to have my private parts touched. I thought it was very irresponsible that there was no security check.

I walked to my middle seat B, row 13, not far from the front. One of the five men in the terminal who wore western clothing had already arrived and was sitting in seat A next to me. He was skinny, like the majority of people in Pakistan, and had a big mustache.

The music flowing through the plane's speaker system was very nice. I started to relax. The pilot announced that it would be a two-hour flight to Peshawar. It was a routine hop. There were 132 passengers and nine crew members on board.

In aisle seat C, next to me, was a father and across the aisle from him were his wife and two children. He was a Pakistani citizen from Ko-hot in the Northwest Province of Pakistan, an electrical engineer working in Medina, Saudi Arabia. They were on vacation visiting their home in Pakistan. It was customary for passengers to introduce themselves. In Pashto he asked who I was. Not wanting to disclose my Afghan identity, I replied, "I am from somewhere," and did not say anything further. The skinny young man with a big mustache to my right, next to the window, said nothing.

The Boeing 720 took off and ascended into the afternoon sky. I started writing my report but noticed that the skinny young man next to me was looking at what I was writing. I thought to myself that most Pakistanis could understand English. Being cautious, I folded my paper so he could not read it. I closed my eyes, laid my head back and dozed off. After a while, the young man touched me on my thigh, which woke me slightly, and I turned to the side so he could get out.

I was awakened by a loud noise. Two men were pushing and shoving a tall American man just a few rows in front of me. They were yelling in English and ordering him to sit down. I was still groggy, waking up from a deep sleep. The pilot suddenly announced over the plane's speaker system, "Please keep calm. The plane is now in the hands of Palestinians." Two minutes later the terrorists declared over the speaker system, "We are not Palestinians. We are like Palestinians but we are the Al-Zulfikar group." That was the first time that I had heard that name. It was not widely known at that time.

We were warned not to make any movements. Unable to find out who the terrorists were and what they were doing, I sat stiffly in my seat. I asked the engineer next to me what his opinion was of the situation. He said it was a complicated political issue. Only later did I learn the identity of the hijackers after the hostage crisis was over. Their leader was Salamullah Tipu, a member of the Pakistan People's Party (PPP). The code name he used on the plane was *Alamgir*. The other two were Nasir Jamal and Arshad Ali Khan Tegi. I don't remember the code names that they used on the plane; therefore, I will refer to Nasir Jamal as *Jamal*, and Arshad as the terrorist at the back of the plane who I did not see or hear during my captivity except when he had initially sat next to me—*the skinny young man*.

There were five terrorists who had boarded the plane. I don't know the names of the fourth or fifth terrorists. Their cooperative relationship to the other terrorists was revealed when I saw them talking to Alamgir after the start of the hijacking and at the Kabul Airport, before they left the plane. At the end of our captivity, I discovered that the hijackers were initially demanding the release of 92 political prisoners held by the Zia regime.

The Al-Zulfikar Organization (AZO) was a Pakistani pro-Soviet terrorist organization headed by Murtaza Bhutto. He was the son of Zulfikar Ali Bhutto, the former Pakistani Prime Minister and pro-Soviet communist. While in office in 1976, Zulfikar had appointed General Muhammad Zia ul-Haq to be Chief of Staff of the Army. Later Zia plotted and deposed Zulfikar from office, declared martial law in 1977, and assumed the presidency in 1978. Within two years the Zia regime executed Zulfikar. General Zia was President of Pakistan at the time my flight was hijacked.

The AZO consisted of members of the Pakistan People's Party who had escaped Zia's persecution. This terrorist group was headquartered in the Soviet-backed communist government in Afghanistan from where it waged an armed struggle against the Zia regime. The hijacking of my flight was part of that struggle. The sister of the Bhutto brothers was Benazir Bhutto. She was pro-West and would later become the Prime Minister of Pakistan and be assassinated in 2007.

Not knowing much about the situation, I thought they would take us to Lebanon. Suddenly the captain announced that we were going to Kabul. It was a shock to me. "Oh, no," I thought. The previous month I had escaped from Kabul. If the Pakistani hijackers discovered that I was an Afghan, I would be a good gift to their Afghan communist comrades in the government and to the Soviets.

As a refugee from Afghanistan in Pakistan, I was still in danger. Afghan communists were collaborating with communists and pro communists in Pakistan, and there were many. The hijackers were among them. I was an anti-communist and had worked for the West all my life, mainly for the US, which was supporting the Afghan mujahideen who the Soviets and Afghan communists regarded as terrorists—the bad guys. Since I worked for the IAC providing aid to the mujahideen, I was considered one of them.

Seat A next to me remained empty. At that time, I did not know

that the skinny young man with the big mustache was one of the hijackers. I did not look to the rear.

In the Kabul Airport

At about 4:30 p.m., we were in Afghanistan; our plane was making slow, wide circles around the Kabul Airport. We touched down, taxied, and stopped about 100 meters in front of the terminal. I could see through my window the control tower and the small, two-story terminal with a restaurant. The photo to the left is the

Kabul Airport control tower years before the 1981 hijacking. In past years I had walked through the terminal many times.

There was a gentle rain outside. We were ordered to pull down the window shades. After an hour the air conditioning system malfunctioned and it became very difficult for us to breathe. All I could think of at the time was how to breathe. Finally the air system was restored and we could breathe normally.

For quite a while I thought that I would be killed. I prepared myself to die. I was seen as an insurgent by the Afghan communists since I was working in Pakistan against the Soviets and the communist Afghan Government. In the past, people like me were brought to the TV station in Kabul and forced to confess. Any of my words of opposition would be censored. I prepared what I would say: "The Soviets have illegally occupied our country. The Afghan communists are puppets and atheists." I had mail from the IAC in my backpack and I would be charged as being a CIA agent. Definitely they would kill me.

Other passengers became hysterical. But I was alert and ready for whatever was to come. I slapped myself on the forehead asking myself, "Is this for real or am I just having a nightmare?" I pinched my thighs hard. "Yes, this is for real."

Within the first couple of hours Alamgir started asking each passenger for either their passport or Pakistani ID card, plus a series of questions. All I had was my Afghan refugee card. The terrorists would presume that I was an Afghan resistance fighter. Alamgir told one of the stewardesses, a Pashto speaker from Peshawar, to stand next to him in the aisle and take notes on a clipboard while he asked questions. He began with the rows in front of me. Alamgir looked at the man sitting to my left and asked him in Urdu for his name, passport or ID card. When Alamgir finished with him, he looked at me.

She Whispered Three Times, "Sit Down."

As Alamgir started to question me and I opened my mouth to answer, he was called to the rear. The stewardess continued the questioning in Pashto. I answered in Pashto in a low voice and told her my name, which I later discovered she had misspelled. I said, "I am from Quetta." She asked for my identification card. I said nothing and just stared at her, which meant I had none. She whispered to me, "Sit down, sit down, sit down." She said it three times. Then she immediately moved to the next row in back of me.

I began to have a severe stomach ache. At about 9 p.m. that first night, an Afghan doctor and a nurse came to check on the passengers. The doctor wore a white doctor's coat over a western suit. He had black, curly hair, was of medium height, and looked pleasant. The nurse wore a nurse's uniform and a white cap. She was short, appeared to be Chinese with a reddish complexion, and was a little chubby. All the cabin lights were on. My stomach was very painful. It felt like my intestines were being cut by scissors.

The doctor and the nurse walked down the narrow aisle talking with each passenger asking, "What problems do you have?" When with Pakistanis, the doctor spoke in English and Pashto. But when the doctor came to me, he spoke in Farsi and I replied to him in Farsi. Because of my pain I was a little blurry minded and thought that he was Dr. Omery from Herat Province, an Afghan doctor whom I had sometimes worked with at the Jamhuriat Hospital in Kabul.

I described my intestinal pain to him. The doctor said that he would bring medicine to me and the other passengers, which he did the same night. I presumed that he recognized me and because he was a doctor, would not disclose to the communists who I was. The doctor literally had my life in his hands. I was naïve. Later in 2001, while in Uzbekistan, I met him again and he revealed who he really was, what he was told to do by the communists, and what he did not do.

We remained parked at the Kabul Airport for six days while the hijackers continued to demand the release of 92 political prisoners from Pakistani jails. I saw one of the five hijackers leave the plane within the first hours after landing. Presumably another hijacker also left the plane in Kabul because there were only three of them at the very end.

On the third day, March 5, late in the afternoon, 29 women, children, and sick men were released from the plane. At the time I did not know why the terrorists decided to release them. Later, after our release, I read in a newspaper that Anahita Ratab zad, the Minister of Women's Affairs for the communist Afghan Government, had appealed to the hijackers for the release of women, children, and sick men. I remember seeing her outside the plane with other women and girls. Anahita Ratab zad was an outspoken, well-known member of the Parliament during King Mohammad Zahir Shah's time. Her brother was a quiet person who had worked for me in 1974 at the Afghan Fertilizer Company.

Within half an hour after they were released from our plane, the engineer sitting to my left began to rapidly jerk and shake. His face tightened and the sounds of ah-ah-ah sprang from his mouth. He started chewing; his tongue stuck out and he bit off the front part of it, and spit it out. He became like a rock and fell into the aisle. He had an epileptic seizure. The hijackers told two of the male passengers to carry him to the rear where he was removed from the plane. I don't know what happened to him after that, but I saw an ambulance drive up to the plane.

After the women, children, and sick men were released, the hijackers cleared all the rows in front of the plane for themselves as a buffer zone. A Pakistani military officer was moved into the seat across from me where the engineer's wife had been sitting before she and their children were released.

One of the hijackers, not always the same one, was constantly walking up and down the aisle, holding a pistol in one hand and a grenade in the other. Sometimes he would walk very slowly, and sometimes quickly.

On the third day, about three times, a young man was led by Alamgir and Jamal from the rear of the plane and taken inside the cockpit and then returned to his seat. I presumed that it was for him to talk on the radio to the tower. He was a tall, handsome, young man with light skin. Later I learned that his name was Tariq Rahim.

In the early evening, for a fourth time, the tall, young man was led forward and again brought inside the cockpit. Then they brought him out. He wore a navy blue jacket, cream-colored baggy pants, and a cream-colored scarf across his shoulders. He bent forward at the waist, did not say a word, did not resist, and did not plead, "Don't kill me!" He did not ask for any help. Alamgir and the other hijacker, Jamal, started beating him viciously. I was in row 13 and only about 10 to 12 feet away from them.

I saw Alamgir then place his pistol against the forehead of the young man and shoot him. The sound was like a pop—not loud. The young man collapsed. It was horrifying. They dragged him down the aisle to the back door which was open half the time. I don't know whether others turned their heads to look, but I did not look. We were told several times during the day not to make any movements. So I did not see him thrown onto the tarmac.

After our captivity we found out that the hijackers had mistakenly believed Rahim was the son of General Rahimuddin Khan, the Governor of Baluchistan, and who Murtaza thought had conspired with Zia to depose his father. The decision to execute Rahim came from Murtaza through the radio after he had consulted with Dr. Mohammad Najibullah (commonly known as Najibullah), then head of the hated Afghan secret police, KHAD, and later president of the Soviet-backed communist Afghan Government. They did not realize that Rahim was a Pakistani diplomat to Tehran and had been a former aide-de-camp of Murtaza's father.

The terrorists then played music over the plane's speaker system. It must have been from a cassette tape that they had brought on board. It was an Urdu song about revenge for Zulfikar Ali Bhutto. The translation was "We will take our revenge/We swear by your head [Zulfikar]."

At 8 p.m. the hijackers had heard the BBC report them as terrorists and that the Pakistani Government had refused to release the prisoners they wanted freed. Therefore, they gave us a death alert. Alamgir announced, "We will kill each one of you like him [Tariq Rahim]." He and Jamal directed us to say our "two verses of prayer" meaning the verses that Muslims pray before they die. I leaned forward and put my head on the back of the seat in front of me and closed my eyes. I did not pray those verses. I don't know why. However, each day I prayed to God, "I am in Your Hands. Whatever is Your Will, I will obey." I did not ask God to free me.

Preparing to Die

Throughout the 13-day ordeal I prepared myself to die. Some people have their lives flash quickly before them when on the verge of death. I slowly reviewed my life from childhood to the present, my relationship with my parents, my brothers and sisters, uncles, aunts, all my family members, friends, and colleagues.

My parents taught us that all people are creations of God and are equal before God. Don't harm any human; try to help others. If you can't help others, at least do no harm to others. My uncles encouraged us to be truthful. At the end of the day, a person who is truthful is successful and can have inner happiness. Always appreciate what you have. I was proud of myself since I had no regrets.

"If I am to go, thank God, I am prepared to die," I peacefully concluded.

"They Cannot Kill You"

In less than a minute I was in a deep sleep. Then all of a sudden I woke up and shook my head because I saw the face of my father which was tense and red. With my eyes closed I heard his voice saying in a commanding way, "What can they do? They cannot kill you!" Three times I heard him loudly say, "They cannot kill you." I understood him to mean that they can beat me up and hurt me, but they cannot kill me. Do not be afraid. Amazed, I opened my eyes, turned my head, and whispered twice to the man sitting next to me who was crying, "They cannot kill us! They cannot kill us!"

On the fourth night, looking through my window, I noticed after 10 p.m. that the Afghan guards at the airport had left and Soviet soldiers had replaced them. A Soviet Airlines (Aeroflot) cargo plane landed. The coffins of dead Soviet soldiers killed in Afghanistan were counted and loaded into the cargo plane. That continued night after night. For six days and nights I could see coffins being loaded into several Soviet cargo planes.

By the fifth night, machine guns of different sizes and ammunition had been transferred from the outside to the terrorists. Alamgir showed Jamal how to use them. I could tell that they were new because they were shiny. I got scared.

After 11 p.m. or midnight, the lights in the plane were dimmed. I could hear people snoring, farting, some crying and grinding their teeth. Passengers talked in their sleep. I remember one person shouted in his sleep, "Don't let them, don't let them, don't let them." Young men in their twenties called out in their sleep in Pashtu, "Mother, mother." Some would groan. It worried the hijackers who would rush over to them. Seeing that they were asleep, they would leave them alone.

I wondered what I might be saying in my sleep. To maintain a low profile I would sleep during the day and stay awake at night. A person asleep was less likely to be asked questions. I was afraid that they would talk to me. I was not fluent in Urdu, the main language in Pakistan. I could speak Urdu, but if they talked to me, they could tell that I was an Afghan by my accent. Also, if they searched my backpack, they would find letters from the IAC and think that I was working for the CIA.

During the day the hijackers would randomly and cunningly interrogate the passengers. They pretended to be nice, sometimes even sympathetic, to extract information. They would intimately address us in Urdu as "hammara bahayon," meaning our brothers. When they asked questions, they were not rough or violent. Sometimes they would give speeches condemning the Pakistan Government.

At other times, though, they threatened us. For example, when a passenger gave a mean look or was thought to have given a mean look to Alamgir, he was asked, "Why did you give me a bad look?" Then Alamgir would badly beat him. The terrorists demonstrated their capacity to act like vicious animals.

Every time the door to the cockpit opened, a *ding* sound would ring. The hijackers constantly went in and out of the cockpit. When they came out, they were usually angry. Their faces were twisted with madness. To this day I do not like the sound of the ding in an airplane.

Alamgir had big eyes and a big mustache. He reminded me of the mean bulls in our family farm in Kandahar with horns that looked like his long handlebar mustache. When I was a child on our farm, the bulls would rush toward us when they would see us. As they approached the fence, they would tilt their head to hit us, but we were on the other side of the fence. As the bulls touched the fence, my siblings and I would taunt the bulls, especially the young bulls, by extending our arms through the fence and slap them on the forehead. Then we would run away.

During the 13 days of captivity the captain of the plane, Saeed Khan, was always in good spirits. He even talked against the terrorists and consoled us saying, "If we are not meant to be killed, they will not kill us. They are terrorists, though." Captain Khan was of medium height and dark-skinned. He had a mustache; it was thick but not as long and curly as Alamgir's. Captain Khan was allowed to walk up and down the aisle in the plane and do stretches because he was needed to fly the plane. But his co-pilot's face and head had been badly beaten. I thought he may have even lost an eye. Captain Khan talked to the passengers and tried to cheer them up.

Two of the stewardesses were also brave and encouraging; the one who helped conceal my identity saved my life. I don't know her name. The other was Naila Nazir who later was given an international Flight Safety Foundation Heroism Award for her courageous handling of this dangerous situation. She cleaned the plane, comforted others and served us as though nothing was wrong. There was a male steward, too, who got badly beaten by Jamal, the terrorist.

Other passengers were having a hard time. After the release of women and children, all were men, except for two women. One was an older mother who would not leave her teenage son. There was also a woman who was not Pakistani. I don't know why she was not released.

I could feel the tension in the air. When my turn to walk to the lavatory came, I looked into the faces of the passengers. They were depressed, angry, disappointed. Some with their eyes open were silently and quickly moving their mouths indicating that they were praying.

A few of the Pakistani passengers confronted the hijackers. Declaring that they were from the Jamaat-e-Islami political party, they called the hijackers *atheists* and challenged them to lay down their weapons and fight them with their fists. Their Islamist party was founded during the British control in India and campaigned to establish an Islamist state in Pakistan. One of them said, "I will knock you down. We are also against President Zia but we are not like you. You are a terrorist." The hijackers ignored the challenge. My guess is that those people were not beaten up or killed because the hijackers feared revenge against other members of their Al-Zulfikar Organization's party, if it came out that they had harmed a Jamaat-e-Islami member.

A Pakistani military officer who was sitting in my row across the aisle was signaling several times to another Pakistani in the row in front of me, gesturing to grab the leg of a hijacker. Fortunately, they did not do anything because the hijackers were at the front and rear of the plane. If they started to fire their weapons, other passengers would have been wounded or killed.

Hostage Advice

Thinking back on my hostage experience, I would like to offer a few short tips for anyone, God forbid, who might become a hostage. First of all, put yourself in the hands of God. Circumstances might be out of your control. Pray! Praying is the best thing to do because it can occupy your thoughts instead of fear. It can give you strength. Be inwardly strong and ready for all conditions; welcome them into your heart. Be patient and be quiet. Don't confront the terrorists.

Do not talk or approach the terrorists. Keep your mouth shut. Don't make a stupid move to put yourself or others in danger unless you are 100% confident in your move. Don't make eye contact with any of them. Don't give a bad look or a good look. I saw several passengers severely beaten because they had given a terrorist an unpleasant face. Be alert all the time. I kept my eyes mostly closed pretending to be sleepy. During the day I would sleep and when not asleep I would close my eyes to give the impression that I was sleeping. At night I was awake, but when the hijackers walked by, I closed my eyes. The lights were dimmed so it was more difficult for them to see my eyes.

Make plans how to use an emergency exit or, if shooting happens inside the plane, how to duck and protect yourself. I had thought about the ways in which I might escape, especially in Damascus. I had no hope of escaping in Kabul, because I would immediately have been caught by the Kabul communist government, which was looking for any Afghan in the plane. People would have presumed that I was an Afghan refugee escaping from the Kabul-Soviet Government.

Terrorists are worse than wild animals. There is no justification for their acts. They will never achieve their goals. At the end of the day, they are losers.

Alamgir and Jamal rotated positions: one would stand at the entrance to the cockpit and the other would walk up and down the aisle with a pistol in one hand and a grenade in the other. I thought they were using us as guinea pigs, training themselves for their next terrorist act. They sought to control us mentally, to show their power as if we were criminals. I did not see them pray daily as Muslims do. The passengers and I would pray.

Alamgir's face was generally pleasant when not writhing with anger. He had an unusually long and curly mustache, large eyes, a short chin, big cheeks, black hair, light skin, large mouth, and broad shoulders. Standing over six feet tall, he was very energetic, very brutal, and often used profanity. Dreaming of ways to escape or fight the terrorists, I imagined grabbing the long mustache of Alamgir and pulling it behind his head.

Jamal was a Pashtun. Had he heard me talk, he would have immediately known from my accent that I was from Kandahar. He was taller than Alamgir, more erect in his posture, had black hair, and was very vicious. He brutalized the co-pilot and a steward.

Alamgir and Jamal made announcements in Pashto, Urdu, English, Punjabi, and Gujarati. They ordered us to write letters to President Zia. They knew that most of the passengers were Pashtun who spoke Pashto and also Urdu because they were from the Peshawar area. I wrote in Pashto, "Dear Mr. President, please accept their demands and please release us from these animals." I knew the hijackers would read it. We did not know what their demands were; but I asked that President Zia would agree to them whatever they were.

We were fed. In Kabul the food came from Ariana Airlines but was cooked in the Kabul Hotel. Today it is called the Serena Kabul Hotel. It was very good. With each meal we were given a coke or a glass of water.

I was young then and did not have a problem sitting for days. I weighed 145 pounds at five feet six inches tall. It was an advantage for me to be so light during that ordeal. Today it would be difficult because I am much heavier. I could see others who were visibly stressed and physically aching from constant sitting. They would attempt to stretch while sitting by rotating their heads, arms, and legs. There was constant movement among the passengers in their seats which angered the hijackers.

Once a day, row-by-row, 100 passengers were allowed to only use the rear lavatory. Some of them stayed inside it for a long time.

The hijackers permitted passengers to smoke which was very bad for my eyes. I don't smoke. The hijackers looked fresh and clean shaven. They regularly washed themselves and changed their clothes.

One day I recognized one of the Kabul workers who came on board to clean the plane. He was a classmate of mine from the third grade and was blind in one eye. I pulled my knees to my chest and folded my arms around my eyes so he would not recognize me.

Suddenly Off to Damascus

On March 8, the sixth night, at 10 p.m. with over 100 passengers, the plane unexpectedly moved and took off from Kabul Airport without any announcement. At first I thought that the plane might be going back to a Pakistani air base where the terrorists would blow up the plane with us in it. Then, as time passed and the plane had ascended to a height that I had never experienced, I presumed that we were not returning to Pakistan. Tears came to my eyes. In my mind was the image of my wife Bibigula and our little, six-year old daughter, Pashtana, and the memories of her rapidly talking to me during the many times we had flown from Kabul to Kandahar. She was a little chatter box.

Before sunrise the plane touched down. When the sun rose, I saw through my window a sign in the airport that read Damascus, Syria. That is how I knew where we were. I could see that there were only a few Syrian soldiers around the runway. They were far from our plane and in foxholes. The plane finally came to a stop on the runway.

Things were different in this airport. In Kabul the rear door was open and people went in and out. Here, in the Damascus Airport, no one came to the plane and the rear door remained closed. In Kabul, nice food was delivered from a Kabul hotel. In Damascus, we could tell that the food came from other airlines like JAL. We were fed, though.

A very bad smell developed in the plane. Passengers were passing gas, the toilets were not cleaned, and body odor was very stinky and strong. There were no sanitation crews to clean the toilets and aisles as there were in Kabul. Naila Nazir, the stewardess, was the only one that I could see who would regularly clean the plane. She worked nonstop and attended to the elderly.

Also passengers were smoking. It was terrible. In the Kabul Airport, air freshener was sprayed in the plane to mask the smell. In Damascus there was no air freshener. The only spray came from the passengers farting.

The terrorists reopened negotiations with Pakistan's Ambassador to Syria. We did not know it at the time, but the Pakistan Government had agreed to release 20 political prisoners named on the hijackers' list. On March 12 the hijackers changed their demand to 55 prisoners.

One night, while I leaned my head against the back of the seat in front of me, I dreamed of my almost two-year-old son, Mirwais. In my dream I stroked the back of his head and gently kissed his head. I woke up and found myself kissing the back of the seat and was so disappointed that I was only dreaming

During our captivity, the terrorists were worried that the passengers would overtake them, so they had zero tolerance for any unpermitted movement. Alamgir and Jamal constantly intimidated us, thrusting their guns at us as though preparing to shoot us.

One night, in the Damascus Airport, while the lights in the airplane were turned off, except for only a light at the front and back of the plane, without thinking and in a kind of daze, I stood up and started walking toward the lavatory in front of the plane. My body wanted to use the toilet. Alamgir, standing in the front, ordered me in Urdu (because all Pakistanis spoke Urdu) to go to the back lavatory. I was sleepy and immediately returned to my seat and sat down instead of going to the lavatory.

To Speak Would Have Invited Death

I misunderstood him, thinking that he had ordered me to go back to my seat. He rushed toward me angrily yelling in Urdu, "Why did you return to your seat when I told you to go to the back lavatory?" Instinctively I did not reply. To speak would have invited death. My Pashto accent would have been discovered and that I was an Afghan. With his rifle butt he repeatedly beat me on my left shoulder. I thought he was going to kill me just like he had killed the Pakistani diplomat. Fortunately, the other terrorist, Jamal, without saying a word pushed Alamgir's forearms to the side to stop him from hitting me.

On the eleventh day of our captivity, the terrorists told us, "If the Pakistan Government does not meet our demands by 8 p.m., we are going to blow up this plane and we will be in it with you." At 7 p.m. they appeared worried. At 7:30 p.m. they became very edgy and prepared ammunition and grenades with trip wires supplied to them in the Kabul Airport.

The atmosphere suddenly changed. Their hands shook as they inserted bullets into their magazines. Grenades had already been put under the tires of the plane. Alamgir was angry as usual. The terrorists stood in three positions: one outside the cockpit in the first class section, one patrolling in the aisle, and the skinny guy in the rear who never rotated with Alamgir and Jamal.

There were only about 10 minutes left. Then 8 p.m. came. Captain Khan walked down the aisle and stopped beside me. With my head bowed down, I asked him quietly, "What are you doing to us?" which was an indirect way of asking what were the terrorists going to do to us. He declared to everyone, "We are free and no longer in the hands of these animals and terrorists."

Alamgir came out of the cockpit smiling. One of the stewardesses held a tray of candies. He followed her and plucked candies from the tray and handed them to us personally. None of us smiled or showed any sign of happiness. Everyone was exhausted. From that moment on we were allowed to move to other seats and talk with other passengers.

Actually, it was not completely over and it was still very dangerous for me. Some of the Pakistanis started to recognize that my accent was pure Kandahari (in Afghanistan). They asked, "Where are you from?" I answered, "Quetta-Baluchistan." Baluchistan is the largest province in Pakistan with Quetta, its capital city, near the border of Afghanistan. Quetta is only about four hours by car from my home in the city of Kandahar. The people there have a similar Pashto accent as in Kandahar.

That was a fearful time. If the terrorists knew that I was Afghan, they would have killed me on the spot. I was not then an American citizen whose international status might have protected me. In Kabul the communists wanted to kill any Afghan on the plane.

Little cultural differences could trip me up and reveal that I was an Afghan. For example, another Pakistani from Peshawar asked me to pass "chini," a sugar packet. The same word "chini" in Pashto from my city in Kandahar means a tea cup. Therefore I passed him a tea cup. He angrily called me "dummy" and grabbed a sugar packet from my tray.

When we were allowed to move and were no longer required to sleep sitting up, the man next to me and I tried to sleep on our three seats. Initially we lay down side-to-side, head-to-toe on the three seats—like packed sardines. We were both skinny and were fine for a few minutes until I passed gas. It was a terrible smell. Passing gas is also a big offense in Eastern culture. Distressed, he said, "Shut your windmill." I moved to the floor. It was hard and narrow. A metal bar pushed into my back as I slept on my side. But it still felt so good after 11 days. The more you have comfort, the more you want. The less you have, the more grateful you can be. I realized how precious it was to lie horizontally, at least on my side and to stretch out.

During the last three days of the hostage crisis while the airplane was parked at the Damascus Airport, international newspapers were brought in to us. The newspapers were printed in various languages. That was when I read that the hijackers had thrown the Pakistani diplomat's body from the plane onto the pavement. The Pakistani newspaper written in Urdu printed our names. My name was misspelled. It was a lucky mistake for me.

On Saturday, March 14, the thirteenth night, the terrorists brought some of their comrades released from Pakistan prisons to show us that they had been tortured by the Zia regime. They wore baggy pants and their shirts were torn, indicating that they had been badly beaten. When their backs, arms and legs were revealed, I saw a mess of different colored bruises. We were told that they had also been tied up on the plane from Pakistan to Damascus.

Later we learned that initially the terrorists had purposely given the Pakistan Government the wrong names of people they wanted brought to Damascus. When they had been rounded up by the authorities in Pakistan, since their names were on the list, they were severely beaten by the authorities who took them to be terrorists. Those unfortunate people begged them to believe that they were not from the Al Zulfikar group. Actually they were innocent people like ordinary shopkeepers. Later, a representative from the Al Zulfikar group told the Pakistani officials that the list of names was not correct and handed them a new list that contained the names of prisoners who were members of the Al Zulfikar group.

Strangely, on the last day the terrorists smiled and said good-bye to each passenger as though we were departing relatives. The young, skinny man in seat A, who never returned to his seat next to me, quietly stood at the rear of the plane. To my surprise he smiled and hugged me as he left. It is my understanding that he did not hurt anyone.

Then the terrorists left the plane holding their weapons pointing to the sky and surrendered to Syrian officials. They were rushed away to a luxury hotel to join the other Pakistani political prisoners. There is a website (http://www.historyofpia.com/hijackings.htm) with photos that documents that moment and other events during the hostage crisis.

My understanding (unconfirmed) is that eventually Salamullah Tipu (Alamgir) fell out of favor with Murtaza and became regarded as a security threat by the Afghan communist government. He was thrown into a Kabul prison and executed by a firing squad in 1984. Jamal and Tegi (the skinny young man) left Kabul for Libya before Tipu's execution.

An American stood up and jokingly declared, "The plane is now in my hands!" After a while, we started to disembark from the plane.

It was nighttime. Standing at the top of the mobile stairway rolled flush against the exit door, I looked out and breathed fresh air for the first time in 13 days and nights. There was a crowd of Pakistani officials and military nurses waiting for us.

Mecca

As we stepped down the stairway, hundreds of photo flashes popped around us like fireflies. Journalists had come from around the world to report about us and our experiences. As we got seated in waiting buses and started moving, the reporters chased us yelling, "What happened on the plane?" The Syrian police beat them back.

We were taken to a military hospital on the outskirts of Damascus located at the foot of a hill. I remember Pakistani military and Syrian nurses with stretchers waiting for us. Many passengers collapsed onto them. The rest of us walked into the hospital. Doctors and nurses quickly screened us. I was taken to a cardiac ward where a nurse pointed and said, "This is your bed." I placed my belongings next to the bed and looked for a shower.

Walking down a hallway I found a washroom but there was no shower, only a big bucket and a small bucket. I turned on a faucet extending out from the wall and filled the big bucket with cold water. In Syria during March it was cold and the water was even colder. There was no hot water. I dipped the small bucket into the big bucket and scooped out water to brush my teeth and shave. Shivering, I washed my body with freezing water and soap. Then I changed into fresh clothes from my briefcase. When I walked back to my bed, I noticed a pill and a glass of water on my bed. I tossed the pill into my mouth, drank the water and lay down. Instantly I fell into a deep sleep after 13 days. I slept that night and all the next day. I don't remember having any dreams.

A nurse woke me. I wanted to get out of the bed, but I couldn't stand on my feet. She steadied my body against the bed while I tried to get up. I had no energy and struggled to move for quite some time. Finally I was able to move, little by little, along the bed. After about two hours I was able to slowly walk back and forth in the hallway.

Then I joined the other passengers in the hospital lobby. There we learned that at the request of President Zia, King Khalid of Saudi Arabia had invited us to his country. The Pakistan Government had sent another PIA aircraft to take us to Saudi Arabia and then to Pakistan. That plane had originally contained Pakistani commandos who were prepared, if necessary, to storm the plane.

The passengers were arguing. Some said that Captain Khan had requested that we fly in the same plane and with the same crew as during our captivity. Others said, "No, we shall fly in a new plane!" Finally we left for Saudi Arabia with a different plane and crew.

We flew into the city of Ta'if. It has a mild desert climate and that day the weather was very pleasant as a light rain cooled the heat. A few American doctors and nurses had boarded the shuttle bus with us to our hotel. They stood observing us.

I initiated a conversation with a doctor who was surprised that I spoke English and with an American accent. The Pakistani passengers were also taken by surprise and thought that I was an American. The shuttle bus drove us to a very nice Sheraton Hotel. It was up on a hill and within sight of a hospital. There we all identified ourselves and registered in a VIP section.

The Pakistan Minister of Higher Education was in a group waiting to welcome us. We chatted and I explained that I was an Afghan working for the IAC. I showed my identification cards. When the Saudi immigration officials realized that I was an Afghan, they shouted, "God is great, you were saved. You are a freedom fighter. God protected you." A crowd of passengers and other officials hurried over when they heard this and I was treated like a celebrity.

In my hotel room I took a wonderful, warm shower. In preparation for our pilgrimage we were given large, white cotton sheets to wrap ourselves in. The sheets form sacred clothing called "ehram" and are worn while walking around the Kaaba, also known as the "Sacred House," the most sacred site in Islam.

The Saudi Government gave each of us a welcome card along with some spending money. In the evening we began boarding buses to the holy city of Mecca for our pilgrimage. One of the hostage passengers stopped me before I stepped into the bus and said, "You cannot go to Mecca, you are an American and not a Muslim." I replied, "I am a Muslim from Afghanistan," and took my seat. He did not think that someone could be an American and a Muslim. Stereotyping is in every culture.

We were driven to a special mosque in Ta'if where we recited a special prayer. From there we reboarded the buses for another almost two-hour ride to Mecca. Inside the buses special Muslim instructors were waiting for us. Along the way they read verses from the Koran which we loudly repeated after them.

We arrived in Mecca, regarded as the holiest city within the religion of Islam and which non-Muslims are prohibited from entering. All Muslims who are physically and financially able are obliged to journey there on a pilgrimage called a "Hajj." It is the religious duty of every Muslim and one of the five pillars of Islam. Mecca is the home of the Kaaba which is the most sacred place within the Al-Masjid al-Haram, the largest and most sacred mosque in the world. There are seven entrances to this mosque. Our entrance was Babl Abdul Aziz where we were greeted by the Governor of Mecca Province and other Saudi officials.

It was midnight and we were surrounded by Saudi police who made sure that we were not crowded. If you have ever seen pictures of many thousands of pilgrims dressed in white sheets prayerfully circling like ocean waves around the cube-shaped Kaaba, you will realize how unusual it was for us to have lots of space around each of us as we walked seven times around the Kaaba. Within the mosque we remained a few more hours while some fellow hostages continued to walk around and pray. Others, like me, sat on the ground and rested.

Captain Khan came over and asked to speak with me. We spoke in Pashto as others listened. I asked him, "How difficult was it to fly into and out of Kabul Airport?" "It was very difficult because the airport is surrounded by mountains," he explained. I praised Captain

Khan for his courage during our captivity. He replied, "I have been trained as a pilot to deal with emergencies." At the back of my mind I was curious and inquired, "How close did we get to being killed?" Captain Khan answered, "More than seven times the terrorists were ready to kill everyone and blow up the plane. God protected you because you were in an especially dangerous position. While in the Kabul Airport the terrorists told the stewardesses to immediately report to them when they identified an Afghan." When the stewardesses served refreshments, they would ask, "Do you want Fanta or Coke?" I would only raise my hand and take whatever they had in their hands and not say anything.

Other passengers who heard my conversation with Captain Khan came over and patted me on the back saying, "God bless you."

Before leaving this mosque, we visited "Abraham's Place," two slightly inclining hills facing one another, called Al-Safa and Al-Marwah, within the enclosure of the Grand Mosque. Pilgrims must run up or jog back and forth seven times between these hills to qualify for completing the Hajj. It is a ritual symbolizing the event of Abraham's wife, Hagar, searching for water to give their infant son Ishmael until God revealed to her the Zamzam Well. I jogged slowly, since I was still exhausted. After hours of prayer, about 7 a.m., we left Mecca.

Upon returning to the Sheraton Hotel, I took a short nap. A few hours later we left the hotel, were bused to the airport and flown to the city of Medina to visit the holy place of the Prophet Mohammed. We remained there for three days. The Governor of Medina was among those who came to see us. Through an interpreter he said to me, "I give asylum to you and your family. You can teach English here." I respectfully replied, "Now, all I am interested in is to see my parents." In the Eastern culture parents represent the entire family; therefore, it was understood that parents included my wife and children.

Off to Peshawar to Meet President Zia

After the tour of holy sites in Saudi Arabia, we were flown to Peshawar, Pakistan. There was a raging storm and the landing was dangerous. I thought that we might all die then and there. The plane tilted sharply from side-to-side as we came in for the landing. The pilot gave several warnings to tighten our safety belts. The Peshawar Airport runway was short, so it forced a jolting stop. I thanked God that we were alive.

When the plane landed, waiting to welcome us with most of his cabinet members was President Zia. At that time we all believed that Zia had made the decision to release 55 political prisoners based on his singular concern to save our lives. Recently, however, I discovered something different. While our plane was in the Damascus Airport, the hijackers repeatedly threatened to blow up the plane if the prisoners were not released. Pakistani and Syrian officials in the control tower had negotiated extensions of time. President Zia, though, was intent on letting the plane be blown up and for us to die. The terrorists made their final warning that there were three Americans on the plane and they would soon be killed. "Be ready to pick up their bodies," they threatened.

It was then, at the edge of the cliff, that former President Jimmy Carter intervened and persuaded President Zia to release the prisoners so the Americans would not be killed. Ronald Reagan had just been inaugurated as President two months earlier. The previous year, in March 1980, President Carter had offered Pakistan $400 million in foreign aid, which Zia had dismissed as peanuts. Zia was after billions of dollars. Afghan refugees were pouring into Pakistan escaping the Soviet occupation. The December 26, 1979 Soviet invasion of Afghanistan was known in Pakistan as "Brezhnev's Christmas present to Zia."

Twenty minutes before the 8 p.m. deadline, President Zia had given the order to release the prisoners and fly them to a sanctuary in Libya where they would be exchanged for us. But that was not the end of the crisis. While the prisoners in a Pakistani plane were in the air en route to Libya, Muammar Khadafy refused to receive them on

Libyan soil. Therefore, we remained in the Damascus Airport until Syrian authorities eventually agreed to receive the prisoners for the exchange.

Now back to my story. As we stepped down the stairway from the plane, it was raining heavily. We walked straight to an open area where President Zia and other officials were waiting. Each of us patiently waited in the rain as President Zia individually shook our hands. An assistant held an umbrella above his head. Oddly, as I approached him, I saw that he was wetter than I was.

Television cameras were filming the event. After I shook his hand and started walking away, the Minister of Higher Education, whom I had met in Ta'if and Mecca, grabbed me by my shirt collar and pulled me back to stand in front of President Zia. The Minister said, "This is the Afghan freedom fighter." President Zia again shook my hand and hugged me. I walked over and stood with others in the rain as the remaining passengers were greeted by him. When that was finished, we were led to a huge tent and sat down on chairs.

We waited for President Zia and stood up as he and other cabinet members entered the tent. When he sat down, the Minister of Higher Education called me over to sit in front of President Zia. With a small coffee table between us, he spoke in Urdu and said, "Please tell me your experience as a hostage."

Not being as proficient in Urdu as in English, I answered in English and told him the story. After I did, he spoke in English and asked, "Which Afghan officials came into the plane?" I answered, "I did not see any of them. I saw only a doctor and nurse and the custodians cleaning the plane." I explained that there was no security checkpoint in the Karachi Airport terminal where we had boarded the plane; that weapons were brought on board, Afghan officials could be seen near the plane, and that sometimes there were PIA (Pakistan International Airlines) small airplanes coming into the airport. Someone was taking notes as I talked.

There were hundreds of relatives and friends of the other hostages and spectators waiting inside and outside the tent. But I was a refugee in Pakistan and no one welcomed me. I had hoped that the folks at the IAC office would have sent a vehicle to pick me up. No one knew what I looked like, though, since that was my first visit to Peshawar. Also no one held up a sign with my name or a sign that read "IAC".

Violent winds knocked down the big tent and the event turned into chaos. I rushed out and hired a gas-powered rickshaw to take me to the old landmark British hotel called "The Deans" where the IAC office was located. Walking into the office, I met the Peshawar IAC Coordinator, a Canadian citizen whose last name was also Dean. "I'm sorry that I arrived late to the meeting," I said. "You must be Sher," he replied. "Yes, I am!" Dean and the other staff members walked over and hugged me. Then I was led to a suite in the hotel.

An hour later an IAC doctor came to my room. His name was Dr. Brown, an Australian. He examined and advised me not to allow a journalist or anyone to talk to me for at least the next three days. He would then examine me again. For the first few hours I was fine; but after that my brain and my body were not friendly with me. I tried to count and couldn't count up to 100. I walked around in my room. It was a large family suite so I had plenty of space to walk and unwind.

On the third day, Dr. Brown visited me again, this time with James Dobbie, the Executive Coordinator for the IAC in Pakistan. The doctor said that I needed more time to recover. James agreed and that I should take time off from work for one month. Two days later I requested time to visit my family. My plan was to travel to Quetta, then to Chaman, which borders Afghanistan. There I would send a message to my family in Kandahar to let them know that I was in Chaman, only about 80 miles away.

"I Would Rather Walk Than Fly"

From Peshawar to Chaman it is about 700 miles. The IAC headquarters staff offered to buy me a plane ticket. I had had enough plane rides, though. "I would rather walk than fly," I said. The office bought me a train ticket instead. It was for a passenger train which stopped at every small town along the way.

It took two days to arrive in Quetta. The hostage experience continued to take its toll on me. I became more exhausted and skinny. From Quetta I rode a taxi to a friend's home in the border city of Chaman. There I thought no one would know that I had been held hostage in a Pakistani airliner. To my surprise my friend knew about it. He quietly sent a messenger on a motor bike to Kandahar to inform my brother, Fazullah, that I was in Chaman.

Fazullah arrived at my friend's home. We sat for a while and talked. Then he walked outside and called me over to a motorbike ready to drive me across the Pakistan border into Afghanistan. I told him, "No, no! It is too dangerous for me to return to Afghanistan." Fazullah insisted, "I have to take you home."

Without saying another word, I agreed and jumped on the rear of the motorbike. We took the back roads across the Pakistan border. After we passed the small town of Spin Buldak, which was about eight miles across the Afghan border, we stopped. Fazullah said, "Wait here." I got off the motorbike and he returned it to a shopkeeper in town. Fazullah came back and we started walking along the Kandahar-Spin Buldak Highway.

After about a mile, a huge truck hauling dirt passed by. It suddenly stopped and slowly drove back in reverse. When the truck eased to a stop beside us, we recognized that the driver was from our village. He was Manan, an elementary school classmate of my older brother, Wahid. Fazullah greeted him and whispered to me, "Don't say that you were across the border." We climbed into the front seat with him since the back of the truck was full of dirt used for farming.

Upon reaching the edge of Kandahar, Fazullah told Manan to drop us off and we would continue to walk or rent a taxi. Since we had approached Kandahar from the east side, and our home was on the northwest side of the city, we still had about a two-hour distance to walk. Kandahar is a large city. Manan insisted, though, that he continue to drive us to our home. Fazullah said, "Okay, take us on the back road." We wanted to avoid the Soviet and Afghan communist soldiers who controlled the main roads. Intense fire fights were common in Kandahar. But at that moment, we were lucky, it was calm.

Manan dropped us in front of our home. When Fazullah and I went inside, I first saw my mother, my wife Bibigula, and our little girl Pashtana. Then I saw Mirwais. They didn't know where I had been and had no idea that I had been held hostage in a Pakistani airliner for 13 days. The only ones who knew were my father, my uncle, and Fazullah. They had been following the news about the hijacked plane, and Fazullah had gone to the Kabul Airport. He was there while the plane sat on the runway for six days. Fazullah had come every morning to the terminal until sunset. He could see the plane from the restaurant on the second floor in the terminal. It is a small airport.

Later I learned that our IAC office had informed the United Nations and the International Assistance Mission (IAM) in Kabul about my captivity. I had worked many years on and off for IAM teaching the Pashto and Farsi languages to their doctors and nurses. Anticipating that we might be released from the plane while at the Kabul Airport, IAM had assigned Ramazan Dehqan Zada to safely guide me away. He would recognize me because we had been colleagues teaching Afghan languages to the USAID, IAM, and UN staffs. Mr. Dehqan Zada and his family now live in Woodland, California.

I wish I could say that my hostage experience was the last of my life and death struggles. Many more would follow, though.

12
KABUL UNDERGROUND RESISTANCE

I returned to my home in Kandahar in April 1981 to recover after having been a hostage. I was feeling depressed after that experience. Kandahar was still a bleeding battleground between the Afghan communists, Soviets and mujahideen. Dozens of my family members in Kandahar had been killed by the communists in the previous three years.

The next month, in May, I traveled to Kabul to withdraw money from my savings account in the Afghan National Bank (Bank Mili). A few days earlier I had explained to my father why I planned to go there: the bank in Kabul was not safe and transferring my money to the Kandahar branch of Bank Mili might be safer. My father replied, "My health condition is not good; don't stay long." Bibigula was also nine months pregnant; so I intended to rush back.

Nothing indicated that he was sick. Every day my father would walk many miles along the Shah Canal. Although he had retired as the Watermaster for Kandahar, he continued for years afterward to monitor the water flow and usage by the farmers. The canals contoured the base of the mountains. Some of them were old and built in the 1700s. My father did, however, appear depressed because of the atrocities caused by the Soviet occupation.

In Kabul, when I spoke with the director of the bank whom I knew, he advised me that the Soviets limited withdrawals of money to 5000 Afghanis per month (about US $63). He warned me, "Even if you merely apply to withdraw your savings beyond that amount, your account would be automatically frozen. It is beyond my control. The communist authorities would presume that you were attempting to escape from the country."

While in Kabul I went to the home of Frances Iliff who was the head nurse instructor for International Assistance Mission (IAM) at the NOOR Hospital. IAM had reopened following five months of suspended operations after two of its staff had been murdered in their homes. Frances called George Terry and said, "Sher is here." George asked me to rejoin IAM when I spoke with him.

After my traumatic hostage experience, I had resigned myself to be a farmer in Kandahar and no longer work for a foreign humanitarian agency. I wanted a peaceful farming life. However, George, Frances, and many other colleagues at IAM were close friends of mine since college and I reconsidered. I told George that I must first speak with my parents before saying "yes." The next day I left by bus to Kandahar.

The Passing of My Father

When I arrived home on May 7 and walked into our family compound, as I rushed past my mother to see Bibigula, I jokingly said to her, "Did you kill my Boss?" I always called Bibigula, "Boss." My mother replied, "Yes, God bless." Immediately that worried me because that meant someone had died. She did not say "him" or "her." Confused and surprised by her remark, I hurried to a special room in our compound where Bibigula had been staying and was expected to deliver the baby. It was nicely furnished with two windows that overlooked our orchards and a rose garden.

I saw Bibigula resting on a specially made mattress and beddings in the middle of a beautiful carpet. Next to her was our new son, Yonus. Relieved, I said, "Hey, Boss, you are alive!" "Yes, I am," she softly replied. It was common for Afghan women to die in childbirth. The memory of Bibigula nearly dying during pregnancy a few years earlier still lingered in my mind.

I bent over to gaze at Yonus and marveled at how special he was. At the same time I was worried about what my mother had said and quickly walked to the house in the compound where my parents lived. In the guestroom I saw my father surrounded by my brothers, uncles, and cousins. He had passed away. Shocked, under my breath I mourned, "Oh no!" My brothers said that I had missed his passing by just a few minutes." My father had had a heart attack.

Shortly afterward my father was carried across the street to our family mosque. It was built on our family land--about one acre. My grandfather, Hajji Rawouf, had built the mosque at the turn of the twentieth century. Our mosque was the first in Kandahar to allow women to pray in it. In the early days it was just for our family--then about 30 people. Later it was opened for everyone and attended by several hundred people living in many surrounding compounds. It is a huge place built with mud and bricks. In addition to a large prayer room, it served as a community center and provided guest rooms. Outside the mosque there is a large terrace for private and public meetings, a large pool and a deep well. At the back of the property there is a permanent running stream with clear water at the base of Elephant Mountain. In 2008 I had our family mosque renovated.

My brothers explained to me the events just before my father's passing. Everyone with him was celebrating the birth of Yonus who had been born just before sunset. The women were across the street in our family compound preparing for a celebration that night. My father had walked to the mosque, finished his prayer and then said, "Take me home, I am not feeling well." A stretcher was brought from our compound and family members carried him back across the street—nearly 100 feet. My father was a big man, about 250 pounds and taller than me.

After he was laid in his guest room, my father said his last words, "I am tired and will rest." Later my step-mother came into the room to check on him and discovered that he had passed away. She cried and shouted out. Other relatives rushed into the room. I had arrived only minutes after that, which was about 2 p.m.

Without delay he was taken to the mosque for ablution, washing his body, and preparation for burial. It was prayer time and the mosque was filled with people. We sent messengers to other mosques to inform the villagers of my father's passing. Within three to four hours more than 500 people came to the mosque and to the graveyard where he was to be buried. They came even though there was a firefight in the northwest edge of Kandahar City between the

Soviet troops and the resistance fighters who, by that time, had come to be called mujahideen. Firefights were a daily occurrence.

About 5:30 p.m., after my father's body was prepared for burial, I announced in the mosque that we would bury him in our family's new cemetery. His will was to be buried there because our old family cemetery was almost filled. The Afghan tradition is for all blood relatives to be buried together; but when the cemetery becomes filled, another location is used.

As we started the procession toward the new cemetery, villagers and my father's friends who had gathered, stopped us and said, "We are taking him to the old cemetery. It is near our home and we can say a prayer when we pass by." "No," I insisted, "...it is my father's will to be buried in the new cemetery. Also there are bullets flying near the old cemetery from the mujahideen and the Soviets who are in a firefight." Several of his friends and leaders of the community replied, "That is okay. He is not only your father, but our father, too." The people protested and against our wishes, took his body to the old cemetery where people started digging a grave between his son and his brother.

About 7:30 p.m. the burial was finished and we arrived home by 8 p.m. During the next three days of *Fatiha*, more than 1000 people came every day to mourn. My father was a respected councilman who had been reelected for many years. He was also a trusted volunteer mediator whom other families and even other tribes sought out to settle their property disputes. They came even from distant provinces like Helmand, Zabul, and Urozgan. My father was very open-minded and friendly to all people, including my Peace Corps friends.

A Great Mediator

He had a good sense of humor and much patience. My father had mentored me how to resolve different types of disputes between tribes. I remember people coming into our home throughout my childhood, seeking my father's services. Visitors ranged from ordinary villagers to tribal leaders and high-level government officials.

My brothers, cousins, and I were required to sit, listen, sometimes take notes, and serve tea and food to them.

As a child the meetings seemed boring to me. Yet the lessons learned in those experiences have served me well in later years. They are a major reason why I have been effective as Senior Cultural Advisor for US and European commanding generals in Afghanistan building bridges of understanding between them and tribal leaders. The military calls this "key leaders engagement" (KLE). Unfortunately, when the military commanders and I left Afghanistan, the cultural bridges of communication and mutual respect that we had built were not maintained.

Since there were many people coming and going in the mosque to pray for my father, we worried that the Soviets would drop bombs on us as they had done before. Kandahar was a bloody battleground. People came by car, truck, and horses to the mosque. Since there were many mulberry trees surrounding the mosque, the Soviets would presume that people were hiding under the trees, having meetings, and plotting against them. Representatives of my family pleaded with the Governor of Kandahar, an Afghan communist, to tell the Soviets not to bomb us because "we would be gathering for Fatiha—offering prayers for Hajji Mahmood." Since 9/11 in Afghanistan, many suicide bombers have walked into mosques and blown themselves up during Fatiha.

The morning after the burial at 4 a.m., I went by myself to the grave to pay my respects. Five people had arrived before me. We took turns reading verses from the Koran, reflected on my father's life and prayed. Bringing flowers to the grave is not an Afghan tradition. After one week, friends and distant relatives invited us to several dinners, which is tradition. At the dinners we talked about my father's life. My mother did not attend the dinners because, according to another Afghan tradition, the deceased husband's wife should not leave the house for 40 days after the passing. Also a baby born inside a compound is not taken outside for 40 days, unless it is for medical reasons. If a baby is born outside the compound, he must remain at the site of the birth for 40 days. Therefore, Bibigula remained in our family compound with Yonus, Mirwais, and Pashtana.

Back to Kabul

Later I discussed with Wahid, my older brother, whether to remain in Kandahar or work for IAM in Kabul. In the fog, death, and complexities of war, one's options become narrowed and decisions may seem contradictory. For the sake of my mental health, I decided that it was better to be actively working. At the NOOR hospital I would be very busy, especially in the new orthopedic clinic. If I stayed in Kandahar and worked on the farm, the slow pace of life would not be good for me. Only one person at IAM knew that I had left Afghanistan and had been a hostage. If confronted by the Afghan communist government, I could argue that I had not left Afghanistan and had gone home to Kandahar when IAM suspended its operations. Now it was reopening and I was returning. The argument was plausible; however, there were no guarantees.

Whispers Away from Death

In Kabul I would be working directly with non-Afghans in the new orthopedic and prosthetic center: they were Dr. Lewis Williams, Ellison Wong, and Sarah Terry, George Terry's daughter-in-law. I could control my working environment, be separated in a new facility and location, and hire local Afghans of my choosing to be on our support staff. That was important because communist informers were everywhere and their accusations could lead to my death. That was how we lived under the communist regime—only whispers away from death.

Considering those things, I returned to Kabul a month later, in June, to work for IAM. Later Fazullah brought Bibigula and our children by bus to Kabul to join me. Kabul was very pleasant in June. The pollution that blankets the city today was not there. The IAM office was reactivated and it was a pleasure to work again with my friend George Terry who continued as IAM's Executive Secretary. A new orthopedic and rehabilitation center was built within the compound of the Wazir Akbar Khan Hospital.

I rejoined IAM as the Deputy Director of the new prosthetic center and had many duties. Dr. Lewis Williams, an American orthopedic surgeon, was its head of operations. As his deputy, I was also his interpreter. He was an orthopedic surgeon who managed the training of Afghan doctors and technicians that constructed artificial arms and legs. I served also as an interpreter for other doctors and trainers. While I was there, we fitted with prosthetics 2700 Afghans who had lost their legs and arms in the war. I remember that number since I administered the project. A training center for Afghan nurses in orthopedics and rehabilitation was also started.

The only way that IAM could operate its hospital was through an agreement with the communist Afghan Government. Dr. Williams and George sat with me and asked that I comply with it. The hospital treated all persons who came for medical assistance whether they were for or against the government. We did not discriminate against any person; at the same time, the communist Afghan Government had agreed not to arrest anyone who came to the hospital if they were anti-government. Fortunately, when I rejoined IAM the government was honoring its part of the agreement.

We were very busy treating both communists and anti-communists. I had a hard time, though, accepting the communists. But I had committed to IAM's agreement so that innocent children, women and men could be cared for. When injured communists came into the clinics for treatment, I made the initial entries into each patient's medical record  asking how and where he or she was injured, and where they lived. The doctors would follow and write their diagnosis on a medical form.

The above 1982 photo is very special because it shows a surprised Dr. Williams watching me talk to two men. One was a bearded mujahideen. He was a messenger representing his commander who had previously sent me a letter requesting personal treatment. Next to him was a member of the feared Afghan secret police, the KHAD, whose hospital had requested assistance. The two men were unaware of the other's identity and it was by chance that they had come at the same time. In a flash of inspiration I thought a photo of them with me and the doctor would be great to show our donors that we didn't discriminate between pro-government and anti-government people. So quickly I asked our Finnish nurse, Sarah Terry, to take that photo.

You can see Sarah in this photo below at the far left. The woman

covered with a scarf was a patient in our orthopedic and prosthetic center. A mujahideen had cut off her arm. It is one example of atrocities committed by many of the "false" mujahideen.

Not all mujahideen committed such barbaric cruelties on innocent civilians. There were true mujahideen and false mujahideen. War is horrible, confusing, and complex.

Underground Resistance

Members of our hospital staff also worked underground to provide medical aid to the mujahideen. Dr. Dolton was a doctor in the Wazir Akbar Khan Hospital. He was a Hungarian who publicly professed to be a communist; however, privately he was a Christian anti-communist. Dr. Dolton had connections with Soviet officers. Through those connections we were provided Soviet military vehicles to travel at night to sites where surgeries were secretly performed on injured mujahideen. Routinely I would travel with Afghan and European doctors from Holland, Belgium, and France to hidden and remote areas of Kabul.

In an area of Kabul called Chowki-Arghandi there is an old ski lodge where we would conduct surgeries. One night, while the doctors and I were returning from a midnight surgery, we saw a Soviet tank and troops approaching. Quickly we hurried away from our Soviet vehicle and ducked under a bridge. Suddenly the tank and troops stopped on top of the bridge. Time stopped for us. If the soldiers had walked around the corner of the bridge, they would have seen us and shot us dead on the spot. Thankfully, they moved on.

We worked throughout the nights and then labored during the days in the hospital. After being deprived of sleep for so long, it felt like sand was in our eyes. Exhausted and with deep mutual respect, we would look at one another and say through our eyes, "We are tired."

A Mistake

Months passed. Bibigula and I built a one-story house in 1982 to show the Afghan Government that we did not intend to escape from Afghanistan. The foundation of our home was concrete and stone. The walls were constructed with alternating red bricks about 12 inches thick. The inside walls were coated with a mixture of sand and cement except for the five bedrooms which were coated in gypsum plaster.

January of 1983 was bitterly cold--a record cold. Many children died. The IAM officers called me in one morning and said, "Here is money to help the poor. Don't discriminate among the people. Manage it to help both needy anti-communists and communists." I bought large quantities of firewood, diesel oil, sugar, and cooking oil in barrels and stored them in our home.

We networked through people that we trusted. Bibigula selected a few friends who identified destitute women to receive supplies. My cousin Haytullah was one of the men I trusted. He traveled by taxi, bicycle, and bus to different districts of Kabul to identify the poor, especially poor women. Many desperate people came to our home within two weeks to pick up the first lot of firewood and supplies.

Four of our neighbors became very suspicious wondering how the firewood and other supplies disappeared so quickly from our home. I came to realize that I had made a serious mistake. I should not have used our home as a warehouse for the supplies. The Soviets and Afghan communist authorities were suspicious of any outside aid given to Afghans that was not controlled by them. Even though the Soviets gave aid to the Afghans in Kabul and a couple of other big cities, it was still not enough for the actual needs of the many suffering people. Although we did not discriminate between pro-government or anti-government people, the Afghan communist authorities chose to interpret any aid to others that they did not control as aiding and abetting the enemy.

About two months later on March 9, at lunchtime, while I was pruning an apricot tree in front of the orthopedic center, a friendly communist informant of ours named Lt. Col. Niamutullah walked up to me. He was also my cousin, about my age, and had been trained in the Soviet Union and in India. Niamutullah worked within the communist Afghan Government commanding a communications department of about 900 soldiers.

"You Will Be Killed"

He asked me, "Why don't you go to America?" Surprised, I answered, "Why?" "I am here to let you know the Afghan Government with Soviet soldiers will search the area where you live. You are on top of the list of people to take away. You will be killed!" I got very worried and said, "What shall I do?" He answered, "Go to Kandahar!" "How can I go there?" I asked. "I will get tickets in my name for you, your wife, and children to fly to Kandahar," he replied. I gave him money and he went to the Ariana Airline ticket office to buy the tickets. It was about two miles from my office. Niamutullah returned in less than two hours with the tickets for my family.

Inside the hospital compound I informed Dr. Williams of the warning. Immediately he called George. It was clear what I needed to do. First they prayed for my safety. Quickly I transferred to them all my office documents and money allotted for the office operation. George calculated for my salary and extra money to be used in case I was captured. "Take this for your safety," they said. In a briefcase I placed 85,000 Afghanis which was about US $1000.

I walked home planning my family's next steps. I could not tell my wife and kids that we were escaping from Kabul in the morning because our kids would right away tell their neighbor friends, who would tell their parents, and who in turn would inform the Afghan authorities.

We Passed Like Two Clouds in the Sky

That night I couldn't sleep. Before sunrise on March 10, I woke Bibigula and told her to put important things in suitcases that we could carry. Surprised she asked, "Why?" Quietly I answered, "We are going to Kandahar," and I explained why. Bibigula then said, "You go first and I will follow after I have sold what I can in the house and put things in order." Looking very seriously into her eyes I said, "You have two choices—me or the household goods."

We woke the children, and quickly packed what we could. I put on an expensive-looking Soviet overcoat and a tie to match with the Afghan colonel's name on the plane ticket. With Bibigula carrying Yonus who was sleeping, Pashtana, Mirwais, and I left our home. We started walking across an open field which separated the front of our home from the Afghan Parliament building and the main road. Suddenly we saw Afghan and Soviet soldiers walking toward us. We continued to walk toward them. They came closer and closer and we passed like two clouds in the sky.

I stopped a taxi and directed the driver to take us to the Kabul Airport. Along the way there were government checkpoints. When our taxi stopped at the checkpoints, the soldiers looked inside, saw my Soviet overcoat and tie, and thought that I was a high-level Afghan official. We were very lucky.

Upon arriving at the airport and slowly moving through the security line, a funny thing happened. An Afghan security man opened my suitcase, fingered through it, and then closed it. Next he opened my briefcase and saw it filled with money. Stunned or scared, he quickly slammed it shut and pushed it back to me. Moving on we then waited in the Ariana Airlines boarding area, still aware that we could get arrested. Yonus and Mirwais slept in our laps. Pashtana rested in another chair. Finally we boarded the plane and settled into our seats. We were so relieved!

Caught in a Crossfire

After 45 minutes we landed in the Kandahar Airport. From the airport we took an Ariana shuttle bus with other passengers to Kandahar City, about 15 miles from the airport. When we arrived around 2 p.m. at the bus station in the city, I looked around and the only movements I saw were swirls of dust. The streets were empty and all the shops were closed. There were no taxis. I felt a light wind. We could hear intense exchanges of gunfire between communist forces and the mujahideen.

My uncle, Dr. Obiedullah, lived nearby, so I decided that we would go to his home instead of to our village which was far away. With Mirwais in my arms and Bibigula holding Yonus, we picked up our belongings and started walking westward to his home. Bibigula was a few months pregnant. Pashtana was able to walk. Suddenly we were caught in a crossfire of bullets. Soviet soldiers were firing from the north and the mujahideen were shooting from the south. Both sides shot at anyone or anything that moved. We rushed and crouched by a nearby wall which provided some protection from bullets whizzing by from the south. But it exposed us more to the bullets from the north. Bullets were hitting in front of us and in back of us like deadly drops of rain. We ran for our lives with three small children. I don't know how we made it alive and uninjured to my uncle's home…but we did! It was beyond my imagination.

When we arrived, Bibigula and I were breathless and couldn't talk. Our kids couldn't talk or cry. When things are so bad, you forget or are unable to cry. Our faces were full of fear and dust. My uncle and his family understood why none of us could talk. The firefight continued to rage outside.

After a while, when things had calmed down, I told my uncle our story. He was a doctor, from my mother's side of the family, and very tall. My plan was to send Bibigula and the children to my parents' home to live while I escaped to Karachi, Pakistan. I had no choice but to go there. I could either work with Hajji Masho or other Western organizations like the IAC (Inter Aid Committee), the USAID or the UNHRC (Office of the United Nations High Commissioner for Refugees). I could send for my family later. George Terry had sent a message by cable to Fred Innis, the Regional Director of the IAC in Quetta, alerting him that I was coming. So I expected to meet him along the way.

We remained at my uncle's home for the night. The following morning I left Bibigula, Pashtana, Mirwais, and Yonus with him. He later arranged for them to be picked up by my brothers and taken to my parents' home in our family compound. It would be the safest place for Bibigula and the children.

Back to Pakistan

I had changed into ordinary clothes in my uncle's home and no longer wore the expensive-looking Soviet overcoat and tie. I took a bus to Spin Buldak, the last stop before crossing the Pakistan border. At the Afghan checkpoint near the Pakistan border, a few miles from the Spin Buldak border crossing, communist Afghan soldiers ordered us off the bus and to sit in a circle on the ground.

Each passenger was questioned while sitting. When the interrogating soldier came before me, I motioned for him to bend down and I quietly said, "I am assigned as the new Director of Spin Buldak Office of Agriculture. Don't tell the others. Keep quiet." The soldier looked at me, nodded, and went on to the next passengers.

We reboarded the bus and continued toward the Pakistan border. Suddenly, after a few minutes, a heavy dust storm descended upon us and stopped the bus in its tracks. Motorbikers were passing by, smuggling medicine and drugs into Pakistan. Not wanting to delay, I stepped out of the bus, flagged down a smuggler and offered to pay him to take me across the border to Chaman. "How can I in this storm?" he responded. "This is the best time when it is difficult to be seen. I will pay you double," I replied.

The smuggler took me the remaining 12 miles to Hajji Masho's home in Chaman. Upon arriving there, his family greeted me warmly. They knew me and my father, who had passed away two years earlier.

From Chaman I rode a bus to Quetta, Pakistan. In the city I took a rickshaw to the office of the International Assistance Committee (IAC). I had previously worked for it a short time in Karachi before being taken hostage. Its operations had expanded and were then providing aid to 1.5 million Afghan refugees in that region of Pakistan.

At the office I met Mr. Fred Innis. He was 74 years old, 6 feet 3 inches tall, had silver hair, big eyes and an Irish/British accent. Mr. Innis was also a retired British officer and an Inspector General in the Pakistan Police Force. Mr. Innis had dual citizenship, British and Pakistani, since he was born and reared in the part of India that was partitioned in 1947 to be Pakistan. He was energetic, very positive, dedicated to the well-being of Afghan refugees, and especially supported good education in the camps.

I explained to him my recent escape from Kabul and experience as a hostage in 1981. Mr. Innis said, "Don't go to Karachi. Stay here in Quetta to be my Deputy and Assistant Coordinator of the IAC. We are opening new refugee camps along the Iranian border." This was in March 1983. I agreed and was officially hired on April 4, 1983.

Then I sent a message to Bibigula to join me in Quetta. Soon afterward in May 1983, my brother Fizullah brought her and our children by bus to Quetta. Their travel to Quetta did not attract suspicion by the communist government because women and children regularly traveled back and forth between Kandahar and Quetta for medical treatment.

Like other refugees, we fled to Pakistan penniless. After we had escaped from Kabul, the communist Afghan Government confiscated all my hard-earned savings at the Kabul bank.

This photo shows us after their arrival. For our protection my family and I were moved from a guarded house outside the Mission Hospital compound to one within the compound. There were three different gates to pass through to get to our home.

Six months after arriving in Quetta, Bibigula gave birth to our youngest daughter, Setara. She was born in November 1983. Setara grew to become a happy child, pleasant, and energetic. She resembles my mother.

Pashtana attended a private British school outside the compound where the children of the Governor of Baluchistan attended. The wife of Mr. Innis was a teacher at that school and also tutored Pashtana in her home. Mirwais and Yonus were not old enough to

begin school.

Mr. Innis was still regarded as a general and had full privileges of a general in the Pakistani police. He assured our safety and assigned Pakistani police loyal to him to guard our children. I kept a low profile and was always escorted by at least two armed bodyguards when traveling outside the compound to protect me from extremists. In this 1984 photo, a former Pakistani policeman served as one of my bodyguards.

13
INCUBATORS FOR EXTREMISM

During the Soviet occupation, Afghanistan descended into another nightmare. It could be called the "Afghan Holocaust." More than one million of 16 million Afghans were slaughtered. Afghanistan became the world's largest landmine field where one of every eight Afghans became an amputee. Almost three million fled to Pakistan and two million escaped to Iran.

My job as an Assistant Coordinator of the IAC was to manage the resettlement of one and a half million Afghan refugees in Baluchistan, the largest province in Pakistan, along the Afghanistan border. Resettlement involved providing them food, shelter, health care, education and vocational training. I also taught Western doctors, nurses, administrators, and politicians about local languages and cultures, provided translation in various languages, wrote grants for funds to operate the programs, and supervised a large number of national and international staff employees.

At the same time, I traveled in pickups and lorries across the Pakistan border to provide humanitarian aid in the Afghan provinces of Ghazni, Urozgan, Zabul, Kandahar, Helmand, Nimroz, Farah, Herat, Badghis, and Ghore. Those trips were often as dangerous or more dangerous than my hostage ordeal. Some of those stories are coming up.

Heartbreaking

There are many accounts of hardship and tragedy experienced by refugees escaping to Baluchistan. Each night we received new arrivals at the Girdi Jungle Camp where 32,000 families lived. I remember asking a father how many were in his family. He said, "Eight." When I counted, there were only seven. He turned to his wife and asked, "Where is the baby?" Miserably she replied, "As we approached the border, the man leading us on a horse warned that the Soviets were nearby to ambush us. The baby started crying. I could not stop her.

The man grabbed our baby and threw her from the mountain."

Many of the families would have one or two dead babies with them. We heard of smugglers (both Pakistanis and Afghans) who would lure entire families with the promise of helping them to escape from the Soviets. Some would kill the male heads of the families and take their wives, children, and property.

Following You to the Graveyard

The resettlement of refugees requires skills that are learned through experience. Working in the 1960s for the US Bureau of Reclamation, helping nomads settle in the Helmand-Arghandab Valley, prepared me for my new job. Looking back, I realize that I have settled many of the same families several times in different countries: in the 1960s in Helmand Province, later when they became refugees in Pakistan, then in the 1980s in Fremont, California, where I also buried members of their families--their final settlement. They have joked with me, saying, "We are following you to the graveyard."

I was very sympathetic for the refugees' losses and trauma since my family and I were also refugees and very familiar with death. Necessity can be a teacher. Knowing that refugees need clothing, a safe place to live, meaningful work, and education, I established vocational training programs in the refugee camps in Pakistan and

 Afghanistan. Those programs included carpet weaving and making clothes. Quilts and hundreds of thousands of garments were sown each year in the Baluchistan refugee camps. They were not only distributed in the Pakistan refugee camps but also within Afghanistan, where displaced Afghans had relocated.

The quilts in the above photo are among those and other supplies

delivered to those displaced children and their families in 1983. They were living at a camp in the Muqur District of Ghazni Province. There and in other camps I initiated agricultural and adult literacy programs.

Refugees need a safe place to live. This photo was taken in 1983 within the Roghani Refugee Camp in the Chaman area just inside the Pakistan border. On one side of those tents, the canvas did not extend to the ground, leaving an 18-inch gap for desert animals, wind, and sand to enter. Not all the tents in the camps were as defective as those. Nonetheless, I required that they be replaced. I brought the supplier of those tents to examine them because they were a big problem for refugee families living in them. His name was Shuwkut, a Pakistani-Pashtun, who had a multi-year contract with the UN and the IAC to provide 80,000 tents for refugees.

After examining those tents, we drove separately to my house to talk. He arrived before me and was waiting in our guest room. When I requested him to replace the tents with correctly-sized ones, he complained that it would cause him to go bankrupt. I explained that the children and families in the refugee camp were from the Arghandab Valley in Afghanistan and were not accustomed to the desert. Most of all, the open side of the tents would expose them to the scorpions, snakes and harsh winds of the deserts.

I appealed to him, "I am Afghan. They are Afghan. I must consider them as my own children. My family lives in a house that protects us." I escorted him to his car and returned to our guest room. Waiting for me was Bibigula who pointed to bundles of money wrapped in cloth which I had not seen. It was a bribe from Shuwkut.

I ran to his car and threw the money inside of it. Soon afterward, he replaced the defective tents. Roghani Refugee Camp was one of the few camps where I was able to establish a full-curriculum school.

Clinics Were Not Sanitary

Refugees need decent health care. The main headquarters of the IAC was located in Karachi, from where it operated aid programs in Peshawar and in Quetta, the capital of Baluchistan, and where I was based. In Quetta, the Christian Mission Hospital was leased and served as our main medical center serving 1.5 million Afghan refugees living in camps within Baluchistan. The Mission Hospital was originally an eye hospital built in 1886 by British missionaries.

Considering the huge numbers of Afghan refugees, the IAC expanded the hospital into a full service hospital. It developed a general surgery unit, orthopedic, women's and children's wards, and a nursing school. The Mission Hospital also conducted residential training for Afghan and Pakistani doctors. It was staffed with experienced medical doctors from Europe, Australia, and America. In addition to medical care, we provided education, vocational training, and other humanitarian assistance.

Branch medical clinics also operated within the city of Quetta and the refugee camps. There were 18 refugee camps throughout Baluchistan. Our main camps were outside the city of Dalbandin near the Iranian border in the Chaghi region, 216 miles southwest of

Quetta. In this photo I am standing outside the gate of a women's and children's clinic in Dalbandin. The

other photo is inside the gate of the clinic. The child in the wheelbarrow later died.

Mobile clinics also traveled across the Pakistan border into Afghanistan to serve locally displaced refugees. We attempted to support other private Afghan and Pakistani medical clinics the best we could by providing them with doctors, nurses, custodians, medicines, and hospital supplies.

Clinics operated by Afghans and mujahideen in the refugee camps were not sanitary. Their surgery rooms were treated like barns. Even in the Mission Hospital, I saw patients walk in with a hernia and after surgery die due to infection. Even though Western doctors were working there, the conditions were filthy. We were always overwhelmed and did not have enough support staff or space to maintain sanitary conditions. Patients were parked in the hallways in beds that were dirty. The infection and death rates were very high.

Some Pakistanis and Afghans had purchased fake medical documents and claimed to be doctors so they could be put on the staff and paid a salary. During surgeries Pakistani doctors would steal the kidneys of Afghans. Those abuses were hideous.

The Afghan and mujahideen clinics were very different from the CARE-MEDICO sponsored hospitals in Kabul and in other provinces of Afghanistan, where the medical staffs were trained to maintain sanitary conditions. At the time of my escape from Kabul, medical facilities there had an exemplary record that was far better than those in India, Iran, or Pakistan. In the surgery room of the Kabul children's hospital, the infection rate had been reduced to zero.

After beginning my job as Assistant Coordinator, I tried to improve the sanitary conditions in the clinics where injuries, sanitation, and malnutrition were the major problems, and where there were not enough doctors. It was an uphill battle to achieve any kind of progress. In a mujahideen clinic I saw a Pakistani doctor with animal dung on his shoes walk into the surgery room. When he came out, I hit him in the head with my shoe and fired him. I had the authority to hire and fire medical personnel in the clinics and I used it when I could. In my first three months I convinced the Afghan doctors and nurses to sterilize the surgery rooms.

There was a lot of resistance by mujahideen commanders to my efforts because the medical clinics were sources of income for them. Improved health conditions would have reduced their funding. The greater the number of patients being treated, the more funding they would receive. Commanders would delay treatment of the wounded to showcase them for visiting Western and Arab donors. I remember discovering that a mujahideen commander had a bullet put back into the body of a wounded fighter when he learned that rich Arab donors were coming to visit. The fighter's infections got worse as he waited to be displayed.

The mujahideen commanders did not like me because I pushed for reform. They opposed me, but I had the support of the Afghan refugees at large. At the same time, commanders would occasionally offer to hire me and pay me twice the salary that the IAC paid me. I refused, not wanting to become their slave.

The Pakistan Government also used Afghan refugees to extract huge sums of money from the US, Europeans, Australians, and wealthy Arabs. Yes, there were clean Pakistani hospitals and clinics comparable with modern, Western hospitals; however, they served only Pakistanis with the exception of some injured high-level mujahideen commanders.

The Arabs operated their own modern, well-equipped, one-stop mobile hospitals outside Quetta, in the Saranon Refugee Camp. They were much cleaner than the facilities in the Afghan refugee clinics. Only Afghans, though, who were Wahhabis, were allowed. Arab hospitals served basically as Wahhabi recruitment centers.

Anyone who came to the Mission Hospital was accepted regardless of their religion, social or political status. We saved many lives even though we were severely overcrowded and could not manage by Western standards. Doctors and nurses came from Holland, England, Sweden, Australia, Switzerland, Austria, New

Zealand, Norway, and the US. I recruited doctors who had worked in Afghanistan at CARE-MEDICO as visiting volunteer specialists (VVS) to serve in the Mission Hospital and in refugee camps. Many brought with them hospital supplies. One of the visiting doctors was Dr. Edward Shortman from Connecticut. He dedicated one year without salary in the Mission Hospital to serve refugees and develop the capacity of the Afghan and Pakistani doctors to perform surgeries. Many gynecologists came from the US, Holland, and Belgium and saved many lives in the women's wards. We also established a nursing program for male and female Afghans and Pakistanis, and a program for lab technicians. First aid technicians who worked inside Afghanistan were also trained.

Cholera in the Camps

Health conditions in the refugee camps were terrible and narrow-minded mullahs there were a problem for us. In the summer of 1984, a mullah named Hajji Mullah controlled a small camp of 2000 to 3000 refugees. It was called Camp Safar. He would not allow any doctor, nurse or teacher to operate within the camp. When we were informed that there was cholera in that camp, Mr. Innis directed me to take doctors there. I replied, "You know the mullah has ordered his people to beat us up if we attempt to enter." Mr. Innis was insistent: "Sher, you are Afghan and must handle the situation. You must do something about the people who are dying there. I want you to do it." I asked for his advice since he was very experienced working with Afghans and Pakistanis along the border regions: "Can you show me some way to handle this mullah?" He replied, "Send him some gifts before you go to see him."

I purchased gifts of clothing, candies, sugar, tea, and food and sent them with my driver to give to Hajji Mullah. I instructed my driver to tell the mullah, "If you are willing, my boss will come here tomorrow to visit you." I added, "Don't talk to him about patients or anything else." After receiving the gifts, Hajji Mullah replied that it was okay for me to visit him and he expressed appreciation for the gifts.

The next day I convoyed to Camp Safar with four ambulances and pickup trucks carrying supplies. Male doctors and nurses filled two of the ambulances, and women doctors and nurses were in the other two ambulances. Sitting in a separate pickup, I told the drivers of the other vehicles to follow me, but not too closely.

When we arrived at the edge of the camp, I sent forward my representative to tell Hajji Mullah that I was near. When he returned, we drove forward. Seeing the mullah come out of his tent, I told my driver to stop. I stepped out of my pickup and walked toward him. From a distance Hajji Mullah called out to me, "I see the light of heaven on your forehead." I thought to myself, "It is not light on my forehead that you see." He could see more gifts that I had brought in my pickup.

We hugged one another as though we were long-lost relatives. When we sat and had tea, I said, "I have heard that there is a sickness that has come to your camp and people are dying." Hajji Mullah responded, "Thirteen children and four adults died this morning." I replied, "It is in the hands of God but we can do our human part. He gives us a brain and wisdom so we can cure the sickness with prayers and medicine. I am sure your people are praying and will continue praying. I am with the International Assistance Committee (I explained that it was an American and European humanitarian agency helping Afghan refugees). You may know that the hospital in Dalbandin belongs to us. We have doctors and nurses and medicines. With your permission, I can bring them to help."

When he gave the okay, I quickly directed my driver to bring them forward. Hajji Mullah thought that they were in Dalbandin; but they were only half a mile away. I gave the green light to the doctors and they set up their tents while I continued to have tea with the mullah.

Refugees rushed to the treatment tents like swarms of ants. Careful to be culturally sensitive, I asked the mullah, "We have women doctors and nurses with separate supplies. Would it be okay to help the women?" The women's tents were already being set up.

Cholera is a terrible disease. People become dehydrated, vomit and lose control of their bowel movements. It was a desperate situation in the camp. People were dying while I was there. It was getting out of control. Yet Hajji Mullah acted as though nothing was seriously wrong. I asked the doctors to prepare a list of food to bring from our Dalbandin warehouse. They advised me, "Don't bring vegetables or fruits because it would only add to the sanitation problems. Bring new clothes for the refugees because their clothes are contaminated."

We worked through the night under the light of kerosene lamps and continuously throughout the week. We saved many lives. The doctors and nurses were very humble and worked very hard to the point of exhaustion. It was necessary to regularly rotate them in shifts so the work could continue nonstop.

By the end of the week I was also able to negotiate two contracts with Hajji Mullah to start a school for boys and a school for girls, each with professional teachers. I asked him whether he had teachers within the camp; if so, they would be the first to be hired. If not, teachers would be hired elsewhere and live in the camp.

Hajji Mullah warned me that if it was discovered that the doctors, nurses or teachers were communists or associated with communists, they would be executed on the spot. I asked, "What if someone makes allegations against them because they have a rivalry?" He replied, "There must be real proof. Accusations are not enough. But remember, your credibility is at stake with the people you bring here."

Hajji Mullah later told me that he had asked many mullahs about me before I had come. Hajji Mullah cautioned, "Stay clean and don't associate yourself with the communists. Be very careful who you introduce." At the same time, I told him that we would test the people that he recommended to be teachers to assure that they were qualified. The teachers were paid extra money as an incentive to be very courteous and good role models for the refugees.

The mullah also signed a contract allowing us to establish two health clinics in the camp—one for males and one for females. In addition, training for midwives was permitted. I told Hajji Mullah that the midwives would be supervised by his wife. A mullah's wife is regarded as the first lady of a village. Mr. Innis appointed Ms. Park, a nurse from Britain, to be in charge of the women's clinic and midwife training. Establishing schools, clinics, and midwife training was the most rewarding part of my job. I was very excited that we could help those people.

The leaders in Camp Safar were the most difficult to convince to accept humanitarian aid for the refugees. Up through 1987, access to the refugee camps was tightly controlled by the Afghans. Previously no other foreign agency had been able to enter that camp and provide needed medical services whether it was from the West or Arab countries. Just before leaving, I asked Hajji Mullah to meet my boss and explained that he was not a Muslim.

A month later I took Mr. Innis to visit the schools and clinics in the camp. I introduced him to Hajji Mullah as "a person of the book." The mullah laughed and said, "He must be either Christian or Jewish. If he is, he is a person of God. Although we have some differences, they are still people of God. You cannot compare them with communists." On a different occasion, Mr. Innis came to Camp Safar with other Western officials. Hajji Mullah treated them very well.

Mr. Innis was a very dedicated, honest man, who strongly advocated for Afghan children's education. He was not an easy person to talk to, though; he was very stern. Mr. Innis was wise and experienced with tribal affairs along the Afghan-Pakistan border. I said to him, "Your advice how to deal with Hajji Mullah was right. The gifts worked." Then he told me a story: "During the British occupation and what is today India, I remember giving gifts to tribal elders and mullahs—shoes that looked nice on their feet. If the tribal elder wore a size ten, I would give him size eight so he could not put them on. He would place the shoes on the outside of his home where shoes are normally located. When the tribal leader's friends came to visit, they would see the shoes and recognize them as British made. They in turn would go to make friends with the British man who gave the shoes, which was me, hoping to get a similar gift. There would be competition among the tribal elders to get British shoes and other gifts."

Mr. Innis would often advise me how to better negotiate with the mullahs. Although I had years of experience helping the USAID and the Bureau of Reclamation with villagers and farmers, working with Mr. Innis better prepared me to work with mullahs and tribal leaders.

In this 1984 photo in Baluchistan at the Saranan Refugee Camp, Mr. Innis is on the right side between two bearded mujahideen. Although he appears to be shorter than me, he was over six feet tall

and was standing on lower ground. Another mujahideen commander in a turban stands between Mr. Innis and me.

You Need a Malala

There was another interesting story that Mr. Innis told me years later when, in 1993, he visited and stayed in our home in Fremont, California. Mr. Innis' father was a British military officer serving in the famous Battle of Maiwand on July 27, 1880. My grandfather, Hajji Rawouf, also fought against the British in that battle. When he shared that part of his family history at a small dinner party in our home, he was asked by another Afghan, "What is the solution to the civil war that is now in Afghanistan?" He answered, "I would like to tell you a secret story."

He prefaced that story with humor and said, "I am old. You may want to kill me for what I say, but I am old, it is okay." Mr. Innis continued: "My father was an officer under General Roberts in the Second Anglo-Afghan War. During the Battle of Maiwand, he was looking at the battlefield with his binoculars. It was summer and extremely hot and gusts of dust were swirling. The Afghans and

British were fighting in hand-to-hand combat. The British soldiers then began chasing the Afghans soldiers. At one point in the battle a young woman named Malala appeared. She picked up the Afghan flag and ran toward the British. That inspired the Afghan soldiers to stop running away. They suddenly turned around and charged the British. The battle ended with the British defeated. But Malala was killed in the battle." Today Malala is an Afghan national folk hero and regarded as the Afghan Joan of Arc. Her story is often told to Afghan school children.

Mr. Innis then said, "With all due respect, you need another Malala." He meant that Afghans needed leadership like Malala who could inspire the warring parties to *stop* fighting among themselves. The Afghans listening understood that.

Madrassas--Radicalizing a New Generation of Militants

Because of the good will we had earned, I knew Hajji Mullah would support my efforts to help refugees in other camps. I could not offer him money for his services because it would appear that he was our puppet and it would compromise his position. However, I gave him gifts--which was perfectly acceptable. He and I traveled to other camps where he was well respected and could speak with other mullahs. In those camps, although doctors and nurses were allowed to provide treatments, teachers were not allowed to teach non-religious subjects. Hajji Mullah explained to the other mullahs that in his camp many people had died of sickness and that "doctors from the IAC saved them. God's hand was with them. They are good people. When the British nurse, Ms. Park, came to our camp, the health of our women improved very much. She is very dedicated and she is a great person."

Hajji Mullah also encouraged the mullahs to allow non-religious subjects to be taught in their camps. Unfortunately, the mullahs in the other camps were afraid of losing their position by doing so. Therefore, the radicalized madrassas continued to dominate in those refugee camps. It was sad that the younger Afghan generation was not provided adequate schooling. They were indoctrinated through the madrassas with extremist thinking. Camp Safar was the first camp where I was able to send professional educators to teach non-religious subjects.

When I first arrived in Quetta and surveyed the refugee camps, the only subject taught in the madrassas was the memorization of the Quran. I proposed to expand the subjects to include history, geography, math, and science--especially chemistry and physics. I wanted to help the Afghan refugees to prosper, not become extremists. As a Muslim I was, of course, not against teaching Islam; but I was concerned that puritanical and narrow-minded Muslims, and radical extremists were preventing the refugees from receiving education necessary to lift their lives from poverty and blind ignorance.

Muslim Scholarship

Acquiring knowledge through the scientific study of the natural world and society has for centuries been an important part of Muslim culture. Such knowledge has been regarded as God-given and the responsibility of humans to develop. When the Muslim dynasties expanded from the eighth century onward, Muslim scholars were living in the Middle East at the crossroads of Eastern and Western cultures. They translated and preserved not only the ideas of ancient Greek works of mathematics, philosophy, science, and medicine lost in the Dark Ages of Europe, but also important ideas from India and China. More important than preserving the Greek texts, Muslim scholars such as Ibn Rushd (twelfth century), known in the West as Averroes, clarified and explained Greek ideas, like Aristotle's philosophy, which were difficult to understand.

Muslim scholars played an important role in Europe's "recovery" of those ideas that form the basis of the Renaissance and the Western intellectual, scientific, and medical traditions. During much of history, madrassas had taught Islamic law, the Quran, languages, natural and political sciences, literature, and in some places, medicine. Westerners have historically downplayed the contributions of Muslim culture.

Now the extremists were forbidding that heritage from being taught in the Afghan refugee camps.

Traditional Afghan Society Weakened

A new type of madrassa was emerging in Pakistan during the Soviet-Afghan War. Its exclusive purpose was to indoctrinate boys and young men to become guerrilla fighters, to battle with the infidels--communists and others regarded as infidels. Madrassas competed with and weakened the authority of Afghan elders and tribal culture. They became a controlling force in the refugee camps. A clear sign of their influence was the new fashion for men to wear beards. Fashion is an indication of what people think. I always shaved.

Extremist Views Promoted

Mujahideen commanders competed to be the dominant authority within the camps. They did that through intimidation and by controlling the distribution of food, medicine, and other essentials provided by foreign donors. Within the refugee camps there was a struggle for the loyalties, hearts, minds, and bodies of Afghans.

As Pakistani authorities favored more fundamentalist groups, and imposed through the madrassas a Wahhabi brand of Islam which was alien to most Afghans, the powers of the warlords and extremist religious leaders increased, and the authority of tribal leaders and village elders decreased. This weakened and reshaped traditional Afghan tribal social structures to be more repressive and similar to the Taliban who would later rise to power. It also encouraged a culture of corruption.

The seven Afghan mujahideen political parties opposed my efforts to hire professional Muslim teachers from Afghanistan to teach basic academic subjects in the camps. They wanted only mullahs to teach and emphasize the religious duty of believers to take on the violent struggle—the outer jihad--against the infidels. The mullahs falsely accused professional teachers, who were Muslims, of being communists and atheists.

Extremist Mentors for the Next Generation

The mujahideen recruited young men from about 40 different Islamic countries with the call to jihad, a holy war. Those men who survived and returned to their countries would become veteran mentors for the next generation of extremists in Africa, Asia, the Middle East, Europe, and elsewhere. They now pose a threat to the international community.

Although three of the mujahideen parties were moderates, they did not want to jeopardize receiving funding from wealthy Arab donors. Also they did not want to anger Pakistani authorities, their hosts. So they joined with the four puritanically oriented parties to require that only mullahs teach in the camps. Because of their desire for money, supplies and weapons, the moderate mujahideen commanders and other influential Afghan tribal leaders acted like they were extremists.

While there may be a standing debate among Muslims over whether jihad means an inner struggle for spiritual perfection or an outer struggle against non-believers, there was no such debate in the Afghan refugee camps and madrassas in Pakistan. The US covertly supported the call for a holy war against the Soviets, and Pakistan was its proxy in the region.

"Why Are You Supporting the Extremists?"

I voiced my concerns about the spread of extremism in the refugee camps to my Western colleagues, especially those in the US Embassy in Islamabad. On one occasion after disclosing that there was a poster in the Sani Clinic in Quetta showing the Soviet and US flags burning side by side, I asked US officials, "Why are you supporting the extremists who equally condemn the Soviets and the US?" They could not give me an understandable explanation. I warned them that supporting extremism would create a threat for them in the future. But who would believe me? None of them asked or discussed what would happen when the Soviet-Afghan War was over.

The way the war was financed and operated developed refugee camps into incubators for extremism. Children were being bred to become guerrilla fighters. The mujahideen imposed a repressive Wahhabi view of life through Saudi-financed madrassas on Afghan society, similar to that of the Taliban, and spread that view to the villages in Afghanistan after the Soviet Union withdrew its forces.

A Chess Game

I could not understand why the US did what it did in those days. Since then, this is how I came to understand it: Former Secretary Albright explained that during the Cold War years of the 1980s, US officials managed foreign affairs as though it was a game of chess where nations were the players who acted rationally to further their national interests. They regarded religion as only causing trouble, as not respecting national boundaries, and as a subject diplomats and government decision makers should avoid.

During the Cold War, the US's strategic objective was only to check the Soviets in a quagmire in Afghanistan to sap their strength and divert their focus away from Europe. The US had no expectation that the Soviets would withdraw from Afghanistan. Pakistan was the only friendly country in the region willing to oppose the Soviet Union during the Cold War.

President Zia maneuvered through the dangerous international chess game to achieve his greatest advantage. He desired to become the leader of the Islamic world and bolster the power of the Pakistan military to counter India. His leadership was recognized by Arab countries because of his confrontation with the Soviets, who were viewed by Muslims as atheists and infidels. The Soviet Union posed a real threat to Pakistan along most of its borders. India on Pakistan's eastern border was pro-Soviet and regarded as an enemy with a nuclear weapon; and Soviet troops occupied Afghanistan on its western border. Invasion of Pakistan was part of the Soviet Union's longstanding "final thrust to the South" to gain access to the oil lanes of the Persian Gulf and Arabian Sea.

Keep the Pot Boiling, But Not Boil Over

Zia reasoned with the US that accepting its aid to support the mujahideen resistance against the Soviets increased the risk that the

Soviet Union would in fact attack Pakistan. He assured the US, though, that he could manage the risk. During the Soviet-Afghan War, Afghan communist forces infiltrated into Pakistan and orchestrated some attacks of retaliation. There were also incidents of Soviet and Afghan bombers that assaulted Pakistan villages along its border.

Zia reportedly told CIA Director Bill Casey in 1982 that his strategy was to "keep the pot boiling, but not boil over" with the Soviet Union. In other words, the mujahideen could be armed enough to harass the Soviets but should not cause such damage to provoke the Soviets to *significantly* retaliate against Pakistan.

Since Saudi Arabia was a major donor and advocated for Wahhabism, an austere, extremist view of Islam, Zia felt obligated to promote Wahhabism in the Afghan refugee camps. It also motivated young men to become jihadist fighters to oppose the Soviets--and the US. What's more, it enabled the Saudi royalty to divert growing domestic unrest among its society to the common mission of jihad in Afghanistan to avenge the killing of Muslim brothers by the Soviets.

Zia needed Saudi support to finance his aggressive military buildup and nuclear development program. More recent intelligence reports indicate that Saudi Arabia's continued generous transfer of funds to Pakistan has been with expectations that Pakistan would provide it with nuclear weapons at an appropriate time.

Zia in turn insisted to the US that the madrassas were the only means to provide authentic Islamic education outlawed by the Soviets and needed to prepare warriors for battle. US officials did not want to upset Pakistan by voicing objections for its support of religious extremism or express concerns that an anti-US movement was developing within the refugee camps. They looked the other way.

Echoes from the Past—"They Are the Infidels"

The US did not learn from Britain's historical mistakes in the nineteenth century when Britain sought to neutralize Russia's power in Afghanistan and in the Middle East. Afghan Amir Abdur Rahman, in the 1890s, provided a model for President Zia in the 1980s, and for Pervez Musharraf after the 9/11 attacks on America. Rahman encouraged holy uprisings against the British while professing to the British that he was completely loyal to them. Britain was regarded as an invader and infidel whose Western ideas and modern progress were opposed. Although Afghans would shift alliances among themselves, they would unite against outsiders.

The Afghans' call to action was jihad. The religious messages extracted from the Koran were essentially the same which justified a holy war against the British in the nineteenth century, and against the Soviets in the 1980s. The messages were "they are the infidels." The same messages are also used against the Americans and Europeans in the twenty-first century.

Like the Soviets, the US did not comprehend the consequences of the extremists, nor the tribal systems, feuds and culture of Afghanistan and Pakistan, nor the mujahideen or the Afghan communists in Afghanistan.

Civil War Continued Radicalization

Following the withdrawal of Soviet troops in 1989, civil war continued the process of radicalizing the next generation of Afghans and fragmenting Afghan culture and tribal authority. Since 1978 Afghans have only known war, poverty, and devastation. Refugee camps and madrassas in Pakistan raised children and young men to become religious warriors to battle the Soviets. They also have produced jihadist fighters for Al Qaeda, the Taliban, and other extremist groups in the world.

The consequences of allowing US funds to support extremism in the Afghan refugee camps in Pakistan continue to haunt the US Government today. During the year prior to 9/11, newspaper articles quoting the Taliban revealed that the meaning of the word "infidel" had been expanded. Previously it had referred to atheists; by 9/11 it also included the US.

The Pakistan Government opposed my efforts to expand education for the Afghan refugees. I argued with the Pakistanis, "You have schools that teach math and science for your kids. Why don't you support the same for the Afghans?" In Baluchistan, where Afghan refugee camps were located, there were only a few secular schools; most schools were the new type of militant madrassas. It was only possible for us to operate small, private schools that taught history and the sciences; but they were primarily in Soviet-occupied Afghanistan, in areas the Soviets could not control by air or on the ground, and in Camp Safar in the Dalbandin area of Pakistan. Mr. Innis supported my efforts to maintain those schools.

Products of 1980s Refugee Camps

One lesson learned from the Soviet-Afghan War is that extremists who live in the villages of Afghanistan today are the products of the 1980s refugee camps in Pakistan and Iran. As US officials were caught off guard by the Iranian Revolution, they did not acknowledge the threats posed by the madrassas and radicalizing influence of Arab extremists in the refugee camps. The West did not adequately realize the importance of religion, tribalism, culture, and the militant education in refugee camps or in the villages of other developing countries. Has it learned that since then?

Syrian Refugees

When I look at the terrible situation of millions of Syrians suffering in refugee camps in Lebanon, Jordan, and Turkey, I am reminded of my days with one and a half million Afghan refugees in Baluchistan, working 18 hours and more a day—seven days a week. There, I literally saw extremist writings on the wall and how the next generation of militant extremists was cultivated. I warned US officials in Pakistan about what was happening. But who would believe me? Now I worry that the Syrian refugee camps will become incubators for extremism, where children are converted into the tools of war, where traditional tribal systems and loyalties are replaced with new loyalties to global terrorism.

Syrians don't have the same advantages that Afghans had during the Soviet-Afghan War. Pakistan was sympathetic to Afghans, especially Pashtuns who lived along their common border.

Today, Syrians are not welcomed in their host countries of Iraq, Jordan, Lebanon, and Turkey as Afghans were in Pakistan. In those countries there are already attacks against Syrian refugees. The big question is "How effectively will extremists manipulate the Syrian refugees to spread extremism throughout the Islamic world?" They were successful in manipulating the *Arab Spring*.

Patient, Intelligent, Genuine Service Needed

If US foreign policy in developing countries is to be effective, culturally intelligent and genuine service must be provided to people where they live. That means understanding and respecting the culture, history, family and tribal systems in those countries. Patience is also needed, because real progress occurs slowly and in measured steps.

Humanitarian aid workers at the IAC did that. We provided unconditional assistance and service which earned the good will and respect of the mullahs who said many good things about us. We were able to train lots of Afghan nurses, first aid and lab technicians who were also refugees from the camps. They learned skills and were paid an income, which greatly helped them and their families. Today those lab and first aid technicians live and work in Afghanistan.

14

THE MUJAHIDEEN

Before continuing with my stories, it is worthwhile to examine the myth that the mujahideen guerrillas were primarily the ones who forced the Soviet military to withdraw from Afghanistan. The myth portrays the mujahideen as brave and selfless heroes romanticized in movies like *Charlie Wilson's War* and *Rambo III*. This myth gained their warlord commanders such as Gulbuddin Hekmatyar and Ahmad Shah Massud Hollywood-style celebrity status. While many mujahideen fought bravely, only a small percentage of the seven mujahideen parties headquartered in Peshawar, and four Afghan factions in Iran, actually fought the Soviets in Afghanistan. The majority of mujahideen used international aid and weapons to bludgeon one another and continue their civil war.

Afghan Communists—Most Strategic Players

This may surprise you, but those who played the greatest strategic role in defeating the Soviets were the Afghan communists. At the same time, most, but not all, of the Afghan communists participated with the Soviet military to commit atrocities against innocent Afghan civilians. Terrible things happen in the fog and shadows of war.

Considering the likelihood that insurgencies and guerrilla wars will continue into the foreseeable future, dispelling the mujahideen myth can provide insight into the nature of insurgencies in a developing country, and hopefully, provide some lessons. If the West is to be a helpful presence in the world to promote stability, peace, and the dignity of life, it must learn from the mistakes of the past, and how to effectively work with developing countries and insurgencies. So let's put the mujahideen, their commanders and warlords, and other major players in the Soviet-Afghan War like the Afghan communists, Pakistan, Saudi Arabia, and the US into historical perspective.

Afghanistan is a traditional and fragmented society, rarely in its history bound together by a strong central government. Loyalty there has always been first local, and based on complex networks of kinship, family, ethnic and tribal relationships. Historically, village chiefs, elders, and tribal leaders provided both civic and military leadership, and usually served as commanders of their militias when engaged in longstanding inter-tribal rivalries and blood feuds. Tribal leaders were elected by members of their tribe on the basis of their merit. Religious leaders, mullahs/imams, most often were in supportive roles and did not lead the militias.

Commanders appealed to time-honored tribal values to mobilize Afghans. For instance, among Pashtuns, the largest of the Afghan ethnicities, commanders would rally their fighters to action by appealing to the Pashtunwali code of revenge. While fighting invaders, Afghans would often turn their guns on one another to settle blood feuds as they had done for centuries. But in the end, Afghans were always first Afghans.

The Role of Religion

Afghanistan is also a traditional Muslim society where decisions are ultimately justified by religion. If a militia was losing a fight, its commander could order a retreat, or ruthlessly make deals and change sides when it was expedient, to minimize loss of troop strength in combat or to gain a decisive advantage, rationalizing that it was God's will. Tribal leaders and regional warlords would mobilize and motivate their fighters by calling them to "jihad" and martyrdom. Threats by foreigners would unite Afghans…for a time.

Tribal Rivalries

That pattern of warfare was waged in the nineteenth and early twentieth centuries when the British had invaded and fought three wars with Afghanistan. Although the British either rented the loyalty of Afghans or defeated them in battle, Afghan loyalties and British victories were temporary and at a terrible cost of lives. Commanders continued their inter-tribal rivalries, switching sides while fighting the British during those wars. The British were eventually forced to withdraw and concede Afghanistan's independence in 1919.

Origins of 1980s Mujahideen and Warlords

When President Daoud was assassinated in 1978, the new Afghan communist government, the *Democratic Republic of Afghanistan (DRA)*, quickly attempted to impose wide-sweeping land and social restructuring which alienated landowners, and religious and tribal leaders. Local village chiefs, elders, and tribal leaders led militias armed with old WWI weapons to counter the murderous attempts of the DRA to coerce compliance with its changes. In March 1979, the city of Herat revolted and many soldiers in the Afghan 17th Division mutinied and joined the revolt. Uprisings mushroomed into a civil war that the DRA could not control. Large-scale mutinies continued in the Afghan Army through the end of 1979 with those soldiers joining the resistance. The freedom fighter resistance was called covertly the *Harakat* (the Movement). Later resistance fighters would be called the *mujahideen*. The revolts were widespread but not coordinated.

When the Soviet 40th Army invaded at the end of December 1979, everything changed. As the winter snow melted in 1980, popular uprisings reached a high point of mass resistance as tribal leaders declared jihad, assembled large bodies of fighters, and attacked Soviet and DRA garrisons. The Soviet military was prepared for those types of attacks and easily crushed the Afghan assaults with their artillery and aircraft. Tribal leaders realized that they were no match for modern weaponry and resorted to guerrilla warfare tactics.

When the Afghan resistance did not collapse and the Afghans resorted to guerrilla attacks from the countryside, the Soviets adjusted their tactics. They conducted a scorched earth policy of carpet bombings, and wholesale blanketing of land mines and destruction of the rural countryside to eliminate any food production and shelter that might be provided to the Afghan insurgency. This forced over five million Afghans to escape as refugees to the border countries of Pakistan and Iran, and two million to be displaced into the suburbs and makeshift shelters around big cities and other parts of Afghanistan. Afghan resistance fighters and their commanders also needed a sanctuary for their headquarters to manage a prolonged war inside Afghanistan.

Pakistan Changed the Afghan Society

Afghan refugees who sought safe haven in Pakistan were corralled into refugee camps where they were further radicalized, if they wanted to survive there. They were required to join an Afghan political party to receive ration cards and aid. Initially there were about 75 Afghan political parties. Pakistan's Inter-Services Intelligence (ISI), which was responsible for Pakistan's national security and managing the refugees, reduced them to seven parties, known as the "Peshawar Seven." They received humanitarian foreign aid and also weapons to fight the Soviets--according to how they followed the directions of the ISI.

Favored were leaders like Gulbuddin Hekmatyar who were fundamentalists and whose authority came from outside the traditional tribal structures. They had become militia commanders by coercing the loyalties of their fighters and by acts of cruelty. Comparable to gangsters in the West, they built organizations outside the tribal communities with near-absolute control because their fighters feared not only that they would be harmed or killed if they disobeyed, but also their families. Those types of militia commanders played a deadly game, changing sides in battle and murdering their rivals. They attained warlord status similar to mafia bosses, as their positions were fortified by Pakistan with foreign aid and weapons.

Other regional powers such as Iran, India, China, and Turkey also sought influence in Afghanistan to further their foreign policy interests by supporting other non-tribal leaders and commanders such as Ahmad Shah Massoud. The Soviet Union did the same, supporting Abdul Rashid Dostum.

Pakistan changed the nature of the mujahideen resistance and the balance of power within the Afghan society by controlling and distributing foreign humanitarian aid and military weapons and supplies to Afghan militia leaders who they could best control.

Power Realigned, Corruption Increased

As a consequence, depending upon the amount of aid and weapons received, the authority, economic and military power of mujahideen warlords and fundamentalist religious leaders were increased, while the power and authority of tribal leaders, elders, and village chiefs were decreased. Unequal distributions also hardened historical ethnic and tribal rivalries, and spawned a culture of corruption as the basis for survival.

In 1981, the ISI gave the name *mujahideen (holy warriors)*, to the Afghan insurgents who fought the Soviets. In the nineteenth century, Afghans fighting foreign invaders were called by a different name— *ghazis*, religious warriors fulfilling their duty for jihad.

President Zia used humanitarian aid and basic necessities such as food, shelter, medicine, and military supplies from the US, Saudi Arabia, and European countries to further Pakistan's foreign policy and his personal ambitions.

Religious Leaders Radicalized

Additionally, Wahhabi-funded madrassas radicalized Afghan religious leaders to become extremists, and educated young Afghan refugees to become jihadist fighters ready to enter the killing fields of Afghanistan.

The following is a list of the seven mujahideen Afghan parties that were based in Pakistan. Three of them were moderate and four were a mixture of puritanical, anti-science fundamentalists and radical extremists. The three moderate parties were:

Party	Led By
Harakat-i-Inqilab-i-Islami (Islamic Revolutionary Movement—IRMA)	Maulana Mohammad Nabi Mohammadi
Mahaz-i-Milli Islami (National Islamic Front of Afghanistan (NIFA)	Pir Sayyid Ahmed Gailani
Jebh-e-Nejat-i-Melli (Afghanistan National Liberation Front--ANLF)	Professor Sibghatullah Mojaddedi

Former President Hamid Karzai's father was a member of

Mojaddedi's party.

The four fundamentalist parties were:

Party	Led By
Hazb-i Islami (The Islamic Party—HIH)	Gulbuddin Hekmatyar
Jamiat-e Islami (Islamic Society—JIA)	Professor Burhanuddin Rabbani
Harakat-e Islami (Islamic Union of Afghanistan—IUA)	Professor Abdul Rasul Sayyaf
Hazb-e Islami Khalis (Islamic Party--HIK)	Mawlawi Yonus Khalis

These four parties were further radicalized when the Arab Wahhabis became involved with them, and especially after the withdrawal of Soviet troops. Professor Rabbani was supported by the US, and Professor Sayyaf was supported by the Saudis and other Wahhabi Arabs.

Hekmatyar Received Lion's Share

The ISI gave the warlord Gulbuddin Hekmatyar's party most of the foreign aid and weapons that it allocated to the mujihideen from its larger pool of foreign aid and weapons covertly received from the US and Saudi Arabia. Hekmatyar received the lion's share because he was the most dependent on Pakistan, having little local support in Afghanistan. The presumption was that he would be Pakistan's man among the Afghans and be the most obedient. Members of Hekmatyar's party were the only ones authorized by the Pakistani authorities to kill Pakistanis opposed to President Zia's regime.

It is important to realize that Hekmatyar and his party fought very little against the Soviets. His military campaigns were mainly against other mujahideen rivals. Hekmatyar's strategy was to weaken them and strengthen his power as a warlord for when the Soviets withdrew from Afghanistan. The Soviet invasion became a Christmas gift for Hekmatyar as it had been for Zia.

The mujahideen parties in Iran supported by the Iranian Government were:

Party	Led By
Shura-i Ittifagh-i Afghanistan (Revolutionary Council of the Islamic Union of Afghanistan)	Sayyad Beheshti
Sazman-i Nasr-I Islami-yi Afghanistan (The Islamic Victory Organization of Afghanistan	Led by a council
Harakat-i-Islami (Islamic Movement)	Shaikh Asif Muhsini
Sepah-I Pasdaran (Army of the Guardians of the Revolution)	Akbari and Saddiqi

The four parties in Iran and the four fundamentalist parties in Pakistan engaged in minimal fighting against the Soviets and directed most of their combat against one another. Like Hekmatyar, they jockeyed for power and prioritized their resources to use after the Soviets left Afghanistan.

Mujahideen Getting Beaten by 1985

After their initial high point of military success, the tribal-led insurgency in 1980 was quashed, and the Soviet-Afghan War shifted into a stalemate. By September 1985, Pakistani General Mirza Aslam Beg, Corps Commander for the Afghanistan-Pakistan border, bluntly reported to Morton Abramowitz, then US Assistant Secretary of State for Intelligence and Research, that the mujahideen were "getting beaten." Nevertheless, in October 1985, the Politburo, led by Gorbachev, resolved to withdraw Soviet troops. Neither the US nor Pakistan were aware of that intention nor did they expect it to happen.

Whether General Beg's assessment that the mujahideen were "getting beaten" was accurate or a ploy to get more weaponry from the US for both the mujahideen and the Pakistani military, there were plausible reasons for it. Let me explain: The US and Saudi Arabia had transferred billions of dollars of aid and weaponry to Pakistan to equip the mujahideen. According to Milton Bearden, former CIA station chief in Pakistan, covert aid escalated during the Soviet-Afghan War, and from 1986 to 1987, the US and Saudi Arabia gave in hardware alone, 60,000 tons of weapons, ammunition, and communication equipment. The ISI gave only a small portion of that aid and weapons to the mujahideen, and only a minority of them actually fought the Soviets.

The defeat of the mujahideen in early 1986 at Zhawar demonstrated that in spite of having received antiaircraft weapons, the mujahideen could not hold a heavily reinforced defensive position or territory against the Soviets' ability to mass and concentrate its air power on that position. The mujahideen could retreat and later reoccupy camps like Zhawar. However, the questions for them were for how long could they hold that position, and was it worth the heavy loss of troops and weapons and supplies?

Zia's "keep the pot boiling, but not boil over" strategy with the Soviet Union enabled the Pakistan military to siphon off major portions of US and Saudi military aid for itself and distribute the remainder to the mujahideen according to a policy that left just enough supplies for mujahideen to disrupt the Soviet and Afghan communist troops.

No Intent to Win, Only Harrass

For most of the war there was no intent to win but only harass and slowly bleed Soviet troops. There were other major factors at play besides the mujahideen resistance that depleted the Soviet's military superiority and caused a stalemate and politically made the war unwinnable for the Soviet Union.

Again, only the three moderate Afghan parties in Pakistan did most of the fighting against the Soviets. Following the Soviet withdrawal in 1989, they disbanded, declaring that the jihad had ended. Mujahideen commanders exaggerated the actual numbers of their jihadists who fought the Soviets so as to increase their financial aid and prestige. The mujahideen who did travel into Afghanistan to fight, did so for varying periods of time: some for only a week, a month, three months, and maybe some for a year. They operated from base camps scattered in remote areas of Afghanistan, where they would venture out to conduct ambush and sabotage operations.

I saw the impoverished conditions of the mujahideen while working in the orthopedic and rehabilitation centers in Kabul in Soviet-occupied Afghanistan, and later many times while reentering Afghanistan from Pakistan, providing humanitarian aid to displaced Afghans, and to the mujahideen.

At a major supply center in western Afghanistan, where I traveled on one of my trips, there were only rations of bread and water, and very low-levels of ammunition. When working in the Kabul hospitals, I saw how a significant number of Afghan communists secretly provided supplies and ammunition to the poorly-supplied mujahideen.

The few commanders who committed their guerrilla fighters were effectively hitting and running, harassing, and disrupting troop and supply convoys on the roads, and sabotaging Soviet facilities. They did not intend, though, to "cause the pot to boil over."

Soviet Strategy

Soviet military officers in the Soviet-Afghan War have revealed that their strategy was to hold key locations and secure the roads and lines of communication (LOC) between them, while the Afghan communist (DRA) soldiers went after the mujahideen to defeat them. The roads and LOC were lifelines needed for resupply. Key locations were a few large cities like Kabul and Masar-i-Sharif, air bases and garrisons, storage depots, and installations.

Plagued by large desertions, the DRA military was unable to meet the Soviet expectations. Therefore, Soviet troops were forced to fill the gap until the Afghan military could be reinforced. That contributed to Soviet strategists underestimating needed troop strength, weaponry, helicopters, and other aircraft. About 85% of Soviet troops were stationed to protect key locations, and the roads and lines of communication connecting them. Only about 15% of troops were allocated for field operations.

A Logistics War—Choking and Bleeding

The Soviet-Afghan War was a logistics war. From the mujahideen perspective, the key strategy to choking and bleeding the Soviet military was disrupting and damaging the roads and their lines of communication. The Soviets were highly dependent on continual resupply of military and economic goods from the Soviet Union, which required transport within Afghanistan by large convoys traveling over damaged or poorly developed road systems. The convoys were extremely vulnerable targets for ambushes, mines, and booby-trapped obstacles.

Afghan Communists Caused Soviets to Withdraw

Militarily, the Afghans that played a greater strategic role in opposing the Soviets were a modest percentage of Afghan soldiers and civilians in the communist Afghan Government (DRA) who worked side-by-side with the Soviets. My experience was that the majority of young Afghan communists did not understand what communism really was. They were idealistic. They were told by the Soviets that the goal of socialism and communism was equality for all people, and the means to that end was revolution. When they discovered the communist lies and that they had killed many innocent people, they turned against the Soviets and their ruthless Afghan communist leadership. Afghan communists who turned on the Soviets were Afghans first and hated the Soviets for invading their country. Ethnicity, culture, and tribal loyalties were much more important to them than Marxist ideology.

Some people will argue that Afghans wanted the Soviets in their country. They point to President Taraki and other Afghan government officials who repeatedly requested the Soviet Politburo to send troops. Those officials, though, were concerned primarily with holding their positions of power. Not all the Afghan communists wanted the Soviets to occupy their country. At the same time, that does not mean that the Afghan communists who opposed the Soviets and helped the mujahideen contributed to the well-being of Afghanistan.

Although their numbers may have been modest, since members of the underground Afghan resistance were insiders in strategic positions, their impact was huge. Winning an insurgency through guerrilla warfare is a matter of willpower, of bleeding the opponent and outlasting him. Preserving limited resources and manpower is critical.

Some Afghans in the government supported the minority of mujahideen actually fighting the Soviets by giving them weapons, ammunition, supplies, and arranging for medical assistance. Especially important, they forewarned mujahideen with accurate actionable intelligence, and disrupted communist operations by giving the Soviets false information. Military analysts recognize that the Soviets suspected members of the DRA leaking operational intelligence to the mujahideen. The Soviets, therefore, became reluctant to share information with them.

Examples of high-level Afghan communist officials and military officers who collaborated with the mujahideen are General Abdul Haq Olomi, and Haytullah Ziarmal, who was the Governor of Urozgan Province in 1978 and in 1983, and who became the Attorney General of the DRA. He also provided me and other mujahideen with assistance.

Soviet cordons and sweeps and raids were conducted based on intelligence reports frequently prepared by the DRA. Russian officers report that the insurgency's intelligence networks were very effective. Often they informed the mujahideen when Soviet units left their base camps, their direction of travel and when the units were near their objectives. As a consequence, Soviet operations targeting suspected mujahideen locations commonly failed. Knowing your enemies' plans allows you to avoid loss and to fight another day.

The lives of my family and me were saved by a high-level Afghan communist officer, Lt. Col. Niamutullah. He warned me of the plan to arrest my family and helped us to escape by purchasing plane tickets in his name. Actionable intelligence from Afghans in the government was essential to counter the Soviets' detection technology. They had remote electronic acoustic and seismic sensors that could detect the mujahideen when they were 20 kilometers away from Soviet and DRA positions.

Keeping your enemy bogged down in a guerrilla war can cause it to lose. The mujahideen disrupted Soviet operations, ambushed their convoys, and sabotaged their facilities. Afghans in the Afghan Government and military, to a great extent, enabled them to do so.

Equally or even more destructive than ambushes and mines were Soviet losses due to disease, injuries, and other noncombat deaths. Hepatitis, typhus, malaria, dysentery, and meningitis had taken their toll on soldiers. As many as 60% of them were hospitalized during the war. Reported noncombat deaths among Soviet soldiers due to disease, accident or other causes averaged 17.7 percent of total deaths. One in every eight Soviet soldiers who served in Afghanistan was either killed, wounded, or missing.

Afghan Communists Who Lived Double Lives

Even though there were no agreements of cooperation between the Parcham and Khalq factions to oppose the Soviets, nationalist-minded Afghans from enlisted men to general staff officers and civilians acted individually. They operated in a compartmentalized manner through trusted third parties so as not to expose their support for the resistance. There were Afghan communist officers who bribed Soviet soldiers with gifts such as hashish (many Soviet soldiers had become drug addicts), gold rings, and the like. The bribes were for weapons, ammunition, and supplies for the resistance. Afghan soldiers also stole weapons from Soviet soldiers and sold them to the mujahideen.

In the photo below I am sitting next to one of my bodyguards, Taj Mohammad, holding his AK-47. It was stolen by Afghan communist soldiers and sold for Soviet rubles amounting to about US $150. We had just delivered humanitarian supplies to that underground mujahideen storage bunker along the Baluchistan, Pakistan-Afghanistan border.

By day, soldiers in the Afghan military were like other Soviet soldiers killing Afghan civilians. They with the KHAD, the Soviet-style Afghan secret police, and the Soviet 40th Army butchered

hundreds of thousands of Afghans throughout the country. At night, Afghan communists supported the mujahideen or conducted sabotage operations themselves. As individuals they would set on fire a storage depot, and in the morning claim that the mujahideen had done it.

Afghans in the underground resistance who were members of the communist Khalqs and Parchams were not united. They were still fierce rivals and informed on one another's support for the resistance. Many were caught and executed. It was complicated.

The desertion rate for Afghans drafted into the Army was enormous—more than 50%. It reflected the countrywide resistance by the Afghan people. The head of the Afghan communist government, Babrak Karmal, followed by Najibullah, resorted to recruiting non-Afghan mercenaries to fight for them. The mercenaries were well-paid, well-trained, and a tough fighting force.

Corruption among the Afghan communists also drained the Soviets' resources. One member of the Politburo complained in a January 1987 meeting that, in 1981, the Soviet Union gave 100 million rubles of aid to Afghanistan. It was siphoned off by the Afghan elite, while Afghan peasants received essentially nothing. The peasants were so poor that they had no kerosene or even matches. Similar complaints would be echoed by Americans and Coalition Forces after 13 years in post-9/11 Afghanistan.

Stingers–the Silver Bullet?

There is a widely held belief that, when the US covertly provided the mujahideen with Stinger missiles in late 1986, they caused such damage to Soviet aircraft that it turned the tide of the war and convinced the Soviets to withdraw. As a matter of fact, the Stingers were effective weapons, but they were not the silver bullets that won the Soviet-Afghan War that most people have been led to believe. People like to believe in silver bullets and quick fixes in war.

Let's consider the historical context for that myth. During the first two years of the Soviet occupation in 1980 and 1981, Soviet military leadership recommended withdrawal from Afghanistan. The Soviet military and Politburo realized that the Parcham and Khalq factions could not run the country. At the same time, Soviet military operations were escalating to counter a growing countrywide insurgency.

Moscow extended cautious peace feelers through the United Nations for a negotiated withdrawal. As early as 1982, the Soviet political leadership wanted to withdraw, but leave behind a government that would not be anti-Soviet. So they contacted King Mohammad Zahir Shah, asking him whether he would be willing to participate in forming a coalition government. The King told them that he would only return to Afghanistan if the people of Afghanistan wanted him, and if the international community would provide security assurances and not interfere in Afghan affairs.

The Soviets were agreeable to those conditions but factions within the US Administration did not and blocked that UN initiative. US officials became more confident that the Soviets were not winning the war and that the Soviet economy was spiraling downwards. They wanted the war to drag on and sap the Soviet Union of its economic and military strength.

Gorbachev came to power in March 1985, one month before I escaped with my family to the US. He desired to initiate Perestroika-- economic and political reforms—in the Soviet Union. That required an end to the war in Afghanistan. However, reportedly before Gorbachev took office, an escalation of Soviet military operations had been planned and he chose not to oppose the hardline generals at that time. Air strikes and air assaults on the villages were increased and 1985 became the bloodiest year of the war.

In October of 1985, though, Gorbachev led the Politburo to set a strategic goal of withdrawing its troops and leave Afghanistan as a friendly, neutral country. Politically it took time to implement. A year later, in a November 13, 1986 Politburo meeting, Gorbachev pushed to practically implement the October 1985 resolution to withdraw troops within the next two years. He stated that the Soviet Union was clearly in a stalemate and acknowledged that economic, diplomatic and political efforts had failed to speed up the process of leaving Afghanistan in a hopefully Soviet-friendly condition.

At the same time, in late 1986, after a lengthy debate among US policy makers fearful of Stingers falling into unfriendly hands, the mujahideen started receiving Stinger missiles from the US to shoot down low-flying aircraft. The prevailing expectation among US intelligence officials, though, was that the Stingers would only further increase the costs to the Soviet military and not defeat it. Even so, the Soviets had already committed to withdraw from Afghanistan.

Soviet helicopters and jets were destroyed by the Stingers. Yet, there is debate whether the *rate* of Soviet aircraft losses *appreciably* increased from the previous years. The Stingers forced the Soviets to shift their tactics. Their helicopters flew at night and their bombers flew higher causing them to be less accurate. Less modern Afghan aircraft were unable to fly at higher altitudes; therefore they suffered greater losses from the Stingers.

Over seven years the Soviet military had suffered huge casualties and could not decisively win the ground war, even though it had improved its ground, air assault and helicopter gunship tactics. The Soviets could not control the rural countryside, the main roads or the Afghan people. They were limited to holding a few big cities and a military draw at best. This led to a process of slow military and economic bloodletting. The Afghan war had become too costly for the Soviets to continue.

A significant number of Afghan communists working in the

Afghan Government and military were committed to the Soviets' defeat. A minority of mujahideen did play a vital role, but not a primary role in the Soviets' withdrawal from Afghanistan. This is not to diminish the value or bravery in battle of mujahideen fighters against the Soviets. The mujahideen field soldiers were not adequately supplied to win. Importantly, the true mujahideen did not commit atrocities against the Afghan people, and after the Soviets withdrew from Afghanistan, they returned to their farms and shops. They did not continue fighting in a devastating civil war that ravaged Afghanistan.

Why They Could Not Win

Politically there could be no victory for the Soviets or Afghan communists. The two feuding Afghan communist factions could not establish a legitimate government of the Afghan people. They were power hungry and in their pursuit of power they failed to respect the Afghan people, their traditions, and the Muslim religion. That largely explains why neither the Soviets nor the Afghan communists could earn the loyalty of the Afghan people or coerce them into obedience.

On April 14, 1988, Pakistan and Najibullah's DRA regime signed the Geneva Accords agreeing not to interfere or intervene in one another's country, and to allow the voluntary return of Afghan refugees. The US and Soviet Union signed as guarantors with an agreement that Soviet troops would withdraw from Afghanistan, which they did by February 15, 1989.

The Politburo's goal of withdrawing its troops was achieved; but the Afghan people at large were not friendly to the Soviet Union: over one million Afghans had been killed, five million were forced to leave their country as refugees, and two million were forced to give up all that they had and live in squalor elsewhere within Afghanistan. The mujahideen were not parties to the Accords and did not agree to comply with its terms.

Why the Soviets Got It So Wrong

The Soviets had made several military and political miscalculations. In hindsight, Russian officers who served in the

Soviet-Afghan War concluded that the Soviet political leaders who ordered the military into Afghanistan "did not consider the historic, religious, and national particularities of Afghanistan." In a January 21-22, 1987 Politburo meeting, Eduard Shevardnadze, then Soviet Minister of Foreign Affairs, reported that "[n]ot one problem has been solved to the peasantry's advantage....I won't discuss right now whether we did the right thing by going in there. But we did go in there absolutely without knowing the psychology of the people and the real state of affairs of the country."

Religion and Tribalism Underestimated

Soviet politicians underestimated the power of religious faith as had US officials. Afghan culture was also misunderstood. Afghanistan is a traditional Islamic society controlled by fiercely independent tribes and rivalries. The Soviet decision to include Uzbeks, Tajiks, and Turkmen from Central Asia as part of the invading Soviet 40th Army further angered the Pashtun tribes who had historically fought those ethnicities in northern Afghanistan.

The Soviet political leaders overestimated their power to control the events in Afghanistan. Afghans are deeply suspicious of foreigners. While their loyalties are local, Afghans have a strong cultural sense that Afghanistan is their home. Although the Soviets had a long history of working with Afghanistan, and prior to the invasion had thoroughly infiltrated the Afghan military with advisers and support personnel, they analyzed the world through a Marxist-Leninist framework and did not understand the core loyalties, tribal systems, and culture of the Afghan people.

Military Technology and Intelligence Overestimated

The Soviet military overestimated the value of its advanced military technology in a guerrilla war, and overestimated the effectiveness of its intelligence networks. The Soviets failed in Afghanistan because they made decisions based on information from faulty intelligence networks. They thought they knew the Afghan people down to the village level because "their Afghans" had infiltrated the villages working as teachers. Afghans born in the villages who became communists and teachers in the villages naively argued that Islam had no conflict with communism--even though Marxism-Leninism is an anti-God ideology. The Afghan teachers told the villagers that communists would provide food, clothing, and shelter to all persons in Afghanistan, equally and not according to merit. As a matter of fact, the villagers regarded the communist teachers as atheists and traitors--they were not trusted.

The two Afghan communist factions, Parcham and Khalq, were communists in name only. Many of them were deeply nationalistic and their attitude toward the Soviets was "we are your comrades, but we don't want you to invade us."

Soviet military officers underestimated the number of Soviet forces and helicopter gunships needed in Afghanistan to counter the guerilla insurgency. Militarily, they became stuck in a stalemate by 1984.

Pakistan's Foreign Policy: Weaken Afghanistan

The warlords and their mujahideen fighters played another important role for Pakistan. They furthered Pakistan's foreign policy of weakening Afghanistan.

The Soviet occupation of Afghanistan was regarded by the military dictator General Zia as an opportunity--*Brezhnev's Christmas gift.* When Zia negotiated with the US to be its exclusive conduit to deliver aid to the mujahideen resistance to fight the Soviets, he was able to divert billions of dollars from the US and Saudi Arabia to build the Pakistan military, its nuclear program started by Bhutto, and to assert his leadership among the Arab world and other Islamic countries. Zia did that through the layered strategy of "keep the pot boiling, but not boil over" policy. It also enabled Pakistan to advance its foreign policy strategy of weakening Afghanistan so that when Soviet troops withdrew from Afghanistan, it would continue to influence or control Afghanistan as a buffer country against India. Zia delegated to the ISI the authority to further that policy.

Soviet & Mujahideen Scorched Earth Policy

Afghanistan was weakened through the mujahideens' mass

destruction of Afghanistan's infrastructure. While transporting aid to displaced Afghans in Helmand Province, I observed that roads, bridges, hospitals, schools, textile factories, irrigation canals, and drainage systems had been destroyed by the mujahideen—in areas that neither the Soviets nor the Afghan communists controlled. When I saw the mass destruction, it did not make sense to me. I asked the mujahideen commanders why they were destroying all the buildings. They said that they were the properties of the communists. But that was not correct. The buildings belonged to the Afghan people. It was very painful for Afghan civilians to lose what they had worked so hard to gain.

The mujahideens' ruin of Afghanistan's infrastructure furthered the Soviet scorched-earth strategy in the rural areas. Ironically, the aim of that strategy was to destroy the Afghan civilians' means of providing aid, food, and shelter to the mujahideen. It also sought to coerce the Afghan people into obedience or to disable or kill them. The Soviet Union caused more destruction in Afghanistan than Germany did to the Soviet Union during WWII. The Soviet-Afghan War led to more than 70% of Afghanistan being destroyed by bombings, 90% leveling of Herat, 70% destruction of Kandahar City, and complete devastation of many other cities. The warlords and their mujahideen contributed to that.

Kabul and Mazar-i-Sharif were not pillaged by the Soviets; on the contrary, they actually developed those cities. The Soviets had brought new construction, food, and clothing to Kabul and cities under its control. They wanted more people to live in the major cities to better control them. After Soviet troops pulled out of Afghanistan, it was the mujahideen who reduced Kabul to rubble and slaughtered civilians during their civil war.

Besides destroying much of Afghanistan's infrastructure, Pakistan and the Afghan warlords weakened Afghanistan and its people in several other ways. The extremist indoctrination in the madrassas, which the warlords supported, weakened the Afghan people. Denying them literacy and vocational education prevented Afghans from improving their way of life. Secondly, by using the distribution of humanitarian aid, weapons, and ammunition as a tool to control people for its purposes, Pakistani officials influenced and weakened the traditional Afghan tribal structure by diminishing the power of tribal leaders, village chiefs, and elders to manage the survival of their people. A residual consequence was that the military and financial power bases of the warlords were expanded within the Afghan society.

Mujahideen Corruption

In a war economy, and in refugee camps where distribution of aid was used to control people, a culture of corruption became a way of life and a way to survive. My experience was that there were three types of mujahideen: 1) those who fought for freedom against the Soviets, a minority of the mujahideen; 2) the opportunists who called themselves mujahideen but their purpose was to enrich themselves; and 3) those who would rob anyone they could—one day they were communists and the next day they were mujahideen. I had problems with the second and third types. Those who were robbing from all sides were the warlords and drug lords. They continue to control the Afghan Government today. That is why little progress has been made since 9/11.

Opportunists can be found today in other conflict zones of the world. They draw upon the symbols and language of legitimacy, whether it is religion, ethnic pride, or a cultural code of honor to justify their grabs for power and wealth. They also manipulate countries who seek to use them as proxies to further their foreign policy objectives.

"They Are Just Robbers"

I had another unpleasant encounter with those who robbed all sides. In August 1984, we had just arrived with three big trucks filled with supplies and driven inside a huge, old fort located in a remote area of Jaghori District within Ghazni Province, Afghanistan. It was about 2 a.m. Inside waiting for us was Commander Hashim, a Hazara, and his fighters. They battled not only the Afghan

communists and Soviet soldiers, but also against other pro-Iranian Hazaras. Suddenly we were attacked with small arms fire. I thought we were surrounded and goners. So I said, "Let's take our picture [...before we die]!" In the above photo the bearded man with the white cap is Commander Hashim. Surprised that they did not shoot back, I asked the commander why they did not return the fire. He replied, "They are just robbers and it is not worth wasting bullets on them." He had fought many battles and knew the importance of conserving ammunition. Those robbers were the scum of the earth, killing and stealing from everyone. They were not Afghan communists or Soviets and eventually left.

In the morning we walked outside and saw the bullet marks from

their small arms fire etched on the massive walls of the fort. The other larger holes in the walls were from previous battles.

Protecting Ourselves From the Mujahideen

We did not know whether the mujahideen commanders would give our aid supplies such as medical supplies, tents, wheat, sugar or cooking oil to needy people, or sell them in the bazaar, or divert them for their exclusive personal use. In Quetta, for example, we had a very large warehouse where we distributed supplies. One day, around noon time, I gave boxes of tents to a mujahideen commander to take across the Pakistan border into Afghanistan. After 5 or 6 p.m., my colleagues and I walked through the bazaar. There we saw our boxes of tents in the shops. They had our IAC identification marks on them. I asked the shopkeeper, "How much?" He revealed a price that was 50 percent less than our cost.

Security Protocols

In addition, we did not know whether the mujahideen would betray and sell our IAC aid workers to the Afghan communists and Soviets. When the Peshawar Seven political parties and their mujahideen commanders requested humanitarian assistance inside Afghanistan, the IAC required them to sign an agreement to provide sufficient security for the IAC representative traveling with the supplies: armed guards back and forth across the Afghanistan-Pakistan border from the IAC supply depot in Pakistan. The IAC would supplement the mujahideen guards with two to four of its own guards. On occasion the IAC would send its security guards in advance as reconnaissance. Sometimes the IAC sent security guards to follow the convoy at a distance. If the IAC representative was injured, captured, or killed in an ambush by Afghan communists or Soviet soldiers, then the IAC would know that the mujahideen were not responsible. However, if the mujahideen betrayed the IAC and collaborated with the communists to turn over the IAC representative as a hostage, then the IAC would know the truth. I was not the only IAC representative to travel with supplies into Afghanistan. There were others.

During my years as a humanitarian aid worker and refugee, I have come to realize that there has always been abuse and corruption in war zones. The challenge is how to minimize it and exposure to hazards that you can't control.

15

WARNING SIGNS TO LEAVE

Danger Transporting Aid

As a Deputy Coordinator for the IAC, I often traveled with convoys to assure that humanitarian aid arrived in the correct locations and to identify new distribution sites. Our convoys were moving targets. We worried about getting ambushed by the communists, especially along the borders and where Soviet aircraft patrolled.

Normally, when transporting supplies from Pakistan into Afghanistan, I would ride in a pickup accompanied by three or four large trucks. In Pakistan I changed clothes frequently to make it difficult for communist enemies to identify me. They were everywhere. Communists had a strong presence in Pakistan. In fact, there were more Pakistani communists in Pakistan than Afghan communists in Afghanistan. The population in Pakistan at that time was between 80 to 90 million. In Afghanistan it was 14 to 16 million (before the killings and exodus of refugees). Only a small percentage of Afghans were communists.

The Pakistan People's Party (PPP) was not friendly to me and was an influential force in Pakistan. Murtaza Bhutto was behind the hijacking of my plane. He was the son of Zulfikar Ali Bhutto, one of the founders of the PPP and the former Prime Minister and President of Pakistan. Zulfikar was deposed by General Zia and executed by his regime. Although the PPP's ideology was socialist-democratic and not communist, it was pro-Soviet. None of those groups were friendly to me.

Inside Afghanistan both the Afghan communists and Soviet troops were indiscriminately killing anyone--not just the mujahideen. The Afghan communist government policy was to enforce absolute control within Afghanistan. If any aid went to villagers and was not from the Afghan Government, it was presumed to be from an enemy.

Cholera in Ghazni Province

The demands of my work were hard on my family. One day in 1984, Mulavi Sher Jan, a mujahideen commander of the Jamiat Islami Afghanistan party, asked for our help to treat a cholera outbreak among his men. My boss, Mr. Innis, asked, "Is there truly a cholera outbreak or is the commander trying to deceive us?" After consulting with our doctors and realizing that Mulavi Sher Jan had been trustworthy in previous dealings, we decided to take the chance. He was regarded as an honest, positive Islamic scholar--not an extremist, and was a member of Ahmad Shah Massoud's party.

I had no choice but to prepare for the long trip. Immediately, the doctors and I started putting together supplies and medicines to take with me to Ghazni Province in Afghanistan early the next morning. It would be a two-day trip to the alleged cholera site.

After making the necessary preparations, by the time I returned home, it was very late. I was met at the door by my children who pleaded, "Daddy, no food!" Bibigula looked at me and said, "We are short of food." It was payday and I had asked her to borrow food from the neighbors. She had done that, but it was just enough food for lunch. She thought that I would be home early enough to buy food for dinner. I jumped on my bicycle and went out looking for food. No shops were open, though. The children went to bed hungry. I asked myself many times, "Did I do the right thing?"

Not knowing for certain whether the mujahideen commander was telling the truth, I traveled with him to his camp with doctors and nurses and we saw the deadly cholera outbreak. Fortunately, we were able to save lives.

Tied to a Tree

In August 1984, Hajji Mohammed Hussan Mojadidi, a very well-known mujahideen commander from the Chist-e Sharif District in eastern Herat Province, traveled to our Quetta headquarters. Initially he met with Mr. Innis requesting assistance to build a hospital within his district. He pleaded, "We have doctors and nurses...we need your help!" Commander Mojadidi is at the far left in the photo below.

When such requests arrived, Mr. Innis would confer with me to evaluate their merits and risks. If it was worth the risk of going to the next step, I would prepare a needs and feasibility assessment. Then it could be submitted to the IAC committee for consideration. We both agreed that I should travel with Commander Mojadidi to the proposed hospital site for further assessment and take medical supplies with me. It was a long, rugged and hazardous trip back into Afghanistan and to eastern Herat. It was more than 650 miles one-way.

On the day of departure I traveled to Dalbandin, 216 miles southwest of Quetta, and waited there for the commander. The IAC had a large depot in Dalbandin which supplied the refugee camps near the Iranian border, and also the displaced Afghans in the western part of Afghanistan. Usually our agency would furnish the supplies and the mujahideen commanders would provide a lorry, a large truck to transport the supplies. I was surprised when Commander Mojadidi arrived in a small pickup truck, and without security guards other than a driver. He assured me, "The pickup is okay." I became suspicious of his intentions. Nevertheless, the driver, the commander and I squeezed into the front seat with the back bulging with supplies. It was a long, dangerous journey. Commander Mojadidi was fat; but fortunately I was a skinny 146 pounds at the time.

I decided to go with him even though he did not comply with the security protocols. Humanitarian aid workers sometimes take risks that they should not. I just felt that I needed to go to help. Medicines and other aid were critical to saving lives.

It was August and the temperature was more than 130 degrees Fahrenheit during the day. Traveling down dusty, unpaved desert roads, zigzagging back-and-forth across the Afghanistan-Pakistan-Iranian borders, we turned north into Afghanistan. Our intermediate destination was Rabath, a small village about 75 miles from Dalbandin. Rabath was a major supply center for the mujahideen in the western provinces of Afghanistan. Today it is a center for opium. Aside from the sweltering heat, we faced the risk of being caught in the crossfire of mujahideen rivalries. Although the mujahideen fought a common enemy, among themselves they were fierce adversaries.

On the way to Rabath, at night, the pickup broke down. We could not fix it. Some mujahideen stopped to help, but they could not fix it either. Just after midnight another group of mujahideen stopped; they also could not fix the pickup. Before departing, though, they said that two of us could go with them to Rabath. When Commander Mojadidi and I said that we would go with them, the driver protested not to be left alone. I told the commander to go ahead and I would follow with the driver after the pickup was running. He agreed and said that he would send another truck back to pick us up. Before sunrise, a group of Iranian Baloch stopped and fortunately were able to fix the pickup. The driver and I were again on our way.

When we entered into Rabath, Afghanistan, we were surprised to see Commander Mojadidi tied to a tree on the side of the road. The driver wanted to pull over and untie the commander, but I said, "Keep going, don't stop. It could be a trap." Our best option was to get to where the commander's fighters were located. They could send a party to release him. Later we discovered that the mujahideen who gave Commander Mojadidi a ride were his rivals from the Hezb-e Islami Gulbuddin Islamist party. Commander Mojadidi was part of the Jobh-e-Najat-e Melli (National Liberation Front) party, a secular group of the mujahideen.

Rabath is a huge area, very hilly, with fruit trees and many streams. There were several mujahideen camps within Rabath. While searching for Commander's Mojadidi's camp site, I happened to meet the nephew of another moderate commander, Abdul Ghafor, who was friendly with me because I had assisted him in the past. He was also friendly with Commander Mojadidi. I informed him that someone had tied "my man" to a tree. I did not say who "my man" was. When I described the location, the nephew recognized it as Gulbuddin's area. He and others on motorbikes carried their weapons--prepared to rescue my man. I advised him not to retaliate and fight the Gulbuddin men. The nephew and others sped off.

When they returned with Commander Mojadidi, I told him that I would go no further since he had no power to assure my safe passage. I asked Commander Mojadidi, "Where is your camp?" He had no proof that it even existed. We took a break and had lunch. It was hard bread soaked in water shared by the nephew's friends.

Then the driver hired by Commander Mojadidi said, "I am returning to Dalbandin." I had no choice but to leave with him; so I left the medical supplies with Commander Ghafor's men and started my journey back to Quetta. Commander Mojadidi returned with us because he also had no other option—it was not his vehicle or his soldier.

An AK-47 Pointed At Us

Danger and surprises did not end there. On the way back, the driver suddenly diverted off the road into a gulley. He stopped, stepped out of the cab, and went to the back of the pickup where he pulled out a Soviet AK-47 assault rifle and pointed it at us. He was shaking and said nothing. I asked, "What do you want? Why do you want to kill me?" Sweating, he nervously replied, "The others pay me more." "How much do you want?" I asked. "Six thousand rupees," he mumbled. Commander Mojadidi was responsible to pay the driver and not our agency. It was useless to argue with him, though. I said, "Okay, I will give you 6000 rupees. But our base is in Dalbandin. When we return there, I promise to give you the money." Thankfully, the driver agreed.

He returned to the driver's seat and drove us back onto the road.

Afterwards no one said a word. However, when we reached the edge of Dalbandin at night, the driver stopped and shouted, "Get out. I don't want the money. I don't want to get in trouble." I replied, "Don't be afraid. I will give you the money. I promised to give it to you." He was still unpredictable and moody. The driver had a positive incentive not to murder us and leave our bodies along the roadside—the money.

We continued and arrived at the IAC office. When inside I asked the treasurer for 6000 rupees explaining that it was to pay the driver. While she was getting it, I asked an IAC driver standing nearby, "How much does it cost to drive to Rabath." He replied, "It is 1500 rupees. And the return trip is 4000 rupees." "Why?" I asked. He explained, "Because opium is usually transported on the return trip." I then suspected that the driver was likely a drug smuggler. I gave him the money and told him not to come back.

Attacked by a Helicopter

The next month, in September 1984, I had another dangerous encounter attempting to provide aid to displaced Afghans in Afghanistan. It again involved Mulavi Sher Jan. He with six other mujahideen and myself crossed the Pakistan border at Badani into a mountainous region of the Waza-khwa Valley in Zabul Province, Afghanistan. We were transporting medical supplies in a large truck to Ghazni Province in Afghanistan. Winding through narrow roads under the canopy of huge trees, we had hoped to conceal ourselves from the ever-present danger of deadly Soviet attack helicopters.

Before beginning the trip, we had discussed the best route to take. Mulavi Sher Jan and the others did not want to travel this Waza-khwa Valley route because it was known to be patrolled by helicopters. Since I had passed through it several times earlier with no problems, I recommended that we use it. So, what happened?

An attack helicopter spotted us and lurched toward us like an eagle after its prey. We jumped from the truck and scrambled into a cave in the side of the mountain. I was the most afraid and the others followed me as far as I could go. We stepped awkwardly through the uneven cave floor. At the end we crouched, waited, and listened. My knees hugged my chest. As my eyes adjusted to the darkness, I saw a huge, poisonous snake staring at me. I asked whether we should be afraid of this snake or the helicopter. "Get out of here," they said. Running out of the cave like a pack of spiders, I jumped onto a tree. "Get off the tree! You are more exposed to the helicopter," they yelled. I quickly shimmied down the tree.

The helicopter had completely destroyed our truck, leaving us without transportation or food. We had no choice but to walk all the way back to Badani at the border, another eight to twelve hours. The helicopter would be looking for us, so we walked at night under the cover of darkness along the sides of the mountain which were very steep. We were hungry, dehydrated, and fearful. The others were upset with me because I had chosen that route. Even if we got to Badani, we did not know whether there would be transportation to return us to Quetta. In the end we were delayed another week. But we were alive.

A Dangerous Elopement

Events between December 1984 and January 1985 convinced me that my family should leave Pakistan and immigrate to the US. During Christmas time one of our male nurses, Abdul, became romantically involved with a refugee girl in the Girdi Jungle Refugee Camp. That triggered a very dangerous series of confrontations.

Abdul was a member of the Hazb-i Islami political party led by Gulbuddin Hekmatyar, and the girl belonged to the political party of Harakat-e Islami. The two political parties were brutal rivals. The girl told her parents that she was going to the Girdi Jungle Clinic. Her parents did not know that the clinic was actually closed--it was a holiday. Abdul picked her up from the clinic and they went into hiding.

A Mob Came Looking for Me

When that was discovered, many refugees from the camp occupied the Girdi Jungle Clinic and held as hostages our doctors, nurses, and other staff members. An angry mob of refugees from the Girdi Jungle Camp drove over 200 miles to Quetta and swarmed through the guarded gate of the Mission Hospital compound looking for me.

It was sunset and I was returning from the IAC office to my home, which was in back of the hospital and separated from it by a huge wall and two gates. Just as I had walked through the entrance gate of the hospital compound and started to step into the hospital, my brother, Zeke, found me. He warned me not to go through the hospital to my home. I asked, "Why?" "There are people there who will harm you," he said. I contacted Mr. Innis, informed him of my brother's warning and that I didn't know who the people were surrounding the compound.

Someone in our IAC headquarters called our Dalbandin regional office. A custodian there confirmed that all of our staff in the Girdi Jungle Clinic had been taken hostage because a male nurse there, Abdul, had taken off with an Afghan refugee girl and had been missing for one day.

Zeke counted a mob of about 30 people inside the Mission Hospital. One of them was a close acquaintance of mine. I later learned that he was forced by the mob to show them where my house was. The mob wanted to force me to find the girl or take me as a hostage since I was the Assistant Coordinator of the IAC, the number two man in charge. If Mr. Innis had been around and seen by the mob, they would have taken him hostage as well.

Mr. Innis called the Pakistani police and the Governor of Baluchistan who controlled the police in the entire province and asked for help. We discussed what to do. My recommendation to him was to call the leaders of both political parties who were in Quetta and bring them to the IAC office to talk. The office was connected to his home in the same compound. My plan was to put them in different rooms but not let them know that the other was there. We knew them very well since we had regularly provided them with aid.

Defusing a Potential Bloodbath

The party leaders came at different times and, fortunately, both were cooperative. From our headquarters the Harakat leader wrote a letter to his staff. One of our custodians took it to his Quetta office. The letter directed his staff there to go to the mob and tell them that his party was responsible for the safety of my family and me, and ordered them out of the hospital and away from my home. At the same time, the Harakat leader made a phone call to the Girdi Jungle Camp and sent notes to his other powerful party leaders ordering them to immediately release our staff. I told the Harakat leader that he must remain until all our staff was released. He was not happy about that. I was afraid that if he discovered that our male nurse was from the Hazeb-e Islami party, he would not release our staff. I also feared that when he would discover the party affiliation of the male nurse, it would trigger large scale killings within the Girdi Jungle Camp between the two political parties. If that happened, the two political leaders would be in our headquarters and we would have a better chance of reasoning with them to stop the fighting. The Soviets and Afghan communists were not far from the Afghan border and they could take advantage of the fighting in the camp.

Mr. Innis said, "Let him (the Harakat leader) go." I said, "No sir!" and explained the above reasons. He agreed. The Harakat leader remained in our compound and we treated him nicely. The leader of the Hazeb-e Islami party in Quetta came later. I informed him that our staff was held hostage; but he did not know what to do.

The next morning at 10 a.m., all our Girdi Jungle staff returned unharmed to Quetta. We sent new staff members to the clinic to replace them. I traveled with them in our ambulances. Along the 200 mile journey we stopped at a rest area. There I saw Abdul, the male nurse, and the girl. He turned pale. I said, "Go to Peshawar to escape because your life is in danger." I gave him some money. We took the girl in the women's ambulance to her family. I began efforts to prevent her from being killed by her family for dishonoring them.

Remember the man who was forced to bring the mob to the Mission Hospital? I convinced him to persuade the girl's father not to stone her to death (an honor killing). He tried to do what he could, but there was no certainty her life would be spared. In the eyes of her tribe, she had dishonored her family by running away with Abdul.

Removing the Shame

Two days later I traveled to the camp and spoke with the father and pleaded with him not to kill his daughter. He said, "If she gets married, she won't be killed because the shame would then be removed." The problem was that, according to his tribe's tradition, no one would want to marry her because the shame would be too great. I told the father, "I will find someone to marry her." One of our custodians in the Girdi Jungle Clinic was an orphan. He had lost his entire family during the Soviet war in Afghanistan. I asked him to marry the girl and offered, "We will pay for the wedding, provide you with a house, and then you will have a family. You could not otherwise afford to pay for a wedding and buy a house to get married." He replied, "If there is nothing wrong with her, why don't you marry her?" I remained quiet. But then he reluctantly agreed.

With some members of my staff, the girl's father and the custodian, we went to the girl. She was completely covered with a burqa. When we were all together, I said to the father, "This boy is willing to marry your daughter." The girl objected, "I want to marry only Abdul, the boy that I left with." I told her, "You know what is going to happen if you don't marry this boy." She replied, "I don't care. It is fine to be killed." I could tell that the father did not want to kill his daughter. He was crying and grieving saying that she was young and innocent and did not know what she was doing. He appealed to her. A few months after I had arrived in the US, I received a letter from one of my colleagues telling me that the girl had been killed by her family.

Escalating Signs to Leave

During that crisis I felt so much stress. I was clenching my teeth and felt intense pain in my mouth. The warning signs were quickly adding up. The leaders of the two political parties regarded me as responsible for the male nurse taking the Afghan girl from the refugee camp because he was my employee. I was afraid that they would kidnap and kill me and my family. The danger that Afghan communists would kill me also increased. The mujahideen commanders did not like me because I tried to reform their practices, which jeopardized their funding. I was also critical of the Pakistan Government's policies toward the Afghan refugees, and they didn't like that I worked for Americans. I was a soft target because I was not a member of any Afghan political party, and the Americans and Europeans could not protect me.

Until that time there had been two reasons for not emigrating to the United States: I was serving the cause of fighting the Soviets by providing aid to refugees in Pakistan and in Afghanistan; secondly, if I went to the US, I would likely work for a humanitarian aid agency in New York City where living in a high-rise apartment building would be very difficult for my disabled wife and four children. However *now*, saving the lives of my family was more important. We *had* to leave Pakistan.

I sent a letter to Doug Atwood who was working as Country Director of CARE-MEDICO in New Delhi, India. I had worked with him when he had been Director of CARE-MEDICO in Afghanistan. I told Doug that I wanted to go to the US. He responded that his office would send a letter to the US Embassy verifying that I qualified as a refugee to immigrate to the US. "Go to the Embassy in Islamabad and introduce yourself," Doug advised. The staff there knew me since I had been a liaison for the IAC with the Embassy for several years. Some of them also knew me from Kabul.

The Embassy contacted me in Quetta and requested that since I was applying to immigrate to the US, "why don't you come and work with us in the meantime?" They immediately put me in touch with the Joint Volunteer Agency (JVA).

Two previous times I had rejected the Embassy's offer in Islamabad to work for its refugee programs in Pakistan. The reason was that my wife needed regular medical care. It could be better provided through the IAC within the Mission Hospital compound where we lived. It was an ideal living situation. The convenience of medical care did not exist in Islamabad. The culture and environment of Quetta was also very similar to our home in Kandahar. That was now in the past.

I was hired by JVA on March 10, 1985, and moved with my family to Islamabad. This photo shows one of my farewell tea parties. From the right was my secretary, an Afghan refugee, Mr. Innis (with gray hair), behind me was my driver, Noor Mohamad, and the others were office staff in the Quetta IAC headquarters.

Each section of the IAC held a separate farewell party for me such as the doctors and nurses, the education, vocational training, resettlement, and humanitarian assistance inside Afghanistan departments.

Mrs. Innis handed me a sealed envelope just before leaving Quetta. I put it in my jacket and did not open it. It was three or four years later in Fremont, while going through my papers, that I found the letter and opened it. It contained some personal money from her and Mr. Innis, and a letter of appreciation acknowledging the things that I had done. I was so moved that I cried.

As we slowly departed Quetta, big crowds of Afghans had come to beg me not to go. When I was hired by the IAC in 1983, I was the only Afghan. When we left Quetta in 1985, I had hired 146 Afghans to be on my staff. It also included Britons, Americans, Dutch, Danish, Swiss, and Australians. The entire area around the IAC headquarters was blocked by refugees. The Pakistani police made a way for my car to go to the train station. The mujahideen commanders were happy that I left.

16
THE HOPE OF A REFUGEE

In Islamabad I began working for the JVA branch of the US Embassy advising the Embassy staff on the geopolitics of Afghanistan, and providing translation and interpretation in various languages. While screening refugees, I understood the hope that they felt. My family and I were like them--refugees.

No one said anything about my status despite the fact that I was working in the Embassy. However, JVA staff members did help me locate a refugee relocation agency in the US that would find a sponsor for my family. I wrote to three of my American friends who had returned to their homes. One was in Napherville, Illinois, another in New Mexico, and the third was Gordon Stinson who lived in Birmingham, Alabama.

All three of them replied agreeing to sponsor my family. Coincidentally, each of their acceptance letters arrived at the Embassy on the same day. I asked a colleague which among the three sponsors' cities most resembled Afghanistan and had a slow pace of life. He said, "Alabama!" So Alabama was where my family would go. Alabama seemed like a good choice because the Stinson family lived there. I had worked and lived with them at different times since my high school days.

Finally, our immigration process was completed and we were approved to leave for the US. Two days prior to departing, while standing in a circle at an Embassy party, Robert Dirra informed the US Ambassador to Pakistan that I was leaving as a refugee to the US. The Ambassador jokingly responded, "Don't let him go. He is too valuable here." He turned his face to me and said, "Do you want to work for Burger King in the US?" That was the first time I heard the name "Burger King" and didn't know what it was. Sometimes when I look at a Burger King, I think of the Ambassador. He was not aware of the serious threats against my life and family. I thought to myself, "I'm glad he was only joking, otherwise I would quit working for the Embassy."

I continued working up to the very last hours in the JVA office. At 8 p.m., as I walked down the stairs to the first floor, I was greeted with a surprise farewell party. There were cakes, cookies, and drinks. Worried that I would be delayed, I said, "I must leave. My flight is at 11 p.m." I cut the cake, said good-bye and rushed home with some colleagues to pick up Bibigula and my children.

When I got home, Bibigula was not ready. She didn't think that we were leaving at that time. We packed in 30 minutes. My colleagues helped us and took us to the Islamabad Airport, which fortunately was not far away. At the airport I was surprised when told that I was in charge of 25 refugee families also going to the US, and was directed to help them.

I had only $146 in my pocket. It was given to me by Dr. Pfeiffer, the Director of Catholic Charities in Pakistan. I had given all my other money and possessions to my mother and brothers who had come from Kandahar to see us off before leaving.

As I was walking to the plane on May 22, 1985, I wondered whether I would be able to return to this part of the world or if I was leaving for good. Other refugee families were happy to be reunited with relatives in the US. My wife and I had no relatives there; but we had a few American friends.

I was so busy with the other families that I didn't have time to dwell on my flight anxiety. In the back of my mind, though, were flashbacks of being held hostage four years earlier in a Pakistani plane just like this one.

We ascended into the Islamabad sky. The first stop was Damascus, Syria, where I had been released as a hostage in 1981.

Next, the plane landed in Istanbul, Turkey, then on to Frankfurt, Germany; there we boarded a TWA flight to JFK Airport, New York.

During the flight I was very tired. My kids continued to ask me many questions and so did members of the other 25 families. They would come to my seat and ask the same type of questions: "What do I do when I get to the US? Will my brother meet me at the airport?" How would I know the answers to those questions? I could not get any rest. I was exhausted.

When we arrived at JFK Airport and exited the plane, I was followed by my family and all the other families. In the crowd I was immediately separated from Bibigula and our kids. When I found them, I shouted at my wife. I was angry. It was the first time that I had shouted at her. Then I looked around me and realized that she had gone with the kids straight to the correct place.

We transferred from the international to the domestic terminal where we would take off to Atlanta and from there to Birmingham. All the other 25 families went to different cities and states. Our family was the only one heading to Birmingham.

At the boarding area for Atlanta, a representative from a refugee agency forced us to run to the buses. It was more than a frustrating experience because his English was terrible and difficult to understand.

When the plane took off from JFK, the sun reflected off the muddy waters around the airport. I felt many things at the same time: worn out, separated, frustrated, disappointed, and lonely. Never before in my life had I felt like that. When we arrived in Atlanta, we were told to remain on board. I changed my shirt in the plane's lavatory, sat down, and relaxed. Bibigula and the kids were sleeping. After a very short time, the pilot announced that we were arriving in Birmingham. From my window I saw huge trees below. I had expected to see sand and desert, like in Afghanistan. It was the opposite of what I had imagined.

Our First Home

As refugees we arrived on May 22, 1985, at 9 p.m. in the Birmingham Airport. We were met by our sponsor, Gordon Stinson, our long-time friend. When I was in high school, I had taught him Pashto. Later I had worked for him when he was Director of IAM in Kabul. During the previous two weeks, Gordon and his family had moved from Huntsville to Birmingham, Alabama. He warmly welcomed us along with his wife, Janet, and their three children. I remembered each child from the day that they were born in Afghanistan. Sometimes I was their babysitter while Gordon and Janet went to parties. Gordon represented one of our two official church sponsors, the Briarwood Presbyterian Church. The other sponsor was Dr. Johnny Long, pastor of the Altadena Valley Presbyterian Church (Altadena Church).

Gordon and his family drove us to our first home in America. It was a big house on 24th Street next to an apartment complex occupied by people on welfare, in an area called Southside, adjacent to Birmingham University. Above us, on the hillside, was where the white middle class and rich people lived. In 1985 the city was divided between whites and blacks.

Upon arrival our four kids were very tired, so were Bibigula and I. There was a huge bed in the master bedroom, a stove, and a refrigerator. Otherwise the house was completely empty. We placed our four children on the bed to sleep. That night, Bibigula and I slept on the floor.

In the morning I walked outside. The front yard was dirty so I swept the sidewalks. A man with a missing tooth approached me and asked whether I had an extra room for him to stay in. I was shocked. I was a refugee and here was a person born in America asking for a place to live. I thought to myself, "God, help me for my future. If he does not have a place to live, what will happen to us?"

During the next few days, families of the two sponsor churches showered us with furniture and other necessities. They were more than kind. We were spoiled. We greatly appreciate them and will never forget them. Wherever they are, we wish them the very best.

It was the middle of Ramadan; that year it was in May. Bibigula and I were fasting before sunrise and until after sunset. When people would offer us food during the daylight hours, we would explain that we were fasting. The rumor spread that there were people who didn't eat while the sun was up. When Ramadan was finished, we celebrated Eid al-Fitr (Feast of Breaking the Fast) and invited the families who had helped us resettle to join us and eat Afghan food. We were very different from others. Many people in Birmingham did not know Afghanistan even existed or that it was at war with the Soviets.

Gordon had my resume and found me a job. Monday was a holiday, Memorial Day. So on Tuesday Gordon drove me to the Walker Drug Company which had agreed in advance to hire me. I worked part-time together with college students stocking shelves and filling medicine bottles that were shipped to retail stores. Starting pay was $3.40 per hour, which was minimum wage at that time. From our home I rode two buses to work. It was my first time in the US and I did not know how to use the bus system. At first it was confusing.

On the second day all six of us waited at a bus stop about three houses from our home. We didn't know that we were required to buy tickets in advance. When a bus stopped and the driver asked for our tickets, I was surprised and replied, "I thought I could pay you when we got on the bus." In Afghanistan we would first step into the bus, take a seat, then a conductor other than the bus driver would go seat-to-seat and collect money for the tickets.

We looked different than other people and the bus driver felt sorry for us, especially with our four small children. He said, "Come on, get on; you are my responsibility." When on board I asked, "We want to ride wherever the bus finally stops. Will you bring us back here?" "No, but another bus will, and I will show it to you," he answered. We had a nice ride through the city and another bus driver returned us home. We paid him with tickets that we had purchased at the bus stop where the other bus ended its route.

It was a very emotional time. Two weeks later Gordon had brain surgery and was no longer able to be our guide. His wife was also going through a difficult time. For 22 years our two families had been very close. I felt like an orphan after Gordon had been incapacitated. We were the only refugee family in Alabama. I thought to myself, "What will I do?" I had no car or a driver's license.

We Were Robbed

During the second week in America our house was robbed and most of our belongings were stolen. It was heart-breaking. Such things did not happen in Afghanistan. It was such a bad experience. The people from the churches treated us very nicely, though. They gave us all the clothes and household items we needed like pots and pans.

While many people brought us things, they did not invite us into their homes. At some point in the first few weeks, though, a neighbor invited our family to her apartment. When we walked in, we saw many, many cats. While we were sitting, it was very uncomfortable for us because in Afghanistan cats and dogs were regarded as the lowest and most unclean creatures and were not allowed inside homes. After about 15 minutes, one of the cats jumped on Bibigula's shoulder. Startled, she grabbed the cat and with both hands threw it away from her. The woman became very angry and told us to leave immediately.

One day while we walked to Piggly Wiggly to shop for food, it started raining. It rained a lot in Birmingham. We were soaked and all of our groceries fell out of the soggy paper bags. After that experience, thanks to members of the Altadena Church, we were provided with rides to buy our basic needs and other assistance to make our new beginning in America easier.

Becky Long, the pastor's wife, was one of those who gave me driving lessons and helped me to get a driver's license. Dr. Doug Heimburger from the Altadena Church and a doctor from another church provided Bibigula and our children with free medical treatment. Tom Jackson, Michael and Karen Payne were also very helpful. I wish that I could remember the names of all those who helped us. Dr. Long and his wife, the deacons, and church families were very good to us.

"I Need to Let You Go"

A month had passed when the manager of the Walker Drug Company called me into his office and said, "I am sorry to tell you that you are overqualified for the job and I need to let you go." He didn't say it, but the real reason was that college students, who were also working there, were constantly surrounding me asking questions about Afghanistan. That caused production to be slowed. I told them to wait until after work when I would answer their questions. I could not stop them, though, from asking me questions during work hours.

To my surprise the manager then said, "We have found a job in another company for you nearer to your home, at Crawford Interiors." That company had made a new contract with the Alabama Power Company to put office equipment and partitions in its buildings. Crawford Interiors had $11 million of inventory. I became its warehouse manager with a salary of $7 per hour. That was a big salary then. As a manager I had to work overtime. I liked that because I was paid extra.

Bibigula's Tasty Bread Business

Mrs. Long sent ladies from the church to teach her English. However, as you know, Bibigula had suffered from toxemia and as a result, she has had difficulty learning new things, especially a new language. That did not prevent them from enjoying one another's company. Mrs. Long took Bibigula shopping. I always saw them laughing together, even though they didn't speak the other's language. Other women from the church helped her to start a small business baking Afghan bread. Bibigula soon became famous for her tasty bread. The demand for it became greater than she could supply.

During the first few months, beginning with the $146 given to me in Pakistan, combined with my salary and money earned from her bread business, we had no financial problems. Our rent for the house was only $300 a month. We were self-sufficient and able to buy a reliable 1978 Plymouth.

As a new refugee in America, however, it took me a while to

learn how to buy things smartly. I would pay full-service for gas not knowing that I could pay less for self-service. Unwittingly I went to a more expensive hair salon not knowing that there were less expensive barber shops to get a haircut. I didn't know!

Crawford Interiors bought a forklift and I was taught the basics of how to drive it. I was not taught, though, how to properly stack large, loaded pallets. More skill and experience were needed. I made a deal with my counterpart, Ray Dickson, who worked with the Alabama Power Company. He did not know how to do inventory. So I offered, "You teach me how to drive the forklift and I will show you how to do inventory."

Developing Teamwork

Crawford Interiors hired 15 more black workers for the warehouse. Working hard and respecting one another, we gradually developed into a tight-knit team and accomplished a lot. Three of the men did not have a car; so every morning I picked them up, and after work, I drove them to their homes which were about seven to ten miles away. They offered me money for the rides but in my culture, since they were my colleagues, I could not take the money. Considering the bus system at the time, I was worried that they would be late for work, get home late at night, and have little time with their families. My teammates were very appreciative.

Taking Good Care of People

I had managed large numbers of workers in the Afghan Fertilizer Company (AFC) and in Pakistan within the refugee camps. From experience I knew that if you take good care of people, work and life will be better for everyone.

In Helmand Province, Afghanistan, for example, in one of the 11 provinces that I had administered for the AFC, I had supervised 140 workers at various distribution warehouses. Most were young laborers who lifted, carried, and stacked sacks of fertilizer weighing 50 kilos, about 110 pounds. It was hard, dirty, tiring work. Fertilizer can burn your skin. The bags were filled with diammonium phosphate (DAP) or urea. Many of the laborers were so poor that they had no shoes. When I arrived at the Helmand AFC headquarters, the workers had only tea and bread to eat for lunch. The manager complained that they moved very slowly. I explained to him that the work was exhausting, especially in the hot sun, and the people were hungry. I proposed to my manager a plan to provide extra food for all the workers. He said that it would cost extra money and did not think the company would agree. Nevertheless, he said, "Give it a try."

Among the 120 workers in the Helmand headquarters site were some elderly people. I could not refuse anyone who asked for work and found something for them to do, like sewing torn fertilizer sacks. I selected some of them to cook: they mixed beef, beans, and greens in big copper pots that were also used to wash clothes. After one week there was a big improvement. Production increased and so did the loyalty of the workers. Soon the managers overseeing the workers had nothing to do. Word got around and we had no problem recruiting workers.

Bibigula's Big Beef Sandwiches

Remembering those experiences in Afghanistan, I sometimes bought pizza with my own money for my teammates in the Birmingham warehouse. They liked that very much. But I would not eat it because I had never eaten pizza in Afghanistan or Pakistan. Also it had pork on it, which I would not eat. I thought that there was only one type of pizza—pork pizza. Not until later, after I had moved to California, did I realize that there was non-pork and non-meat pizza. My team members laughed that I would not eat pizza. At other times I would bring my teammates very thick sandwiches made by Bibigula with her homemade bread. She would cook ground beef mixed with chopped onions and greens and wrap it in individual pieces of bread. They resembled burritos, only much larger. My black friends loved them. Later I discovered that they would have liked them even more if the sandwiches had included cheese. They never told me that, though.

Since our warehouse was on the outskirts of Birmingham, there were no nearby restaurants. When there were many trucks to be unloaded from Dallas, Chicago, Madison, and Atlanta, we were rushed and given little time to unload. We had only one forklift to move and stack many pallets of equipment. So we ate on the run. Bringing homemade sandwiches saved time and brought us closer together.

Racial Misunderstanding

Throughout the first few weeks at the Walker Drug Company at break times, the white and black college students would sit in different places. I was left to sit alone. I asked one of the black workers, "During the day whites and blacks work together. But, during break times, why do whites and blacks sit in different places?" He said, "Because I am black." Puzzled, I asked him, "What difference does that make?" He had no answer. This young college student and I were wearing T-shirts at the time. So I said, "Close your eyes and stretch out one arm." I rubbed my arm against his bare arm and asked, "What color do you feel?" He laughed and replied, "None!" Then I asked, "What is the difference between whites and blacks?" That was the beginning of my gradual discovery of the racial barriers and tensions in the US.

Among my 15 black teammates was Mike Pollack who was a forklift driver. Mike and I became friends and sometimes went bowling. We both liked to tell jokes. In Afghanistan it was common to make jokes about ethnicities. There, black people are considered brave, strong, and honest. My daughter, Pashtana, and my son, Yonus, are considered black in Afghanistan; but in the US, they are not. That was my Afghan experience which is different from the American experience.

Not understanding the racial history in America caused me a big embarrassment. One day we were rushed and working very hard. We laughed and joked with one another to relieve tension. I have always laughed in difficult times, especially after 1978 when Bibigula almost died from toxemia. Mike started joking with me. He said, "Are you one of those people who singsong lu-lu-lu?" *Lu-lu-lu* was spoken in a high-pitched voice. He was referring to a cheer that Arab women do at weddings and games. While laughing, I joked back and said, "Hey, nigger, get to your work!" When I was in high school, I read a novel in which the word *nigger* was used. I thought it was an ordinary word meaning a black person and not meant to be derogatory. I did not know otherwise. Another black worker heard what I said. His name was also Mike and he was very muscular. Ray, my counterpart with the Alabama Power Company, was white and also overheard it. He was quiet and mumbled to himself; but it was clear that he did not like what I said.

Not knowing that Ray had called my supervisor, Mike Bern (another Mike), phoned me from the company headquarters and said, "Come to my office ASAP." He was also the human relations officer and vice president of the company. Ray had informed him that I had called Mike a nigger. Mike asked me, "What did you say to Mike?" I said, "Nothing." Mike pressed further asking, "Didn't you call him a nigger?" I laughed and replied, "He is a nigger." "Do you know what nigger means?" "Yes, it means a black person," I answered. "Do you know it is against the law?" he asked. Very surprised, I said, "No! When I was in high school, I read a novel that used the word nigger and I did not think that it was a bad word." When Mike explained, "It is against the law and a racial slur, and you are lucky that your nose is still on your face," I was shocked. I did not want to hurt Mike (Pollack). Coming from Asia, I did not know the racial history and laws in the US. As a refugee I made mistakes because I did not understand the American culture.

When I returned to the warehouse, I was very embarrassed before my teammates. I did not realize that nigger was such a bad word. No one said a thing and acted as though nothing had happened. While they were standing near Mike, I apologized to Mike. He said, "No, no, it was nothing at all." My teammates were very surprised, though, that someone had complained about me. "Who was it?" they asked. I did not know at the time, but it was Ray. Mike continued and joked, "Lu-lu-lu, you camel jogger." A camel jogger is someone who leads camels.

Mr. Tornado Is Coming

Another example of cultural and language misunderstanding occurred one day in June or July at the Crawford Company when all my colleagues were listening to the radio. The news reported that a tornado was approaching. I thought a tornado was a high-level company official. I was not concerned about him coming. Later I was told that the tornado had passed. When I arrived home, and watched the news on the TV, I saw the destruction caused by the tornado. Then I discovered what a tornado was. Returning the next day to work, I told my teammates, "I'm sorry that so much damage was caused. I didn't know what a tornado was." Then I explained my misunderstanding. One of them replied, "So that is why you were not worried about the tornado." Jokingly I said, "From now on when an official from company headquarters comes, I will say Mr. Tornado is coming."

Meeting Afghans in Atlanta

My days were full. I was busy at work and daily took the kids to school. They quickly learned to speak English because they had received English instruction in Afghanistan and Pakistan. Bibigula was busy, too, with her baking business; but she had no friends who spoke Pashto, and she was very lonely. Bibigula cried a lot. We did form friends with Afghans who lived in Atlanta; but that was some distance away.

It is a funny story how we first met Afghans in Atlanta. One day a young man from the Altadena Church drove us to the refugee services agency office in Atlanta that coordinated our immigration into the US. There I asked for a list of other Afghans in the city. The secretary said that she was not permitted to give it to me. I said, "Here is my name, address, and phone number. You can give it to any Afghan." She picked up the phone, called an Afghan man, explained that I was trying to make friends, and handed the phone to me. When I talked to him, he recognized my Pashto accent and that I was from Kandahar. He asked, "Are you from Kandahar?" "Yes, I am," I replied. He continued, "You are welcome in our home at anytime. Here is a phone number of Abdullah, an Afghan from Kandahar." It was getting late; so we drove back to Birmingham.

When I returned home, I immediately called Abdullah. His voice was high-pitched and a little unusual. After explaining that my wife was bored and we were looking for other Afghans to associate with, he asked, "Then why did you leave Afghanistan?" I replied, "We are coming to your home next weekend." "No, you cannot come to our home," he insisted. "Yes we are...we are coming!" I said.

Afghan Hospitality

The principle of hospitality in Pashtunwali, the Afghan code of ethics, is deeply engrained in the culture of all ethnicities in Afghanistan. It is an obligation to open one's home to someone if they come in need or ask to come to visit. The expectation is that you offer hospitality because God wants you to help his creations. The guest need not say "thank you" for the hospitality given, which may be a meal or other assistance. If someone's car breaks down, you help where you can. In a similar manner, if service is provided in your home, the guest or stranger need not extend verbal appreciation for it. At least the courtesy of saying "God help you" is expected. It means that the guest hopes that God will somehow help you in your life. The expectation is also that the guest or stranger would provide even more hospitality or assistance to others.

I again told Abdullah, "We are coming; what is your address?" Abdullah answered back, "You are a strange man. We are living in only a one-bedroom apartment." From the perspective of Pashtunwali, it was strange that he refused us. I knew that if other Afghans discovered this, he would be shunned. No one would even go to his funeral. I joked, "Okay, I will bring a tent with us and pitch it on your street." Then he agreed, and we scheduled to visit him and his wife Rahila the following week. Since I did not have a driver's license at that time, I informed him that an American from a church that sponsored us would drive and be with us.

The next week, as we approached Atlanta on the way to Abdullah's and Rahila's apartment, the young man who drove us suggested, "You told me that you don't know the family we are going to visit. Why don't we eat something before we get there?" "No, we will eat there," I said. In disbelief he replied, "But you don't know them!" He did not understand the Afghan culture.

When we arrived near their apartment, we called Abdullah from a phone booth. He came to our location and guided us from there. We were all warmly greeted. Bibigula and Rahila immediately became great friends. It was as if they had known one another all their lives. Our girls helped them bring out a beautiful spread of food enough for 20 people, and in the Afghan tradition, placed it on a long tablecloth on the floor. Our young American friend was more than surprised to see how well we were treated. We visited for several hours and returned after sunset. It was Sunday and the next day I had to work and the children go to school.

The young man who drove us to Atlanta later explained to members of his church our experience visiting Afghans that we had never met before: "If I could find a job for Sher in Atlanta today, I would move him and his family there tomorrow. When I saw how his family was embraced by the Afghan family, and how Bibigula came alive with joy with Rahila, it was amazing."

"Come to Chicago"

After about nine months, I was almost ready to move to Atlanta when another American friend, David Leatherberry, contacted me by telephone and inquired, "How are you folks doing there?" I replied, "Bibigula needs Afghan friends." He told me that his church would like to be our sponsor and relocate us to Chicago. We had worked together in the International Assistance Mission (IAM) and I had helped him learn Pashto. David was on a short visit to Chicago and would soon return to Pakistan. He said, "Here in Chicago there are many Afghans." I replied, "First I would need a job in Chicago."

A few days later, David's local pastor invited me to Chicago to search for a job. I agreed and took two days off. Because I was still reluctant to take trips by plane, I traveled there by Greyhound bus. The pastor gave me a tour of the city. I saw Hispanics and Greeks on the streets and presumed that they were Afghans. "Oh," I thought, "there are many Afghans here!" I looked in the phone book and saw Afghan names. Upon returning to Birmingham, I submitted my resignation. My boss at Crawford Company said that if I was not happy with my job in the company, I would be given a new job with more pay. I explained that I was not leaving because I was unhappy: "The problem is my wife. She is lonely, bored, and crying. She needs Afghan friends. We need to go to Chicago where there are Afghans."

I informed Gordon that we were moving. He discouraged me from going there, "Chicago is not the place for you and your family. I lived there for three years."

When we moved to the Chicago area, David's pastor found us a home to rent on Chestnut Street in Hammond, Indiana, which is on the border of Chicago. Through the newspaper I found a temporary sales job.

Not long afterward an Afghan friend, Qayium, said, "I am going to California to attend a friend's wedding. There are many Afghans living there." Seeing an opportunity, I responded, "I want to go with you on the condition that I do not fly. We must take a Greyhound bus." He agreed.

The wedding was in Redwood City, California. There I met many former Afghan classmates and friends. I decided then that my family must move to California. We stayed with another Afghan friend, Azim. I asked him to rent an apartment for my family, and gave him money for the rent. He advised me that before doing anything, he would wait until I had returned with my family.

Upon arriving back in Hammond, I resigned my job after working there for only four months. We gave all our household items to the church that helped us, and to our Afghan friends. The six of us crammed into our five-passenger Plymouth with a few possessions. After traveling three days, we arrived on September 24, 1986, in Redwood City. Azim led us across the Dumbarton Bridge to

Fremont, on the other side of the San Francisco Bay. There, in its Centerville District, he had located an apartment for us in a 14-unit complex.

17
A NEW BEGINNING IN FREMONT

When another Afghan friend in Chicago learned that I was renting an apartment in Fremont, he asked me to also rent an apartment there for him, which I did. Word quickly got around the Afghan community about that area of Fremont and many Afghans moved there. In the apartment complex where I lived, I arranged for eight other units to be rented by Afghans. The owner of the building soon asked me to manage the apartments for him, which I did. I had no previous experience, but I learned quickly what to do. Afghans continued calling me, asking for help to find a place to live in Fremont.

Since the mid-1980s, Northern California has attracted the largest concentration of Afghans within the US. Afghans were simply looking to live near other Afghans. In Fremont, the clustering of Afghans in the Centerville District came to be known by many people as "Little Kabul."

"I Can Do That"

Children from one of the Afghan families in my apartment complex were enrolled in American High School on Fremont Boulevard. During the first week after driving them there, while walking past classrooms, I observed an instructor teaching English as a Second Language (ESL). I thought to myself, "I can do that!" I asked the secretary of the school, "Do you hire people to teach ESL?" She said, "We don't hire directly." However, she put me on the phone with the School District ESL Director. Over the phone I was interviewed and asked, "Would you be willing to take a test at our office?" "Sure," I happily answered.

While taking the four-hour test with others, I saw only white, Anglo-Saxon faces. I asked myself, "Why am I taking this test? I am competing against native speakers." I passed the test and surprised, a week later was hired as an ESL teacher. The Fremont School District assigned me to teach in three schools: Azevada Elementary School, Chadbourne Elementary School, and Kennedy High School. I was also asked to coach and tutor the parents of the ESL refugee students. I invited the parents to Kennedy High School in the evenings to learn English and to bring their children there to do their homework.

Hot Dogs Filled With Dog Meat?

Life in a new country can be very confusing for refugee families. On Central Avenue, across the street from the Department of Motor Vehicles and next to the Centerville Presbyterian Church, there were 60 Afghan families living in an apartment complex. An elderly lady on the second floor, intending to visit her daughter-in-law, walked down the wrong hallway and stood in front of the wrong apartment waiting for her. Another family with seven children had no car. I took them shopping at the Lucky grocery store in the Brookvale Shopping Center. At the checkout counter I noticed the items that they had put into their cart. When they placed cans of dog food on the counter for the cashier to handle, I asked, "Do you own a dog?" "No," they replied. The parents were unwittingly buying dog food for their children thinking that it was food for humans. They could not read the labels. Simple misunderstandings about food can continue for a long time. Let me tell you that even at that time, and for many years afterward, I believed that hot dogs were filled with dog meat. I would not eat them.

I thought to myself, "How can I help the Afghans? There are too many of them." I walked into the Centerville Presbyterian Church and spoke with its co-pastor, Gordon Wilson. I appealed to him: "You and I have different religions. But here next to this house of God, there are people who cannot even find their way within the building they live. There are people there who select dog food from the grocery store shelves thinking it is food for their children." "What can I do?" he replied. "Ask your congregation to volunteer to teach them to read and write," I answered. He invited me to a church meeting where he requested volunteers. Many raised their hands and

I wrote down their names. I was very encouraged and grateful.

The Plight of Refugees

It is extremely challenging for people from non-Western traditional cultures like Afghanistan who have lost everything to resettle into America or Europe. Many Afghan refugees have suffered unspeakable tragedies. Refugees are people who were threatened with death or torture, war or disaster in their home countries due to political, religious, racial, or other types of persecution. Immigrants are different. They are people who leave their countries for better economic opportunities. Refugees usually do not have time to plan their escapes. They leave their countries with very little or nothing. When they arrive in America, the stresses of communicating with people who speak a different language, finding a place to live, to work, locating food that looks familiar to eat, and health care can take a huge toll on one's emotional and mental health.

During the same period of time, by coincidence, I ran into Jim Lamar. He was a VISTA (Volunteers in Service to America) volunteer assigned to work with Literary Volunteers of America (LVA) for the state of California headquartered in Berkeley. Jim said, "Your Afghan volunteer program would be a great program." We met several times and I asked him whether he would be willing to go to the Centerville Presbyterian Church, where I would introduce him to the co-pastor. Jim agreed but encouraged me to set up my own program. He said, "You have the ability to do it. VISTA and LVA would help you." I said, "Okay! I will call it Afghan Tutorial Services."

Jim made appointments for me to speak in a classroom at the University of California, Berkeley, to recruit volunteers. I asked Pastor Wilson to provide a room at the church to start the adult literacy program. There Jim trained 45 volunteers from the Centerville Presbyterian Church and students from UC Berkeley to tutor Afghan refugees in their homes. I personally matched the volunteers with refugee families that I felt could best work together.

Founding of International Refugee Services Inc.

While teaching ESL in the schools, I realized that lack of literacy was a problem not only with Afghan refugees but also for other refugees and immigrants such as Vietnamese, Latinos, and Eastern Europeans. There were 2.6 million legal refugees and immigrants from various countries in California. I told Jim that I was going to expand the nonprofit to be *International Tutorial Services Incorporated*. Later the name was changed to *International Refugee Services Incorporated (IRSI)*. Jim advised me that I also needed a board of directors, by-laws, and articles of incorporation.

In 1987 Jim assisted me to formally establish a 501c3 nonprofit organization and serve as its Executive Director. It began from a small room in my apartment on Glenmoor Drive in Fremont. But it needed money to operate and I needed to provide for my family's livelihood. So I started a landscaping and painting business. Soon I had enough money to buy a van for $800, which also became my mobile office. I paid for the gas to recruit volunteers, travel to match and introduce them to Afghan clients in their homes, and paid the typical communication and administrative expenses of a nonprofit. In 1988 our family was able to move from a small apartment to a

home on Hudson Place in Fremont. An office was set up in our garage.

IRSI grew rapidly. Our first board of directors consisted of Bob Darr, founder/director of the Afghan Culture Center in Berkeley, Dr. Julienne Lipson, a professor at the UCSF School of Nursing, Patricia

Omedian, assistant professor at the School of Nursing, Jim Lamar, and Pastor Gordon Wilson. Later joining our board were Dr. Greg Roth, pastor at the Centerville Presbyterian Church, Connie Guidotti, a photographer, Randy Fewel, a social worker, Terry Cotter, a Paralympics coach, and Ken Hardman, a real estate broker.

The first grant we received was from the ARCO Foundation in 1990; then there was the James Irvin Foundation, which sent three ladies to interview me in my garage office. Several federal and state grants  followed. In addition to the ESL programs, we initiated programs teaching adult literacy up to the eighth-grade level in math, reading and home economics. Also taught were job readiness and placement, and computer training. Our literacy program expanded throughout California, from Eureka to Blythe on the Arizona border, and we had a branch office in Bakersfield. ESL was also taught to farming migrants.

We provided interpreting services for law enforcement agencies, schools, and immigration offices. Interpreters and translators in hospitals were especially important—they saved lives. Mistakes are often made by health care providers who misunderstand what non-English speaking immigrant and refugee patients say. We served the Hewlett Packard Children's Hospital in Stanford, the Washington Township Hospital in Fremont, the San Francisco Health Screening Clinic, and many more.

At the same time, I was employed as a VISTA Coordinator for California.

Over time I recruited, trained and supervised more than 400 volunteers, interns and staff, and implemented public relation services for governmental bodies, churches, mosques, and community-based organizations. It was a busy time. I appeared on Coast to Coast TV in Concord and in many cultural awareness programs to discuss refugee issues. My work took me across the US, Europe and to the Indian subcontinent where I conducted 413 presentations on various topics including cross-cultural awareness in the workplace, schools and hospitals, as well as family values, youth awareness, interreligious

dialogue, and geopolitical issues between Afghanistan and the former Soviet Union.

Being a Father and a Husband

Managing IRSI and its many projects on a bare-bones budget and living on a meager salary put a lot of stress on my family. I did my best, though, to teach important values to my children. I sought to instill in them the value of being loyal and kind to their mother. Bibigula was disabled by toxemia in Afghanistan. She has had difficulty counting and is a little slow with certain things. I have always respected my wife. I have never tried to go back in time and ask "what if?" There is no sense in doing that. I submit to God's will.

I did not allow our friends to disrespect Bibigula. One day in our home, a friend blurted out in front of our children, "Your wife is not a good match for you. Why did you marry her?" I called him outside and scolded him, "Don't you ever do that again and never say anything bad about my wife, especially in front of my children." Children are sensitive to even the smallest criticisms against their parents and between their parents. Disparaging remarks weaken the home. One of my worries, when our children were young, was that if they thought their mother did not have full capacity, they would be fearful that there would be no one to care for them if I passed away.

At heart I am a farmer. Often I would take my children and other Afghan families in my van to pick cherries, apricots, peaches, pomegranates, vegetables, okra, and strawberries in Brentwood, Oakley, Tracey, Modesto, Gilroy, areas east of Manteca, Lodi, and as far south as Fresno. We had picnics in those places and swam in the large drains in Novato, Santa Rosa, Napa, and Sonoma. In the orchards and farms I would rub the soil in my hands, and analyze the drainage systems as though I was their manager.

In Afghanistan it is common practice to pick fruits and vegetables in neighboring farms in areas designated by farmers for the public to pick. In wheat and corn fields we would pull the weeds and grasses between the stems and use them to feed our cattle. We were careful not to pluck the stems of the wheat and corn. Removing the weeds and grass was a benefit for the farmers. It increased their yields. In the US, chemical weed killers are used which pollute and contaminate the soil and food.

I made friendships with farmers in Newman and Merced. Most of the time, I paid them more than they would ask for the fruits we picked. That was because as we picked the fruits, we would eat them. If they asked for "x" dollars per pound, I would pay for two more pounds estimating for what we ate. Although the farmers said that it was not necessary, I did it anyway. I knew what it was like to be a farmer. Sometimes I would help prune the trees, especially pomegranate trees. People picking fruit carelessly break branches on the trees. I always advised parents and children not to break a branch, and while walking through the fields, to be careful not to step on the strawberries and tomato plants so as not to smash them.

Blowback: Growth of Extremism

Now let me discuss the trends that I observed within the Muslim communities in northern California since the mid 1980s. Those trends are connected to the events in Afghanistan after the 1989 withdrawal of Soviet troops, and the events leading up to 9/11.

Following the withdrawal of the Soviets from Afghanistan in 1989 and the collapse of the Soviet Union, there was a global rise of Islamic extremism, increasing anti-Americanism, and anger against Western countries. Analysts call the growth of Islamic extremism "blowback" from years of the US financing and training mujahideen extremists in Pakistan during the Soviet-Afghan War. In Pakistan, extremist views of Islam had been advanced through Saudi-funded madrassas in the refugee camps. Madrassas were part of President Zia's efforts to realign Pakistan along Islamist ideology (Islamization), and train Afghans to fight the Soviets in Afghanistan. He believed that only religion could keep Pakistan from splintering apart.

Oil-rich Middle Eastern countries were funding the spread of extremism into poor developing countries and also into economically advanced developed countries such as the US.

Young Americans Converting to Islam

In 1988, in the mosques that I attended in the San Francisco East Bay Area, I began to see more young Americans converting to Islam. Many of them were students of high school age who were romantically attracted to Muslim girls and boys. They attended American High School, Washington High School, Newark High School, Kennedy High School, Logan High School, and Hayward High School. College-age students were less likely to convert. I observed more girls converting to Islam than boys. The girls wanted to marry their Muslim boyfriends. Most of the non-Muslim girls came from families where the parents had separated or divorced or had no religion. Generally, the Muslim families would reluctantly accept the non-Muslim girls. On the other hand, it was very different for non-Muslim boys. The Muslim religion could accept male converts; but Middle Eastern cultural pressures worked against the marriage. Although a non-Muslim boy may be infatuated with a Muslim girl, it was unlikely that he would convert to Islam. There were exceptions, though.

There is a funny story about a young man who wanted to marry a Muslim girl. I will change his name to Bob. He was a volunteer at IRSI teaching ESL (English as a Second Language). Bob had graduated college by that time. One day I asked him, "How is it that you are fluent in Pashto and Farsi?" Bob explained that during high school he had fallen in love with an Afghan girl and learned how to read, write, and speak both Pashto and Farsi to communicate with her parents. He had even converted to Islam. Bob said that he had desperately pleaded with the Afghan girl to allow him to come to her home and meet her parents. She said, "No, don't come to my home. My parents would be very upset." Bob was insistent. He explained: "Without her knowing, I went to her home at nighttime. I jumped over the locked side fence and without realizing it, I had fallen into a garbage bin and got trapped in it. That made a lot of noise. Her family members rushed out and started hitting me with sticks. They thought that I was a burglar. I pleaded in Farsi, 'Don't beat me up!' But they hit me even more. I escaped and suffered many bruises on my arms and back." That is how Bob came to convert to Islam, and learned Pashto and Farsi. His bruises were the result of his foolishness and falling in love.

Even if a man converted to Islam, within the Afghan community, the parents of the girl would not give their permission for her to marry him. Those were my observations of conversions during the late 80s and 90s in the Bay Area.

There are many other reasons why people convert to another religion. It is a very touchy subject. I won't make judgments about conversion from one religion to another. Nevertheless, the practice of extremism is wrong in any religion whether it be the three Abrahamic religions of Christianity, Judaism and Islam, or Buddhism, Hinduism, or any other.

American Converts Becoming Extremists

I was afraid that American converts would be taught by extremists and eventually become extremists. John Walker Lindh, known as the American Taliban from Marin County in the San Francisco Bay Area, is an example of that. More recently a Florida young man, Moner Mohammad Abu-Salha, was reported to have joined an Al Qaeda-linked opposition group in Syria and was part of a four-man suicide bombing against Syrian Government forces. He had traveled to Syria, returned to the US around May 2013 without US officials knowing that he had received training from a terrorist group, and returned six months later to Syria to perform a terrorist suicide attack. In more recent weeks there are reports of dozens or possibly over one-hundred American converts to Islam who have traveled to fight with the Islamic State group.

Early Stages of Radicalization

While living in Birmingham in 1985 we became acquainted with an Egyptian and Turkish family, and two Pakistani families. The father in one of the Pakistani families was a top engineer for the Alabama Power Company. He was a rigid extremist. The Turkish father was a retired colonel and during discussions I discovered that he, too, was an Islamic extremist. One day they told me that Islamic preachers had come from Pakistan, India, Arab countries, as well as from within the US and were meeting in Atlanta. I was curious and rode with them to Atlanta to listen. Among the preachers were high-level scholars who were moderate but leaning toward extremist views.

When we returned to Birmingham, I stopped going to the homes of three of those families. The reason was that while the men and women would sit separately, the children played together. I was afraid my kids would be negatively influenced by their kids. Islam teaches respect between Christians, Jews, and Muslims. Those families did not believe that and were separating themselves from the American community. We visited the churches of our sponsors. The extremists told me, "Stop going there; the churches will brainwash your kids." I thought to myself that those families would brainwash my kids. We continued to visit one of the two Pakistani families, though.

Google sponsored a conference in 2011 called the *Summit Against Violent Extremism,* which brought together former extremists (an American neo-Nazi skinhead and a British Islamic radical), victims of terrorism, academics, and intelligence analysts. The panelists all agreed that the early stage of recruitment of youth into extremist groups, when they are looking for acceptance, is a neglected problem. The issues of radicalization are usually compartmentalized and not seen as part of a whole. They may be narrowly viewed as gang, religious extremist, nationalistic, or racist extremist issues.

Fear of Losing Their Children

Afghan and Iranian refugee parents came to me distressed that they were losing their children. They explained that their kids were doing poorly in school, were becoming more disrespectful, and were rejecting the traditional values of their culture. I, too, was worried about young Muslim refugee students in the San Francisco Bay Area; especially those whose parents were not fluent in English, gainfully employed, or self-sufficient.

Students who fail in school are very vulnerable. They can be marginalized, withdraw into themselves, or be attracted to bad influences and join criminal or violent extremist groups.

Tablighi missionaries who preach extremist views in the mosques search for young people who will join them. "Tablighi" refers to those traveling from village to village, city to city preaching a particular view of Islam. During the 80s and 90s, while Tablighi missionaries were based primarily in India and Pakistan, they also operated in the US and were financially supported by wealthy donors from the Middle East. One of the reasons I took my kids and other Afghan children with me everywhere possible was to keep them away from bad influences.

BAAR Story

Now hold that thought about the spread of extremism in northern California and globally. Next I will tell you the story about our competitive Afghan amputee bicycle team. It is connected with our discovery of Osama bin Laden's location in Afghanistan in 1996.

In 1991 Howard Williams was one of our volunteer tutors at IRSI who periodically traveled to Pakistan and to Jalalabad, Afghanistan, to volunteer in rehabilitation centers helping amputees. He proposed that I join him to form a nonprofit that would help amputees in Afghanistan learn to ride bicycles. He knew that I had worked fitting amputees with prosthetics in Kabul. At first I expressed doubt that amputees could be trained to ride bikes. Howard insisted, "As a bicycle messenger in San Francisco I know how to do it." I said, "Okay, let's talk about it."

We met later to discuss the feasibility of training amputees. What he said sounded workable. Howard urged me to find an additional person to be on a board of directors with us. I met Dr. Julienne Lipson and brainstormed the idea with her. She agreed to participate because it was related to her mental health specialty.

The three of us decided to establish *Bicycles for Afghan Amputees and Rehabilitation* (BAAR) as a nonprofit to train Afghan amputees in Afghanistan and Pakistan to ride bicycles commonly used where they live. Those bicycles are different from western racing bicycles. They are very simple and don't have multiple gears. Later the program was expanded to include vocational and literacy training, as well as fitting amputees with prosthetics.

Dr. Lipson and I were not paid a salary. All funds raised were used to pay the program expenses. Howard was the executive director and was paid a nominal fee. He was very dedicated and would periodically travel to the two service sites. BAAR was funded by the Refugee Foundation in Los Altos, California, the Sandy Gall Foundation in London, and other donors.

The Devastating Civil War

BAAR started its programs in 1992 and operated during most of the horrific Afghan civil war (1992-2001), a nightmare that bludgeoned Afghanistan far worse than the Soviet occupation. We managed an amputee rehabilitation center in Jalalabad in Nangahar Province, Afghanistan, and one in Peshawar, Pakistan. By that time Afghanistan had been forgotten by the world.

Najibullah had been installed by the Soviets as the Afghan communist president in 1987. After the Soviet withdrawal in 1989, his regime stubbornly resisted the Afghan mujahideen assaults. The US continued to fund the mujahideen mistakenly thinking that they would quickly defeat Najibullah. The Soviet Union supported Najibullah until it dissolved. In 1992 Boris Yeltsin, head of the new Russian Government, formally ended Russia's support of Najibullah. Losing that vital support, Najibullah expressed his willingness to resign and make way for a neutral interim government.

The United Nations sought to broker a deal through the Peshawar Accord with Najibullah's administration and the Afghan mujahideen political parties for a post-communist coalition government. Just as Pakistan had decided which Afghan political parties were allowed to operate and be funded in Pakistan, its civilian leadership, headed by Prime Minister Nawaz Sharif, took a directive role by shepherding the Afghan parties to sign the Peshawar Accord. The draft agreement created an interim two-year coalition government, the *Islamic State of Afghanistan*, to precede general elections. The positions of president, his cabinet, and supreme court were assigned to the warlord leaders of the Afghan parties. The Peshawar Accord was signed in April 1992 by the major mujahideen parties, except for Hekmatyar's party. Unfortunately, the agreement was weak and lacked integrity, as each Afghan party tried to out-maneuver the other and promises were broken. The UN is partly to blame for the Afghan civil war that followed.

Hekmatyar had been offered the position of prime minister in the interim government, had agreed to it and the format of the power sharing agreement. However, when he learned that north of Kabul Massoud had formed an alliance with the Uzbek communist general, Abdul Rashid Dostum, and was negotiating with Najibullah's administration to transfer power to their alliance, Hekmatyar rejected the drafted Peshawar Accord. He raced from the south to compete against the other mujahideen warlords to occupy the city and its government ministries, loot the banks, and capture military hardware.

Afghan Military Dissolved

When Najibullah expressed his willingness to resign and Dostum shifted his alliance to Massoud, Najibullah began to lose control, and the Afghan military broke apart. Top Afghan communist generals escaped to the Soviet Union; other officers and troops joined the mujahideen; but most returned to their homes. Soviet planes, tanks, weapons and hardware were abandoned.

Tragically, dissolution of the Afghan Army and Air Force left Kabul and its innocent civilians exposed to looting, raping, and indiscriminate rocket bombardments by the warlords and their militias. Disbanding the Iraqi army in 2003 also had disastrous consequences. The mujahideen militias were undisciplined, quickly changed their loyalties, and randomly robbed and destroyed public properties.

It is important to realize that up to that point, even though the Afghan military forces were very cruel to the civilians, they were disciplined and not looters. During the previous 60 years the Afghan military had been expanded and modernized by King Nader Shah and afterward by his son, King Mohammad Zahir Shah. The Afghan Army would not be resurrected until after 9/11 and by NATO forces.

Overthrow of Najibullah

When the warlords and their militias overthrew Najibullah, he was placed under house arrest in the United Nations compound in Kabul. The Peshawar Accord first designated Professor Sibghatullah Mojaddedi as president. After serving as president for two months, and according to the terms in the Peshawar Accord, he stepped aside for Professor Rabbani to assume the presidency. Since the Afghan parties were at war among themselves, they were unable to collectively agree on who would continue to fill the government positions for the Islamic State of Afghanistan. Therefore, Professor Rabbani continued to fight and hold his position as president. His authority, though, would be limited to only a portion of Kabul.

Warlords' Plunder of Kabul

Pakistan's military continued to support Hekmatyar as he launched attacks in Kabul against the other warlords and civilians. Hekmatyar's indiscriminate bombardments alone accounted for most of the destruction of Kabul. It was plundered because that was where the nation's wealth and foreign embassies were located. Public buildings were arbitrarily rocketed because the warlords viewed it as their right as conquerors to loot and pillage the capital city. Kabul was a modern city before the Soviet invasion and was further improved by the Soviets after the invasion. The warlords' civil war reduced Kabul to rubble. Many tens of thousands of innocent people were massacred by the warring mujahideen in Kabul. The civil war also devastated my hometown of Kandahar and Mazar-i-Sharif.

The warlords and militias called themselves mujahideen to appear respectable as they fought for military supremacy during the civil war. Tragically, the mujahideen committed atrocities against the Afghan people and battled for resources and power--not for religion or ideology.

Another fact to remember is that following the Soviet withdrawal from Afghanistan, the three moderate Afghan parties disbanded, declaring that the jihad had ended. The true mujahideen returned to their farms and shops.

Although the US had agreed to stop sending arms to the mujahideen, the horrible civil war continued as other powers competed for regional dominance by providing weapons to the warlords. It was basically a proxy war between Pakistan (Sunni) acting on behalf of Saudi Arabia (Sunni/Wahhabi), and Iran (Shia). Turkey (Sunni) and Uzbekistan (Sunni) who were competing for influence and dominance in Central Asia also provided arms.

Hekmatyar failed to deliver what Pakistan wanted--renewed influence over Afghanistan to further its political objectives. Pakistan wanted a Pakistan-friendly government in Afghanistan that was unstable and dependent upon it, and not an India-friendly government on its western border. Afghanistan was viewed as a fallback country in the event of a war with India. Secondly, Pakistan desired, and still does, to draw upon the rich resources of Central Asia to which Afghanistan is the doorway.

Growth of Taliban

Pakistan next turned its support to the emerging Taliban. What is known today as the Taliban began in 1994 as a small group of former mujahideen fighters in my hometown of Kandahar. They were Pashtun Islamic fundamentalists fed up with the abuses of local warlords. Mullah Omar organized them to defeat a warlord militia post, which in turn led to another successful military skirmish, another and another. As the Taliban ventured beyond Kandahar into other provinces, they encountered greater resistance but grew into a militia movement. When the Pakistani ISI heard about this, it infiltrated its agents into the fast-growing Taliban force. As the Taliban expanded, the ISI increased its support providing military hardware, trained soldiers, and leadership.

The Taliban took the city of Herat in 1995, and in 1996 ventured forward to take Kabul, the capital, and most of Afghanistan.

18

MY WARNINGS BEFORE 9/11

Paralympic Bike Team

BAAR had organized a bicycle team of Afghan amputees consisting of former mujahideen fighters. They competed in local events in Jalalabad, Afghanistan. Beginning in about 1994, the best competitors were selected to participate on an Afghan team in world bicycle championships in London, Toronto, Atlanta, San Francisco, and Barcelona. Howard Williams supervised that project during his periodic visits to Jalalabad. I was unable to go there because I needed to be near my wife who was not well and my kids were still young. Besides that, BAAR had only a bare-bones budget and travel to and from Jalalabad was expensive.

In Atlanta, the 1996 International Paralympic Committee

RENEE' HANNANS / Staff

MISTER JIMMY: Terry Cotter (left) coached three amputees (on bikes, from left) — Gul Afzal, Zabit Khan, Bahadur Khel — as they trained in Afghanistan for competitive biking.

assigned Terry Cotter to ready our team for competition. Terry was also one of our IRSI board members who had extensive experience coaching mentally and physically disabled athletes, as well as participating with

them in international athletic events, which have been recorded in award-winning films.

Back to Pakistan

In April of 1996, in preparation for the Atlanta Paralympic Games, I flew to Islamabad, Pakistan, to arrange the visas for the Afghan bike team and a group of Afghan musicians who would entertain other Paralympians in the Olympic Village. Commander

Syed Hussan Sadaqut, head of the Afghan Disabled Department in Nangarhar Province (Jalalabad is the capital) and a highly respected former mujahideen commander, served as the captain of the team, even though he could not be a rider. Both his legs were paralyzed.

It was the first time in 11 years that I had been in Pakistan. I did not go into Afghanistan because there my life would be in danger. At that time, if you were an Afghan, you were forced to choose sides, either the Taliban or the Northern Alliance. I did not support either. Therefore, each side would regard me as an enemy presuming that I belonged to the other side.

While speaking with ordinary Pakistanis and Afghans in their homes, I was shocked to hear their anti-American verbal attacks. I was asked whether I had American citizenship. That question was rapidly followed by, "Those bloody Americans." I did not take that well and replied, "Yes, I am one of them. What do you mean bloody Americans? They protected you from the Soviets. Now they are bloody? I am an American and I don't want to hear your talk."

Upon returning to the US, I did not go to the Atlanta Paralympic Games because I was needed in Fremont to plan the Afghan bike team's next competition in San Francisco. I did, however, send Bibigula and my teenage daughter, Setara, to Atlanta. Setara is in the above photo. The Afghan team needed help. The team members spoke only Pashto and could not communicate with other Paralympians in the Olympic Village. It was also difficult for them to eat Western food. Therefore the team was moved from the Olympic Village to stay with our Afghan friends in Atlanta. Bibigula cooked tasty Afghan food for them and Setara interpreted and coordinated their activities with the Paralympic Committee. Terry Cotter and Howard Williams provided them with coaching at the Village.

Ambassadors for Afghan Amputees

It was a very emotional and proud moment for the Afghan team and Afghans throughout the world. For the first time Afghan amputees would participate in the prestigious international Paralympic Games. They were ambassadors for the more than two million faceless amputees in Afghanistan. The team was very well received by the international community. After the Games, the Afghan community in Atlanta held a celebration party in the Olympic Village. Afghan volunteers from the Atlanta area cooked Afghan food, not just for the Afghan Paralympians, but for all the Paralympians.

Then the Afghan Paralympic Team flew from Atlanta into the San Francisco Airport and was brought to our home in Fremont on Hudson Place. The team stayed with us for several weeks and participated in a San Francisco bicycle championship, which was not an event exclusively for the disabled.

Daily many Afghans came to visit their Paralympians in our home. There were so many visitors that we organized them according to the provinces in Afghanistan. The Afghan amputees were showered with gifts, varying from cash to wheelchairs, and jewelry for women in their families.

Treating with Respect

The captain of the Afghan team, Commander Sadaqut, was an open-minded Islamic scholar. He expressed his appreciation for the American Paralympic Committee, other Americans, and Afghan-Americans who treated him and his team so nicely. He said, "In Afghanistan we are constantly fighting one another and destroying things. But here in America, people are developing themselves and the world around them. From the religious perspective, you can tell who will be going to heaven. They treat one another with respect and as human beings." Since Commander Sadaqut was paralyzed, he had no feeling in his legs and wore no shoes or socks sitting in his wheelchair.

The airlines in America would not allow him to travel without at least wearing socks. A stewardess brought him socks and put  them on his feet. Commander Sadaqut was very impressed by her act of service and said that in Afghanistan or Pakistan no one would provide him that courtesy. "That is the sign of those who go to heaven," he stated.

Osama bin Laden

In late August, while the Afghan bicycle team stayed in our home, we heard the news that Osama bin Laden had issued a fatwa printed in a London-based Arab newspaper. It declared war against Americans for occupying Saudi Arabia with its air bases. It was called *Declaration of War against the Americans Occupying the Land of the Two Holy Places*. When Commander Sadaqut heard this, he said, "The sheikh is in my district." The sheikh is what bin Laden was called in both Afghanistan and Pakistan. Commander Sadaqut explained that earlier, in May, President Rabbani had granted bin Laden refuge and had arranged for him to be flown from Sudan into Afghanistan. Bin Laden was living in Commander Sadaqut's district within Nangarhar Province. Bin Laden's fatwa received little media attention then, and it is debatable how seriously the US regarded it.

I called the US State Department's Afghan Desk and spoke with Roberta Chew. She quickly flew from Washington DC and came to our home in Fremont. I interpreted for her as she interviewed Commander Sadaqut for over four hours. On the same day, members of the Afghan bike team and Ms. Chew were invited by Mahmood

Karzai to his restaurant in San Francisco on Broadway Street. He is the brother of former Afghan President Hamid Karzai.

While driving them to San Francisco I said, "I am at this moment not speaking in the role of an interpreter. You now know where bin Laden is located. He could be easily caught." She answered, "We have no legal grounds to capture him."

Formation of Northern Alliance

During the same time that the bike team remained in my home, the Taliban were engaged in a major offensive against the government of President Rabbani. We heard that on September 27, 1996, the Taliban had entered Kabul. That forced Rabbani and his Islamic State of Afghanistan Government to retreat to northern Afghanistan. While in exile there, he continued to claim that he was Afghanistan's lawful head of state. The Northern Alliance was then formed with Rabbani as its leader. Officially known as the *United Islamic Front for the Salvation of Afghanistan* or the *United Front*, it was organized by former mutual enemies: Abdul Rashid Dostum, Ahmad Shah Massoud, and Abdul Rab Rasool Sayaf. It included Tajiks, Uzbeks, Hazaras, and Pashtuns.

After debating whether to return to Afghanistan, in early October the Paralympic team finally decided to return.

Two years later in August 1998 bin Laden was linked to the US Embassy bombings in Tanzania and Kenya. It was then that he came to the attention of the American public. Anticipating that the US would bomb bin Laden's terrorist training camps in Afghanistan, we closed the BAAR rehabilitation center in Jalalabad, fearing collateral damage to our workers and to the center.

Educating 7000 Child Workers

The next year in 1997, through a mutual Afghan-American friend, Syed Abdullah Kaghaz, I developed a working relationship with Hajji Muhammad Naeem Walizada, an Afghan carpet manufacturer in Peshawar, Pakistan. He employed 7000 Afghan children--eight to sixteen years old--in several factories within the Northwest Province of Pakistan. As a native Afghan, Hajji Naeem desired to help poor families living in Afghanistan. That is why he hired only Afghan boys whose parents sent them to work in his factories. The money earned by the boys in the factories went to their parents in Afghanistan. Hajji Naeem also provided the boys housing, food, and clothing.

I made Hajji Naeem a deal. As an agronomist I am an expert in judging the quality of wool that he used to manufacture his carpets. He agreed that if I would advise him how to maintain good quality control of his wool, he would supply time and facilities for me to provide educational programs for his child workers. Hajji Naeem also agreed to pay for the cost of my travel, hotel, and food while in Pakistan. Using IRSI's English as a Second Language (ESL) materials, the children received instruction in reading and writing Pashto, Farsi/Dari, English, and simple math and science.

Taliban-US Relations

From 1997 to May 2001 I made several trips to Pakistan to supervise the education of the 7000 Afghan children in the carpet factories. During that time I spoke with ordinary Afghan Taliban in Pakistan. They did not express hatred toward Americans or the West. They were upset, though, that the US Government did not recognize or support the Taliban as the legal government in Afghanistan, known as the *Islamic Emirate of Afghanistan.*

At that time the Taliban controlled about 90% of the country and was at war with the Northern Alliance. During their civil war both sides committed atrocities against one another and against innocent civilians. The Taliban regime had been recognized by Saudi Arabia, the United Arab Emirates (UAE), and Pakistan. Saudi Arabia recognized the Taliban Government to prevent the Shia from exerting further influence in Afghanistan and Central Asia. Saudi Arabia is primarily Sunni; the Taliban are Sunni, and Iran is primarily Shia. The UAE recognized the Taliban because it (UAE) had territorial disputes with Iran. The Northern Alliance was supported by Iran, Russia, and India.

The Taliban gained early popularity among the Afghan people because they brought an end to the civil war in the areas it controlled, enforced lawfulness, ended corruption, and enabled the roads to be safe for traveling and commerce. There was hope that the Taliban would be a stabilizing force. However, when it gained control of most of Afghanistan, it ruled with an iron grip and imposed an austere interpretation of Sharia Law that most Afghans did not share. Girls were not permitted to attend school, women were forbidden to hold jobs and were required to wear the burqa. The Taliban were only a small percentage of the Afghan population.

The US condemned the Taliban's treatment of women as abusive. The Taliban argued that they were applying Sharia Law to protect women and pointed to the chaos of the civil war where rival warlord troops committed terrible crimes against women.

Initially the Taliban were not anti-American. They had negotiated with the US and United Nations to lift the economic sanctions against them. The Taliban wanted to be recognized as the legitimate government of Afghanistan. In 1999, Mullah Omar, the leader of the Taliban, ordered farmers to end their poppy cultivation. The expectation was that the UN would in turn recognize the Taliban's government. When the UN did not do so, the farmers were told they could continue their production. In fact, ordering the farmers to stop growing poppies had not stopped the drug trade in Afghanistan because the drug lords had huge drug reserves to satisfy the demand. Also, the Taliban's government did not own the poppy fields. It could only collect a tax on the production of poppies.

Rising Anti-US Feelings in Pakistan

In contrast to the Taliban, ordinary Pakistanis and Afghans in Pakistan with whom I talked expressed growing anti-American feelings. Later, under pressure from the US and because of bin Laden's presence in Afghanistan, Saudi Arabia and the UAE withdrew their recognition of the Taliban. Pakistan continued, though, to support the Taliban in their civil war.

Warnings to the US: the Stockton Boy

In early 2000, while in the San Francisco Airport on the way to another visit at Naeem's carpet factories in Pakistan via London, I met a young Pakistani-American boy, about 19 to 21 years old. What drew my attention to him was that there were two tall, bearded men-- 35 to 45 years old--with him wearing traditional Pakistani clothing: clean, white, long shirts extending below the knees over white baggy pants, with nice black jackets and white Muslim prayer caps. Looking at them I sensed something was wrong. I walked up to the boy and in Pashto asked, "Where are you from?" "I am from Stockton," he answered in Pashto. His handlers became suspicious and motioned to him not to talk to me.

In the London Airport I again approached him. The boy looked depressed. Although the two men were nearby, I asked, "Where are you going?" "To Pakistan, I am going with them to do God's work," he replied. Then I asked, "Have you been to Pakistan before or traveled outside the US?" "No," he said. But his parents were from Pakistan. "Are you sure you want to go to Pakistan? Do you know the situation there?" I asked. He said, "No, it's my first visit." The boy was shy and not very quick-minded. Seeing his US passport sticking halfway up from inside his shirt pocket, I could tell that he was a US citizen.

Then the two men walked over to us and moved the boy away. I strongly suspected that he would be indoctrinated with extremist ideas and returned to the US to influence his friends. As US citizens these boys could do big damage. When I saw the Stockton boy, I remembered the Pakistani engineer and retired Turkish colonel in Birmingham. Both were extremists. I think of their children.

In my mind I thought, "How can I identify who the boy is and let the US Embassy know? What would I say? The Embassy personnel would ask, 'What is wrong? Who are you? Where is the boy?'" At that time there was little public suspicion of terrorist activities in the US. Who would listen to me?

A Pattern Was Developing

All those experiences were adding up. I became more curious to find out what was happening and started asking more questions to ordinary Pakistanis. In Pakistan I purposely avoided speaking with Pakistani government officials. There was no need, in any case, to get their permission to manage the children's education program at the carpet factories. It was a private program.

I was faced with big dilemmas. I was concerned about marginalized Afghan, Pakistani, and other refugee/immigrant young people in America who were not doing well in school and were involved in gangs. They could be indoctrinated with extremist ideas and be manipulated to do very bad things. But who would believe me and what proof could I provide of the dangers that I was observing? At the same time, the Muslim communities were negatively stereotyped in the US and it would become worse after the 9/11 attacks.

But Who Would Listen to Me?

Since 1987 I had given hundreds of intercultural seminars to local and regional communities and businesses. Anyone involved in community relations knows that dispelling negative stereotypes about Muslims or other religious and social groups is a long-term process. Positive images and voices of the stereotyped groups need to be seen and heard by the larger public.

I lived in the Tri-City area of Fremont, Newark, and Union City. By and large there were few voices representing the diverse Muslim, Hindu, and Sikh communities. In the Muslim communities, especially among marginalized youth, negative stereotyping added further to their challenges of integrating into the American society. That also made them more vulnerable to Tablighi missionaries who came to their mosques.

Immigrant and refugee Muslims from different countries attended local mosques: they were South Asians, Arabs, Afghans, Pakistanis, Africans, Asian/Pacific Islanders, Bosnians, Croatians, Serbians, and Iranians. Leaders--the mullahs/imams-- in the mosques were usually immigrants who did not speak English. When I asked some of them to participate in the local interfaith association, the Tri-

City Ministerial Association (TCMA), now called the Tri-City Interfaith Council (TCIC), each responded, "I don't speak English." But when I offered to send them English tutors, they expressed no interest.

My friend Ken Hardman, a member of the IRSI board of directors and TCMA, observed that there was a similar reluctance from priests in the local Hindu temple and Sikh Gurdwara to join the interfaith association. They were also immigrants and their English was limited. Their reluctance may have been because they did not speak English, or did not regard interfaith discussions as part of their role as a religious leader; or it may have been simply the apprehension of joining an unfamiliar group. It is fair to say that many local Christian leaders who spoke English were also reluctant to join interfaith groups. Historically it has been difficult for leaders of different religions, often using different words to talk about religious ideas, to build bridges of understanding and cooperation, and to learn from one another.

Eventually, civic-minded lay representatives who were not imams, mullahs, or priests from the Muslim, Hindu and Sikh communities joined TCMA and other local public organizations to represent their faith communities.

Warnings to the School District

In early 2000, after meeting the boy from Stockton, Ken supported my efforts to speak with people who might listen. He arranged a meeting with Linda Garbarino, Educational Resources Director at the Fremont School District headquarters. We both had previously collaborated with the school district on various projects.

I explained to Linda the dangers that I saw for marginalized youth. As an ESL teacher for many years and an advisor on the school district's Affirmative Action Committee, I had noticed increasing percentages of refugee (as distinguished from immigrant) students skipping classes, doing poorly and then dropping out of school. I would see them at a mosque, wearing Arab-style clothing and growing beards. They would argue with their parents and other adults. In my other capacity as the Executive Director of IRSI, many of the parents of those students, particularly those who were enrolled in our literacy and ESL programs, came to see me. They asked for advice on how to deal with their children's rebellious and disrespectful behavior.

Linda referred us to Fred Turner, the Director of Pupil Personnel Services concerned with at-risk students. What I told Fred was totally new to him and he did not know what to do. Ken and I also addressed the TCMA where I too was a longtime member. At a monthly meeting I conveyed my warnings and observations about the Stockton boy, at-risk students, the anti-American sentiments in Pakistan, and concerns about bin Laden. What we said was also completely new to them and must have sounded very strange—dangers of local youth becoming indoctrinated as Islamic extremists.

Warnings to Government Officials

In late 2000 we next went to local legislators. But again, my warnings were not on anyone's radar screen. So without them saying so, I was sure they were thinking, "Who are you?" I was not working for any intelligence agency. No agency had contacted me. I was just an Afghan-American. Who would believe me? Jo Cazenave, District Director for Congressman Pete Stark, listened closely and tried to be supportive. Ken and I continued on and spoke with the district representatives for Assemblyman John Dutra and State Senator Liz Figueroa. They were respectful, but again, apparently all that they could do was listen.

We intensified our efforts to sensitize our local school and government representatives of the dangers that I was observing. There were indications that foreign extremists were operating in Northern California. Muslim youth in the Bay Area were attractive targets for extremists because American citizens can become much more effective terrorists. There were signs of radicalization in Pakistan and in Afghanistan where the Taliban were becoming financially dependent upon bin Laden.

Countering Extremists' Arguments

The major argument that Muslim extremists advance is that America and other Western countries seek to destroy the Muslim culture. Extremists seek to exploit misunderstandings, weaknesses, resentments, and rivalries between families, tribes, ethnicities, religions, and nations. Countering those efforts requires accurate cultural intelligence, authentic service, and systematic cultural bridge building. Our many IRSI programs with the refugee/immigrant communities provided working models for such efforts.

A Bridge-Building Conference

I felt that I had to do something else. Ken and I organized a conference to promote bridge building and bring warning. I invited from Pakistan Hajji Naeem and his friend Waliullah Ghulam to meet with US Government and local officials in Fremont. They could be important cultural intermediaries in Afghanistan since, although they were affiliated with different political groups that opposed one another, they had strong common interests.

Hajji Naeem was from the Northern Alliance which was supported by Russia, India, and Iran. Waliullah, although not a Talib, was sympathetic to the Taliban, which was supported by Pakistan. The Northern Alliance and the Taliban were enemies. However, Hajji Naeem and Waliullah were friends, Afghans, businessmen, and anti-Al Qaeda. Both wished to preserve their business interests and both recognized that Al Qaeda was trying to cut them off from the Western world, especially the US.

They agreed to come to Fremont and testify how Al Qaeda was gaining increasing influence in Afghanistan. They hoped to convince US officials that it was a mutual benefit for the US to have trade relations with moderate Taliban who were willing to engage in business, were anti-Al Qaeda, and were not anti-West. Encouraging trade with the US could minimize the influence of Al Qaeda and other extremists that sought to completely sever Afghan relations with Westerners. That seemed to be the best strategy *at the time*.

Need for Refugee/Immigrant Partnerships

The US needs the partnership of Afghan, Pakistani, Indian,

African, Middle Eastern, and other refugee/immigrant communities in the US to neutralize extremists and terrorists operating in their native countries. Those extremists seek to radicalize and make their families opponents of the US and other Western democratic countries. Beneficial partnerships can be developed by supporting refugees and immigrants in the US to become self-sufficient and responsible citizens, which was one of the objectives of IRSI. Encouraging positive trade and cultural exchange between the US and their native countries also contributes to strengthening bridges of cooperation and friendship. It makes good sense.

Next, Ken and I met with representatives of our local legislators. They agreed to meet with Hajji Naeem and Waliullah to hear their testimonies, warnings, and to discuss the possibilities for trade. Considering the difficulties of arranging separate meetings between them and Hajji Naeem and Waliullah, we scheduled a conference called *Building Bridges for Peace to Central Asia*. There, after listening to Hajji Naeem and Waliullah, the officials could decide whether to further meet with them.

Conference Purposes

We explained to the officials that the conference purposes were to warn of the dangers of Islamic extremists recruiting young people in Northern California, and about Osama bin Laden and Al Qaeda. Specific initiatives would be proposed to promote local commerce and international trade with moderate elements of the Taliban, those who were pro-business, anti-Al Qaeda, and not anti-West.

Prime Minister David Cameron in 2013 lamented that it was a mistake after 9/11 not to have included the Taliban in the December 2001 Bonn Conference. Based on what I said earlier about moderate Taliban, you would think that I would agree. On the contrary, I respectfully disagree. Everything changed after the 9/11 attacks. Let me explain.

Everything Changed

Before 9/11, I thought there was still the possibility that US trade relations with moderate elements of the Taliban could neutralize its economic dependency on bin Laden and Pakistan and serve as a bridge for Afghanistan to eventually become a stable and responsible member of the international community. The majority of the Taliban were moderate in their thinking at that time, which means that even though the Taliban did not like US policies which did not recognize their government, they were still not anti-West. However, the Taliban became increasingly financially dependent upon bin Laden and Pakistan after the US had forced Saudi Arabia and the UAE to sever relations with the Taliban, and when the US had imposed sanctions and froze Taliban assets in foreign banks. The Taliban did not want to be dependent on bin Laden. Their culture was different from Al Qaeda, although the Western world viewed them as the same. Remember, too, that the Taliban represented only a small percentage of the Afghan people. Most Afghans did not share the Taliban's rigid interpretation of Islam.

After 9/11, the Taliban had been completely compromised by bin Laden, Al Qaeda and Pakistan. There were very few moderate Taliban remaining, and they had no influence among the other Taliban who had become instruments of Al Qaeda.

Warnings to Interfaith Leaders

Meaningful dialogue between Islamic and non-Islamic leaders is important to counter the propaganda spread by extremists that the non-Muslim world is attempting to destroy Islam. Extremists exploited the simplest cultural differences. Realizing the importance of interfaith dialogue and cooperation, I invited the members of TCMA (the interfaith association) in their March 2001 meeting to co-sponsor and participate in our planned August conference.

In that meeting I explained the nature of the Taliban's government and that international extremists were spreading rumors that the non-Muslim world was trying to destroy Islam. Therefore Muslim and non-Muslim leaders must publicly stand together to demonstrate mutual respect. In my presentation I explained that Taliban government officials in Afghanistan were not religious scholars or mullahs; they were mainly young men educated in the madrassas, influenced by Arab extremists and other extremists from Pakistan.

In the same month of March, the Taliban destroyed two ancient Buddhist statutes in Bamiyan Valley, Afghanistan, condemning them as idols that violated Islam. Taliban officials asserted that it was not done in retaliation to the international community for economic sanctions against the Taliban Government.

The next month, in April 2001, Ken and I met with Fremont Mayor, Gus Morrison. After explaining the purpose of the conference, he agreed to convene it in a city meeting room. August 30, 2001, was selected as the conference date since that was when a room would be available and most of the conference participants could attend. It was 12 days before 9/11.

Meaning of Infidel Was Expanded

In April, 2001, Pakistan's pro-Taliban Jamiat Ulema-i-Islam party held a conference and large public gathering near Peshawar. It repeated Mullah Omar's message urging Muslims globally to unite against the "infidel world." The pro-Taliban party extended the term "infidel" beyond communists and atheists to include the Western world. In Omar's message he argued that infidels were oppressing Muslims through the United Nations by falsely accusing the Taliban of terrorism and human rights violations. He condemned UN sanctions imposed on the Taliban for not handing over Osama bin Laden to the US for trial.

In the same month of April, Massoud, a political and military leader with the Northern Alliance, addressed the European Parliament where he appealed for humanitarian aid for the Afghan people, and warned of Al Qaeda and the Taliban.

Swat Valley--Followers of the Sheikh

In May, 2001, I traveled once more to Islamabad and to Peshawar, Pakistan. It was part of my ongoing supervision of the Afghan children's education program and consultation for Hajji Naeem's carpet factories. This time, as appreciation for my work, Hajji Naeem provided me a Toyota Land Cruiser with a driver and guide to tour the Swat Valley for sightseeing. In those days it was a tourist area like Lake Tahoe except that it didn't have a large lake. The Swat Valley had many beautiful trees, hills, and mountains from which snow-melted water flowed over rocks into the rivers. While in the valley, my guide quietly explained, "Here there are many followers of the *sheikh*." The sheikh that he referred to was Osama bin Laden. The Pakistani and Afghan people did not refer to him as bin Laden. While driving through the Swat Valley it was apparent in the small towns and villages who the extremists were by their beards and clothing. They were farmers and ordinary shopkeepers who posted extremist writings on their shop walls. I traveled as a tourist and said very little. We stayed in a nice but modest hotel. Driving further to the remote area of Mingora, I saw more Al Qaeda graffiti written on walls and trees.

"How Is It Possible...?"

When we returned to Peshawar and then proceeded into the Haripur area, I saw even more Al Qaeda graffiti on big rocks, walls, and trees. Although I understood that the Arabic word "Al Qaeda" literally means base or the foundation of a building, at that time I did not know that it referred to the terrorist group that people know of today. In Haripur I went to meet an Afghan Turkman (an ethnicity) who was a carpet expert operating a factory for Hajji Naeem. He knew that I was coming and arranged a huge dinner for me. After traveling a great distance in very difficult mountainous terrain, I was very tired and hungry. During the dinner the guests complained that Islamic extremists in Uzbekistan were worse than Afghan extremists in Afghanistan and that Uzbek extremists were working with Arabs in Afghanistan. I asked the factory manager, "How is it possible that there could be Islamic extremists in Uzbekistan since it has been a communist country?" He said, "I am personally aware that it is so."

From Haripur we drove along the twisting back roads to Islamabad where I continued to see Al Qaeda graffiti. As we approached the bigger cities, the graffiti disappeared.

Extremist and anti-American feelings were on the rise since my visit in 1996. As anti-American emotions were escalating in Pakistan in 2001, when people would ask if I was a US citizen, I would reply that "I am living in Quetta." It was for my own protection. The West was sleeping. Ordinary Americans did not realize that other people in the world hated them.

Arabs Flowing into Afghanistan through Pakistan

Pakistani business people were telling me that there were thousands of Arabs in Afghanistan. They said that there were two types of Arabs who had come to Pakistan: "those who do business here and those who go to Afghanistan." When Arab fighters arrived at the Karachi Airport, they changed into Afghan clothing and were escorted into Afghanistan. Later, when ready to leave, they were escorted from Afghanistan back to the Karachi Airport. The Arabs were very secretive. Pakistan was allowing bin Laden's Al Qaeda fighters from Arab countries and Central Asia to travel into Afghanistan to fight with the Taliban against the Northern Alliance. Al Qaeda trained them to export terrorism and prepare for 9/11.

Al Qaeda Control

That was consistent with what my brothers living in Afghanistan were reporting to me. Bin Laden's Al Qaeda fighters were imposing their mafia-like control on local villages in Kandahar. For example, if Al Qaeda fighters saw a male villager whose beard was, in their opinion, too short, they would take a rock, smash it against his face and break his jaw. The Taliban did not oppose Al Qaeda's abuse and intimidation of the Afghan people. My brother in Afghanistan communicated to me that the Afghan villagers were beginning to think that the Arabs were taking control from the Taliban.

A Surprise in Uzbekistan

Three months later, in August, I flew to Tashkent, the capital of Uzbekistan, where other Afghans in Pakistan had informed me were Islamic extremists. Why did I go there? By chance I had met a minister in the Uzbekistan Government at an international interreligious conference in Virginia. She was the Minister of Women's Affairs. When she learned of my experience helping

Afghan refugees during the Soviet occupation of Afghanistan and later in America through the nonprofit IRSI, she invited me to Uzbekistan to explore what I could do to help Afghan refugees in her country. Most of them were communists who had come to study during the Soviet occupation of Afghanistan and remained after the Soviets left Afghanistan. She asked for my help to enable Afghans, especially women, in her country to qualify for refugee status with the United Nations Refugee Agency (UNHCR), and to start adult literacy and vocational training, which were my areas of expertise.

In Tashkent, at a large Afghan party held in my honor, Afghans in casual conversation admitted that they were former mid-level communists before and during the Soviet invasion of Afghanistan and regretted their brutality toward fellow Afghans. They complained that, in the villages of Uzbekistan where they lived, Islamic extremists were harassing and beating them. "How does that happen?" I asked. One Afghan explained, "If I go to the butcher shop and wait in line, and the owner of the shop and other customers are extremists, they would push us to the side and we would be the last to be served. The same thing would happen in buses and trains. In the villages where we once were called comrades, we are now condemned as atheists." At the same time, I met other Afghans who were not aware of any Uzbek Islamic extremists.

I Was Stunned

At the party I told my hostage story. An Afghan man listening asked me, "Do you remember the doctor who treated you on the plane in Kabul?" "Yes, I remember," I replied. "What did his hair look like?" he continued to ask. I answered, "It was Dr. Omery from Herat. He had black, curly hair." "No. It was me, Dr. Zufar," the man declared. But the man in front of me was almost bald with a few gray hairs on his head. I was stunned. He went on to say that he was originally from Jalalabad and was not a communist; yet, he had been a close friend of Najibullah who during my hostage was head of KHAD, the Afghan branch of the Soviet KGB. Najibullah was the most hated man in Afghanistan responsible for the torture and execution of tens of thousands of Afghans. He was the last communist President of Afghanistan who was tortured and hanged by the Taliban in 1996 in the first hour after they had taken Kabul.

Dr. Zufar told me that when I was a hostage, he was head of the KHAD hospital in Kabul and ordered by Najibullah to determine whether there were any Afghans on the plane and report them to him. Dr. Zufar then explained what happened afterward when he saw me inside the hijacked plane: "As I looked over the rows of passengers, when I first saw you in your Kabul-made suit, I guessed that you were an Afghan. When I spoke with you purposely in Farsi, there was no doubt in my mind that you were an Afghan. Pakistanis would not understand Farsi. That night I could not sleep. I woke up at midnight and your innocent face was before my eyes. I asked myself, 'What does this mean?' My wife next to me asked, 'Why are you so uncomfortable?' Before dawn I woke up two more times and the same thing happened. I saw your face. It was so unusual. I decided not to report you to Najibullah."

Dr. Zufar invited me to his home where he introduced me to his wife and children. He then said to his wife, "Do you remember when we were in Kabul in 1981 and I woke up several times? This is the man that I was troubled about." That was the first time she had heard this story from her husband. So that is how as a hostage I had survived the first night in the Kabul Airport.

August 30, 2001 Conference

In mid-August I returned to Fremont for the conference. Hajji Naeem and Waliullah had their visas and flew into San Francisco Airport. On the morning of August 30, the *Building Bridges for Peace to Central Asia* conference was convened in a Fremont City meeting room. Ken formally introduced me to those attending: Mayor Gus Morrison, Gloria Ritchie from the Office of State Assemblyman John Dutra, Jeff Barbosa from the Office of State Senator Liz Figueroa, Fred Turner from the Fremont School District, and Dan Meyer, President of the Tri-City Ministerial Association. Jo Cazenave from

Congressman Pete Stark's office was not able to attend.

I provided a geopolitical overview of Afghanistan, and explained the opportunities and benefits for building bridges of trade and culture between the City of Fremont, the US and with moderate Taliban (those who were not anti-West, were pro-business, and were anti-Al Qaeda) in Afghanistan. Hajji Naeem and Waliullah were introduced and confirmed what I said. Then I explained the threats from expanding global extremism and from bin Laden, the story of the Stockton boy, and threats to refugee/immigrant communities in the Bay Area.

Specific goals, projects, and counterterrorism strategies were proposed to address and neutralize extremism in the local communities; among them were efforts to affirm that non-Muslims were not out to destroy Islam, and that the practices of extremist Taliban did not speak for all Muslims; also initiatives to encourage cooperation with the local mosques were recommended.

Emphasized was the importance of supporting the school districts to provide education programs for marginalized youth to minimize the chance of them becoming influenced by extremists. Today savvy online recruitment videos from the Islamic State group and other terrorist groups have successfully targeted and persuaded disaffected youth to join their extremist ranks.

Afterward the participants, except for Mayor Morrison, rode to the Afghan Village restaurant in Newark and had lunch. Sadly, in the days that followed, no one invited Hajji Naeem, Waliullah, or any of us for further discussions. On September 10, Ken and I met with Jo Cazenave in her Fremont office and reviewed our warnings and proposals voiced at the August 30th conference. Jo then asked me, "Sher, don't you think the CIA is aware of these things?" I replied, "The CIA is sleeping."

The next morning Jo called me at my office asking whether I had watched the TV and heard the news. I said, "No, I have not." "The World Trade Center has been hit," she said. I was shocked. It was beyond belief. It was really hard on me. My heart was with those passengers, the pilots, and their families. As a former hostage, I could sense how they felt. I knew the fear. I started praying for God to give them strength and President Bush wisdom. I thought how difficult it was for a President to deal with this tragedy. "God give him wisdom to make the right decisions." The terrorists wanted the US to overreact and beat up the Islamic world. That would cause a raging fire that would engulf most people in the world.

Forced into a Corner

In the days that followed, while watching the news on TV, I heard the announcement that Pakistani ISI Director, Lt. General Mahmood Ahmed, was to be the liaison between the US and the Taliban who would convey the US ultimatum to hand over bin Laden or to face the consequences. Being an Afghan-American I knew the mentality of Afghans. If the Taliban complied with the US ultimatum, it would be a violation of Afghan honor. The Taliban are Afghans and they would rather die than hand over their guest, whoever it was. Afghan loyalty to the ethical code of Pashtunwali is strong. Mahmood was dishonest with the US and knew the Taliban would not agree. The code of Pashtunwali had been a political dilemma for the Afghans in WWI, WWII, and now at 9/11. Mahmood knowingly forced the Taliban into a corner, and made the Taliban victims of their own code of hospitality.

At a party in Kabul in 2006, I met Mullah Wakil Ahmed Mutawakal. He had been the Minister of Foreign Affairs for the Taliban Government from 1996 until the US forced the Taliban out of power in December 2001. When we were sitting alone, I asked him, "I heard the story back in 2001 that in the morning time Mullah Omar was ready to ask bin Laden to leave Afghanistan. However, when General Mahmood came in the afternoon, he at first conveyed the US's ultimatum to turn over bin Laden; and then he privately discouraged Omar from doing so. Is that story correct?"

Mutawakal answered, "Yes," and explained that he had been in the cabinet meeting with Mullah Omar. Omar favored that bin Laden be asked to leave Afghanistan since the US had helped Afghans during the jihad to remove the Soviets, and had helped Afghan refugees. He argued, "We don't want to fight Americans. We are weak and not a strong country. Bin Laden is not a guest. He is causing lots of trouble for us. We should ask him to leave." Omar's cabinet had agreed with him. General Mahmood came in the afternoon to meet with Omar, who informed him of his cabinet's decision. Then Mahmood asked, "What kind of Muslim are you?" After prayer time, Mahmood met privately with Omar. Mutawakal was not in that meeting.

The 2001 Bonn Conference

The United Nations convened the Bonn Conference in December 2001 after the US invasion of Afghanistan and after the Taliban had been driven from power. Tragically, many of the Afghans who had been invited to represent the Afghan people were former warlords and drug lords who had plundered Afghanistan and its people during its devastating civil war. It was an ill-conceived "quick fix" approach. The US asked Russia's help to bring the Northern Alliance leadership to the bargaining table. Russia was pleased to "do the favor" considering the US role in the Soviet-Afghan War. The Bonn Conference participants were united only in their opposition to the Taliban. The warlords were experienced in manipulating Western nations, particularly the US. Their skill would continue to this day. The Bonn Conference plan to rebuild Afghanistan was like a plan to build a mud wall with no foundation.

If the US and the UN would have understood the nature of the Afghan culture and tribal affairs, and learned from the painful lessons of recent and not too distant history, like the previous US foreign aid development efforts in Afghanistan during the Cold War, and the Soviet-Afghan War, they could have acted wisely and led Afghanistan to a far better place than it is in today.

A Better Alternative

The Bonn Conference could have formed an interim transitional council composed of UN representatives, and an equal number of credible Afghan representatives not controlled by warlords or drug lords. They could have included Afghan intellectuals in Afghanistan, the US, Europe, and Australia, and genuine Afghan tribal elders and religious leaders.

Initially the UN could have selected Afghans who would temporarily serve in those positions until a Loya Jirga could convene to vote and select others to replace them. The Loya Jirga through the centuries has proven to accurately vote for the collective will of the Afghan people. Customarily, Afghans desiring to serve in the Loya Jirga assembly would volunteer, and from among them villagers would select their best representatives to send forward to vote in the assembly.

Rebuild from the Ground Up

UN representatives could have collaborated with the Afghan leaders to stabilize and gradually rebuild from the ground up the foundation for Afghanistan's continued growth and stability. National elections could have been held after five years. The five-year period would have served many purposes: it would be a period to gradually cool the tensions between rival ethnicities and political parties; and it would be a time for a war-time mentality to transition to a peace-time mentality among the people.

Lessons from the US Cold War foreign aid investments in the HAVA project could have guided development. A bottom-up approach could have been implemented. International foreign aid through the UN could slowly be provided to villages at a rate that they could realistically absorb to become self-sufficient, and develop social and political structures that would be consistent with their tribal and religious traditions. Since 9/11, top-down planning and overriding control by warlords have prevented US foreign aid dollars from being absorbed into Afghanistan's economy. Through massive corruption foreign aid has been channeled into the pockets of drug lords and warlords.

Measured inputs of monies and aid into the villages would enable more enforceable verification, accurate assessment, and minimize corruption. That could have created a manageable framework for village, district, province, and national level development. On that foundation Afghanistan could become a stable, democratic, and responsible member of the international community.

According to this plan, at the same time, the UN could have warned the Taliban, warlords, and drug lords that, if they were to act like Al Qaeda, they would be opposed by the international community.

Building from the grassroots up in Afghanistan with credible representatives is a better foundation than building from the top down with people who have blood on their hands.

In my next book I will continue with more personal stories of survival in post-9/11 Afghanistan, the complexities of working with multinational organizations and governments in Afghanistan, and strategies and projects that have actually helped the Afghan people.

EPILOGUE

Do global leaders learn from the past? The historical record does not look good when it comes to their dealings with the country of my birth, Afghanistan. The lessons from the twentieth-century Cold War, the Soviet-Afghan War, and Afghan civil war that followed were disregarded or forgotten:

1. Increasingly it appears that we are descending into a twenty-first century Cold War-like confrontation between Russia and the US. Even former Soviet leader Mikhail Gorbachev brings this warning.
2. After 9/11 the US continued to support the same warlords who plundered Afghanistan during the Soviet-Afghan War and afterward in their civil war.
3. During the Cold War and before the Soviet invasion of Afghanistan, as the US had formed no genuine partnership with the Afghan Government while providing it foreign aid, neither has the US done so after 9/11.
4. Enriched with Western foreign aid, Afghan warlords may launch another devastating civil war as they did after the Soviet Union withdrew its troops from Afghanistan in 1989.

When the connection between the past, the present, and the future is disregarded or forgotten, mistakes of the past will be repeated.

21st Century Cold War

Russian President Vladimir Putin is pursuing an expansionist dream of a *Greater Russia* which has led him to send mercenaries into the Ukraine and to support separatist groups there. It is a mirror image of "The Great Game" played by former General Secretary Brezhnev, who sought to expand the Soviet Union's borders and control its neighbors. Over 35 years ago in 1979, he and other Politburo officials decided to invade Afghanistan. Ten years later, stuck in a military stalemate and realizing that it could not win politically, the Soviet Politburo withdrew its troops from Afghanistan. The Soviet Union paid dearly for its invasion—vast amounts of capital and the lives of men were squandered. Disillusionment spread like poison throughout Soviet society. Soon to follow, the Soviet Union collapsed and the Cold War ended.

Russia should think twice about invading or putting other countries under its control. As the Soviet Politburo attempted to use proxy Afghan communists to maintain control over Afghanistan, Putin will discover that using proxy separatists in neighboring countries will backfire. Separatists and insurgents can be undisciplined and fiercely disunited, and turn against their foreign benefactors whom they resent. Renting the loyalty of separatists, mercenaries, and tribesmen is not reliable or sustainable. The Soviets in the past also miscalculated the role of Islam.

Brezhnev feared Afghanistan would drift into the Western sphere of influence. Putin similarly fears that Ukraine and other neighbors could do the same. Attempting to ruthlessly manipulate client states will eventually drain Russia of its human and financial treasure. As the Russian economy suffers, and Russians die in Greater Russia military campaigns, there will be severe blowback from Russian mothers and fathers, Russian youth, and businessmen.

Soviet politicians made many miscalculations about Afghanistan, largely because they did not listen to cultural experts who understood Afghanistan and its people, or because short-sighted political presumptions took priority over cultural intelligence. The US has unfortunately made the same type of mistakes since 9/11.

I hope that the Russian leaders and people will learn from the past and not continue to coerce their neighbors into submission. In the twenty-first century that will not lead to a Greater Russia. Their present actions will, in fact, lead to a lesser Russia despised by the international community. Russia can become an economically and culturally greater country by becoming a contributing member of the international community.

The Soviets failed to gain the hearts and minds of the Afghan people. They benefited only a small elite, who the Soviets complained were corrupt. From the perspective of the Soviets' objective of stabilizing their influence in Afghanistan, they failed. Aside from violating the human rights of the Afghan people, they supported the wrong people to govern the country. The Soviet Politburo slowly recognized the corruption and sabotage by Afghan communists.

The US and the Soviet Union had less control of events in the Soviet-Afghan War than they thought. In actuality they were being manipulated. Proxy wars are unpredictable and the dangers of unintended consequences are high.

Continued US Support of the Wrong People

Part of the US Cold War foreign policy of containment was to make the Soviet Union bleed while it was in the Afghan quagmire. A side effect of the bleeding policy was prolonging the Soviet occupation. It also extended the training of international jihadists in Afghanistan, and funded the training and recruitment of Islamic extremists through the radicalized madrassas in Pakistan's refugee camps. US and Saudi funding further filled the war chests of the Pakistani military and of the Afghan warlords, who in their civil war power grabs weakened traditional Afghan tribal systems, expanded Islamic extremism, and slaughtered tens of thousands of innocent Afghan civilians.

The consequences of that policy have surfaced in the form of the Taliban, Al Qaeda, and next generation terrorists operating in dozens of countries. The US must also worry about home-grown extremists. Ryan Cocker, former Ambassador to Iraq, has written that as many as 2000 Westerners with passports, including those from the US, have volunteered and fought in Syria and Iraq with terrorist forces like the Islamic State group. As foreign volunteers they are used for the most vicious acts because they tend to be the most ideologically motivated and do not regard their acts as terrorism but rather noble and heroic acts of justice and liberation. A reasonable fear is that they will return to their home countries in Europe, Australia, and the US and bring global terrorism with them.

At the December, 2001 Bonn Conference, by supporting the same Afghan warlords from the Soviet-Afghan War to lead the reconstruction of Afghanistan, the US and NATO perpetuated Afghanistan as a failing state.

No Genuine Partnership Then and Now

During the Cold War the US invested at least $111.5 million in foreign aid into the HAVA project. That approaches US $1billion in today's dollars. Although the project was economically unsound, the overriding US foreign policy priority was to maintain a strategic relationship with Afghanistan so it would not become a satellite nation of the Soviet Union. Tragically, most of the capital investments in Afghanistan were destroyed through the Soviet invasion and civil war that followed.

For similar foreign policy reasons, after 9/11 the US and its allies pumped billions of dollars into Afghanistan to prevent it from again becoming a safe haven for terrorists. Today there is little to show for it. Afghanistan is still among the least developed countries in the world. The US Government Accountability Office (GAO) reports that from 2002 through 2013 the US Departments of State (DOS) and Defense (DOD), and the US Agency for International Development (USAID) gave about $100 billion of aid to Afghanistan. That does not include the billions that other countries poured into Afghanistan. Yet, Afghanistan is ranked as one of the poorest countries in the world, 175 out of 186 countries in the Human Development Index.

Corruption

How could that be? Corruption! It's no surprise. The GAO identifies widespread corruption as one of the three continuing "challenges" operating there. Afghanistan has been ranked by Transparency International as among the most corrupt countries in the world--at the bottom with North Korea and Somalia.

No Enforced Accountability

US politicians, the US military, the USAID, NATO, and other foreign donors have been deceived and manipulated in Afghanistan.

That is to a great extent because they have not consistently enforced the requirement for Afghan political leaders and government agencies such as ministries and district councils, businesses and nonprofits--as well as US contractors--to be accountable. For "fiscal year 2013 the USAID had provided about $900 million of its Afghanistan mission funds in direct assistance" to the Afghan Government. The GAO disclosed that a Special Inspector General reported that the USAID "may have approved direct assistance to some Afghan ministries without mitigating all identified risks."

The disastrous result has been that only a small percentage of Afghans in need have received US and other international aid. That in turn has bred jealousy and anti-American resentment. The US has not learned from its Cold War history of foreign aid in Afghanistan. The good will that American and NATO countries had earned has been squandered.

Another Afghan Civil War Might Follow

After the Soviet Union withdrew its troops in 1989, a civil war led by warlords followed. Warlords are "lords in war." They fought for territory and believed that as victors they were justified to loot Afghanistan's banks and museums, military installations and armaments, and justified to destroy irrigation systems, roads, factories, public buildings, and schools. The majority of the warlord factions in Pakistan and Iran had prepared for that moment by diverting and conserving the monies, weapons, ammunition, and supplies given them through Pakistan and Iran by Western and wealthy Arab nations. Only a minority of the mujahideen had actually fought the Soviets in Afghanistan.

After 9/11, Western nations blindly supported warlords and drug lords to occupy main positions in the new Afghan Government. They were the same few who had previously destroyed Afghanistan's infrastructure. During the next 13 years foreign aid continued to be diverted into their war chests, as during the Soviet-Afghan War.

US and NATO troops have been dramatically drawn down and

the winner of the 2014 Afghan presidential elections, which were plagued with voter fraud, agreed to sign the Bilateral Security Agreements permitting a small US and NATO military presence in Afghanistan after 2014. Their presence is limited to supporting and training Afghan forces, and counter-terror operations. If a civil war occurs, it would, however, not be because the US and NATO military presence was small.

The Civil War Trigger

The trigger for civil war could be a Taliban offensive that tips the scales of security. Warlord militias would respond to the security threat to restore order—their order and their power.

Even before 9/11, Pakistan trained, supplied, and led the Afghan Taliban. Today it continues to be controlled by Pakistan, although Pakistan would deny it. Pakistan's foreign policy has been to keep Afghanistan weak and unstable as a buffer state.

The Taliban, though, could turn against Pakistan. They have learned how to make bombs to destroy bridges and people. The Taliban can now use those bombs to retaliate among themselves to settle clan and tribal rivalries, and against Pakistan. At some point extremist Taliban will become an unmanageable threat for Pakistan.

As Russia should think twice about destabilizing another country for the purpose of moving it into its orbit of influence, so should Pakistan rethink its policy toward Afghanistan.

Don't Abandon the Afghan People
They Are Hostages

The international community should not abandon Afghanistan. It could again slide into civil war and chaos, and become a safe haven and training center for terrorists, as it was before 9/11. Conflict favors extremism.

As of the writing of this book, there are a few good things that have resulted in Afghanistan: a new constitution, which is similar to the 1964 constitution of Afghanistan, and some coed schools, although they are mainly in the big cities of Kabul, Mazar-i-Sharif,

Herat, and Bamiyan. In most of the country, unfortunately, especially in the villages, education is in the hands of the Taliban who enforce the strict Cold War madrassa style of education.

The majority of the Afghan people are hostages of poverty, the corruption of Afghan officials, warlords and drug lords, the Taliban, and of Pakistan's foreign policy.

Learn the Lessons of History

Western nations have not learned how to effectively help the majority of Afghan people nor maintain their trust. The US and NATO forces in Afghanistan have relied on technology and air strikes, which did not eliminate the insurgents who regularly escaped and then returned to the villages. The bombings hurt the villagers, though. At some point, Western countries must learn that technology has its limitations.

Hopefully, they will also learn to support the right people-- Afghans of all ethnicities who genuinely desire to build the country rather than those who just enrich themselves.

Corruption can be countered by enforcing a policy that money will stop when proof of delivered services is not provided.

Be Patient

During the Cold War, US policy makers, Afghan government officials, and the US private contractor hired to make a desert area bloom in Helmand Valley, each had different priorities and sought quick solutions without proper research and planning. They did not understand the needs of the Afghan people, the unique characteristics of the Helmand-Arghandab Valley, and therefore, the wise application of technology and US dollars to that region. Short-term progress was made but it was unsustainable and stagnated. In the end, only a small percentage of needy people gained temporary benefits.

Developed countries want underdeveloped countries to quickly operate at the same level as they do. They rush and short-circuit a necessary and measured process of agricultural, social, cultural and political development.

A Pashto proverb says that one rose does not bring a spring. It means that if you see a rose in the cold winter, it does not mean that springtime has arrived. Short-term benefits do not mean that they will last.

In the twenty-first century with rapid technological breakthroughs, the American public is conditioned to expect quick solutions. Americans and their policy makers expect Afghans to immediately have democratic elections and function as a democracy. Prior to 9/11 the Afghans were under Taliban rule for years. Then, after 9/11, there were elections. What kind of elections were they? Although Afghans showed purple ink on their fingers after voting, the elections were manipulated. Warlords and drug lords, and foreign powers such as Iran, Pakistan, India, China, and some Arab countries bought the votes of those who were able to vote. The majority of the people who live in villages in the countryside were excluded from voting because the Taliban controlled their areas.

Sometimes US officials say, "Underdeveloped countries don't like our democratic ways of thinking." Well, they don't like it because they don't have it, or understand its values. They have not experienced it. The elections after 2001 were not fair.

In terms of realistic expectations for development in Afghanistan, consider this: If I have a handicapped foot, and you have normal feet, do you expect me to race with you? Be patient with me!

Countering Global Terrorism

In terms of economic development, the US can learn from the Cold War HAVA project and the example of people like Sanford Caudill to support bottom-up development efforts in Afghanistan. Other nations can learn to do the same. Enabling the Afghan people and impoverished people in other developing countries to be self-reliant, healthy, educated, and secure at the village level is fundamental for their well-being, and for countering terrorism globally and locally.

NOTES

CHAPTER 2: STINKY ESCAPE FROM THE KABUL MILITARY
        SCHOOL

21   *"badly defeated by local Bajaur Pashtun tribesmen,"* Louis
Dupree, *Afghanistan.* 3d. (Karachi: Oxford University Press, 1997), 539.

CHAPTER 3: LESSONS FORGOTTEN OR DISREGARDED

25   *"directed through the Helmand-Arghandab Valley Authority
(HAVA),"* Cynthia Clapp-Wincek and Emily Baldwin, *The Helmand
Valley Project in Afghanistan. Evaluation Special Study* an *A.I.D. Evaluation
Special Study No. 18,* USAID (December 1983), 9,
http://pdf.usaid.gov/pdf_docs/Pnaal028.pdf.

26   *"bloom for nomads (Kuchis) and landless farmers to farm,"* Lloyd
Baron, *Sector Analysis:Helmand–Arghandab Valley Region,* for USAID,
(February   1973),   9,   12.
http://pdf.usaid.gov/pdf_docs/PNABR280.pdf .
"negative ecological and human impact, and its costs," Ibid., 13,
24.
"irrigation project into a rural development program," Clapp-
Wincek and Baldwin, *The Helmand Valley* ..., vii.

27   *"massive dams which would eventually flood their villages,"*
Baron, *Sector Analysis,* 13, and Dupree, *Afghanistan,* 501.
"not on the central government's drawing boards," Dupree,
Afghanistan, 501.
"land distribution and title transfers," Ibid., 502, 503.
"Reluctantly MKA agreed," Ibid., 483.

28   *"wrongly located for proper gravity water flow and drainage,"*
Baron, *Sector Analysis,* 14, and Clapp-Wincek and Baldwin, *The Helmand
Valley...,* 2, 5.
*"20 percent margin of error in estimating the acreage or water
supply,"* Aloys Arthur Michel, "The Kabul, Kunduz, and Helmand
Valleys and the National Economy of Afghanistan: A Study of
Regional Resources and Comparative Advantages of Development"
from *National Academy of Sciences: National Research Council,* no. 5
(Washington, DC, 1959), 153; and Clapp-Wincek and Baldwin, *The

Helmand Valley..., 2; and Baron, *Sector Analysis*, 14.

"*not the long-term benefits for the people of Afghanistan*," Clapp-Wincek and Baldwin, *The Helmand Valley...*, 8.

"*salvaging the efforts of MKA, a private contractor*," Ibid., 9.

29 "*defects to be further aggravated and fester*," Baron, *Sector Analysis*, 15.

30 "*housing and utilities, communications, agricultural research and extension*," Ibid., 45.

"*national airlines of Afghanistan, and Kandahar Airport*," Nick Cullather, "Damming Afghanistan: Modernization in a Buffer State," in *Journal of American History*, 89 *(Sept. 2002)*, *512-537*, http://www.journalofamericanhistory.org/teaching/2002_09/article.html.

"*US Export-Import Bank were poured into the HAVA from 1949 to 1979*," Clapp-Wincek and Baldwin, *The Helmand Valley...*, xi.

32 "*by using fertilizers, improved seeds, and tractors*," Baron, *Sector Analysis*, i.

"*blocked progress for the following two years*," Cullather, "Damming."

"*and the HAVA's funding was continued*," Cullather, "Damming,". and Clapp-Wincek and Baldwin, *The Helmand Valley...*, 6.

"*the HAVA project was terminated*," Clapp-Wincek and Baldwin, *The Helmand Valley...*, 12, 13.

33 "*[HAVA] intended to gain, and how they [were] to be gotten*," Baron, *Sector Analysis*, 46.

"*failures in the Helmand Valley that occurred after it left Afghanistan*," Ibid., 31, 32.

34 "*Corruption, often, is a matter of cultural definition*," Clapp-Wincek and Baldwin, *The Helmand Valley...*, Appendix B-1.

"*regarded as a "Golden Age" in those two provinces*," Monica Whitlock. "Helmand's Golden Age," *bbc.co.uk*, 7 August 2014, www.bbc.co.uk/news/special/2014/newsspec_8529/index.html.

"*tacit H[A]VA policy not to communicate with farmers*," *The Helmand Valley ...*, 24, 25.

37 "*useful compromises could be found*," Ibid.

CHAPTER 6: THE 1973 BLOODLESS COUP

59 *"dress codes and equal rights for women,"* Dupree, *Afghanistan,* 458-461. Dupree provides an excellent review of this period in Afghanistan's history.

CHAPTER 8: THE DARKEST DAY

84 *"unmarked mass grave was discovered,"* Abdul Waheed Wafa and Carlotta Gall, "State Funeral for Afghan Leader Slain in '78 Coup," *www.nytimes.com,* March 18, 2009, http://www.nytimes.com/2009/03/18/world/asia/18afghan.html?_r =0.

CHAPTER 10: THE SOVIET INVASION

96 *"Amin's purges reached 50,000 people,"* Alexander Antonovich Liakhovsky, "Inside the Soviet Invasion of Afghanistan and the Seizure of Kabul, December 1979," *Cold War International History Project Working Papers Series. Working Paper # 51,* trans. Gary Goldberg and Artemy Kalinovsky, The Woodrow Wilson International Center for Scholars (January 2007), 3, http://www.wilsoncenter.org/sites/default/files/WP51_Web_Final.p df.

97 *"look like aggressors to the Afghan people,"* William R. Polk, "What the Russians did in Afghanistan And What We Can Learn From It," in "Will We Learn Anything from Afghanistan? William R. Polk, Part 1," intro. James Fallows, *The Atlantic,* February 23, 2013, http://www.theatlantic.com/international/print/2013/02/will-we-learn-anything-from-afghanistan-william-r-polk-part-1/273448/. Polk provides Sir Rodric Braithwaite's (*Afgantsy: The Russians in Afghanistan 1979-89*) summary of Andropov's recorded objections to the invasion. *"and what to do about it,"* Madeleine Albright with Bill Woodward, *The Mighty & The Almighty* (New York: Harper Collins: 2006), 39-41. *"undervalued the role of religion in Iran,"* Ibid.

98 *"Eastern Bloc countries, which in fact it did,"* Zbigniew Brzezinski, interview by Paris Le Nouvel Observateur. "The CIA's Intervention in Afghanistan," trans. Bill Blum, January 15-21, 1998, from *Global Research.ca, Centre for Research on Globalization,* www.globalresearch.ca/articles/BRZ110A.html.

"because there appeared to be no better alternative," Polk, "What the Russians did in Afghanistan And What We Can Learn From It".

99 *"inadvertently killed by another Soviet soldier,"* Liakhovsky, "Inside the Soviet Invasion of Afghanistan", 64.

CHAPTER 13: INCUBATORS FOR EXTREMISM

171 *"government decision makers should avoid,"* Albright, *The Mighty...*, 8.

172 *"keep the pot boiling, but not boil over" with the Soviet Union,"* Robert Gates, *From the Shadows: The Ultimate Insider's Story of Five Presidents and How They Won the Cold War* (New York: Touchstone, 1996), 252.

"nuclear weapons at an appropriate time," Mark Urban, "Saudi nuclear weapons 'on order' from Pakistan," *BBC*, November 6, 2013, www.bbc.com/news/world-middle-east-24823846.

173 *"they would unite against outsiders,"* David Lyon, *In Afghanistan: Two Hundred Years of British, Russian and American Occupation* (New York: Palgrave Macmillian, 2009), 6.

CHAPTER 14: THE MUJAHIDEEN

182 *"Mujahideen Getting Beaten by 1985,"* Diego Cordovez and Selig S. Harrison, *Out of Afghanistan: The Inside Story of the Soviet Withdrawal* (New York: Oxford University Press, 1995), 196 from digital copy in Alameda County Library system. Diego Cordovez, an Ecuadorian diplomat, was appointed a United Nations mediator in the 1980s to negotiate the withdrawal of Soviet troops from Afghanistan.

"resolved to withdraw Soviet troops," An excerpt from the November, 13, 1986 Politburo meeting discloses that Mikhail Gorbachev referenced an October 1985 Politburo policy and goal to withdraw Soviet troops over two years. "Gorbachev and Afghanistan," ed./annotated Christian F. Ostermann, in *Cold War International History Project Bulletin Issue 14/15,* The Woodrow Wilson International Center for Scholars (Winter 2003 to Spring 2004), 143, 144, http://www.wilsoncenter.org/sites/default/files/CWIHPBulletin14-15_p2_0.pdf. Notes from that meeting were provided by Anatoly Chrnyaev from the Gorbachev Foundation, Moscow, and trans. by Gary Goldberg, (Hereafter *Cold War International History Project Bulletin*

Issue 14/15 is called *Cold War 14/15.)*

183 *"ammunition, and communication equipment,"* Christian Friedrich Ostermann, "New Evidence on the War in Afghanistan: Introduction," in *Cold War International History Project Bulletin Issue 14/15,* The Wilson Center, (Winter 2003 to Spring 2004), 140, http://www.wilsoncenter.org/sites/default/files/CWIHPBulletin14-15_p2_0.pdf.

"heavy loss of troops and weapons and supplies," Cordovez and Harrison, *Out of Afghanistan,* 200.

184 *"15% of troops were allocated for field operations,"* Lester W. Grau, "The Soviet-Afghan War: A Superpower Mired in the Mountains," from the "The Mature Insurgency" section, Foreign Military Studies Office, Ft. Leavenworth, Kansas previously published in *The Journal of Slavic Military Studies* 17, no. 1 (March 2004), http://fmso.leavenworth.army.mil/documents/miredinmount.htm.

186 *"reluctant to share information with them,"* Ibid., from the section "The Government of the Democratic Republic of Afghanistan."

"when Soviet units left their base camps," The Russian General Staff, *The Soviet-Afghan War: How a Superpower Fought and Lost,* ed. Michael A. Gress and trans. Lester W. Grau (Lawrence, Kansas: University Press of Kansas, 2002), 116, 117. Russian General Staff officers report their experiences in the Soviet-Afghan War.

187 *"from Soviet and DRA positions,"* Ibid., xiv.

"was either killed, wounded, or missing," Ibid., 309.

188 *"had no kerosene or even matches,"* "Notes from Politburo Meeting 21-22 January 1987 (Excerpt)", *Cold War International History Project Bulletin Issue 14/15,* 145.

189 *"not interfere in Afghan affairs,"* King Mohammad Zahir Shah disclosed this to his close friend, Senator Abdul Qados, from Kandahar.

"its economic and military strength," Cordovez and Harrison, *Out of Afghanistan,* 103.

190 *"a hopefully Soviet-friendly condition,"* *Cold War International History Project Bulletin Issue 14/15,* 144.

"costs to the Soviet military and not defeat it," Cordovez and Harrison, *Out of Afghanistan,* 201. Ronald Krueger, director of the Afghan Task Force at the Defense Intelligence Agency, is cited.

"greater losses from the Stingers," Ibid., 199, 200.

192 *"the real state of affairs of the country,"* Cold War International History Project Bulletin Issue 14/15, 144-145.

193 *"they became stuck in a stalemate by 1984,"* Grau, *The Soviet-Afghan War,* in the "The Insurgency Matures" section.

CHAPTER 17: A NEW BEGINNING IN FREMONT

235 *"to perform a terrorist suicide attack,"* Lee Ferran, 'Troubling': Suicide Bomber Hung Out in US After Terror Training," *www.abcnews.com,* July 31, 2014, http://abcnews.go.com/Blotter/troubling-suicide-bomber-hung-us-terror-training/story?id=24790407&google_editors_picks=true.

236 *"racist extremist issues,"* Michelle Shephard, "Ex-skinhead, former Islamic radical open summit against extremism," *www.thestar.com,* June 28, 2011, http://www.thestar.com/news/world/2011/06/28/exskinhead_former_islamic_radical_open_summit_against_extremism.html.

CHAPTER 18: MY WARNINGS BEFORE 9/11

254 *"Prime Minister David Cameron in 2013,"* Steven Swinford, "David Cameron: Talks with Taliban should have begun a decade ago," *www.telegraph.co.uk,* June 29, 2013, under www.telegraph.co.uk/news/worldnews/asia/afghanistan/10149983/David-Cameron-Talks-with-Taliban-should-have-begun-a-decade-ago.html.

256 *"not handing over Osama bin Laden to the US for trial,"* Reuters, "Afghan Taliban urges Muslim unity versus 'infidels,'" *www.afghanistannewscenter.com--www.aol.com* appears to no longer show this article, April 10, 2001, http://www.afghanistannewscenter.com/news/2001/april/apr10h2001.html.

"warned of Al Qaeda and the Taliban," Henry Schuster and Mike Boettcher. "How much did Afghan leader know?" *www.cnn.com,* November 3, 2003,

http://www.cnn.com/2003/US/11/06/massoud.cable/index.html.

EPILOGUE

266 *"Mikhail Gorbachev brings this warning,"* Rob Broomby, "Mikhail Gorbachev warns of 'new Cold War'," *www.bbc.com*, November 8, 2014, www.bbc.com/news/world-europe-29970275.

268 *"bring global terrorism with them,"* Ryan Crocker. "It's Not Too Late to Engage Iraq," *www.washingtonpost.com*, June 19, 2014, http://www.washingtonpost.com/opinions/its-not-too-late-to-reengage-with-iraq/2014/06/19/d2a437d6-f644-11e3-a3a5-42be35962a52_story.html.

269 *"gave about $100 billion of aid to Afghanistan,"* US Government Accountability Office, *Afghanistan: Oversight and Accountability of U.S. Assistance.* Testimony Before the Subcommittee on the Middle East and North Africa, Committee on Foreign Affairs, House of Representatives (Washington D.C.: US Government Accountability Office, GAO-14-680T, June 10, 2014), 1, http://www.gao.gov/assets/670/664034.pdf. (Hereafter GAO).

"175 out of 186 countries in the Human Development Index," United Nations Development Programme, *Summary Human Development Report 2013: The Rise of the South: Human Progress in a Diverse World* (New York: United Nations Development Programme, 2013), 15, http://hdr.undp.org/sites/default/files/hdr2013_en_summary.pdf.

"most corrupt countries in the world--at the bottom with North Korea and Somalia," Transparency International, *Corruption Perceptions Index 2013,* (Berlin, Germany: 2013), http://www.transparency.org/cpi2013/press#en.

270 *"without mitigating all identified risks,"* GAO, 6.

BOOK COVER PHOTOS

Three Mujahideen,

http://commons.wikimedia.org/wiki/File:August_1985_Muja.jpg.

Two Attack Helicopters,

http://commons.wikimedia.org/wiki/File:Afghan_Mil_Mi-35.jpg, These Mi-35 attack helicopters in Afghanistan are export versions of the Soviet Mil Mi-24 attack helicopters used during the Soviet-Afghan

War.

Soviet Main Battle Tank,

http://commons.wikimedia.org/wiki/File:T54A_and_T55_at_Bagram _Air_Base.jpg. Soviet tanks like this litter Afghanistan.

Soviet General Leonid Brezhnev Signing Document,

http://commons.wikimedia.org/wiki/File:President_Ford_and_Soviet _General_Secretary_Leonid_I._Brezhnev_-_NARA_-_7162417.jpg. In 1974 Brezhnev signed with President Gerald Ford a Joint Communique on the Limitation of Strategic Offensive Arms.

Burning World Trade Center Towers,

https://www.google.com/search?q=9+11&tbm=isch&tbs=simg:CA QSZRpjCxCo1NgEGgIICQwLELCMpwgaPAo6CAISFPMYnSGCG fAdnxvJHZQf5BP1IsYlGiAHZMDMr0Irx4EBZ66c4KjNIWBcr1V2 s9GI9jDhtrPC7QwLEI6u_1ggaCgoICAESBKssW2AM&sa=X&ei=t m9nVO- GHo2fyATklYAg&ved=0CBsQwg4oAA&biw=960&bih=541.

Airliner,

http://en.wikipedia.org/wiki/Boeing_720#mediaviewer/File:Bo eing_720-048_EI-ALA_Aer_Lingus_1965.jpg. This photo is of a Boeing 720 similar in appearance to the one within which I was held hostage.

Afghan Refugee Camp,

https://www.google.com/search?q=afghanistan+refugee+camps&tb m=isch&tbs=simg:CAQSZxplCxCo1NgEGgQIAwgJDAsQsIynCBo8 CjoIAhIU1xrcI7MayCPDJMYj2yPeGtoarxoaIDtyC9_14x3GjebKa0fz pa4duBZwUAMQBg71D3oZBDy1UDAsQjq7- CBoKCggIARIEKq54_1ww&sa=X&ei=G3FnVOPhAsLwyATQvILI Dw&ved=0CBsQwg4oAA&biw=960&bih=541.

General Muhammad Zia ul-Haq,

https://www.google.com/search?q=muhammad+zia+ul+haq&tbm=i sch&tbs=simg:CAQSZRpjCxCo1NgEGgIIQgwLELCMpwgaPAo6C AISFJQilyKJGOohlSLIDsoYtR6SIuMhGiDo- JnEllS5iT_1RYTTDv7gsCvU5FyEiRvLWl9A- u6UgrgwLEI6u_1ggaCgoICAESBHXowsEM&sa=X&ei=EfhxVPD4 EfSMsQTzv4DICQ&ved=0CBwQ2A4oAQ&biw=960&bih=541. National Security Adviser Zbigniew Brzezinski in this 1980 meeting shook the hand of General Muhammad Zia ul-Haq with President Jimmy Carter looking on.

Made in the USA
San Bernardino, CA
22 January 2020

63492304R00180